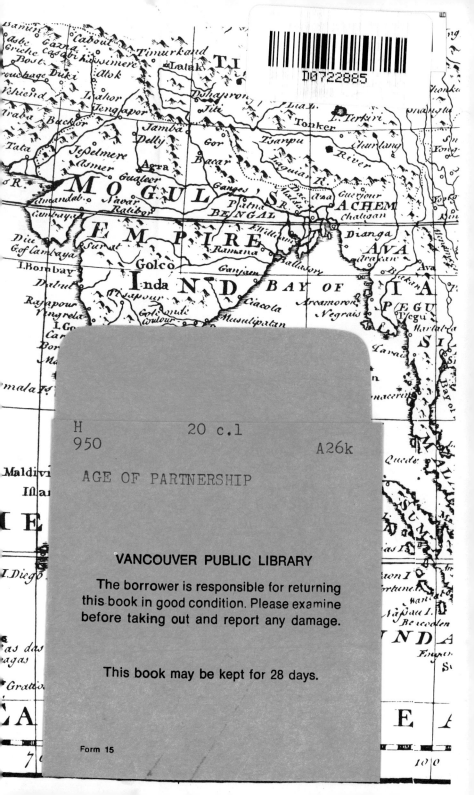

H
950   20 c.1
              A26k

AGE OF PARTNERSHIP

VANCOUVER PUBLIC LIBRARY

The borrower is responsible for returning
this book in good condition. Please examine
before taking out and report any damage.

This book may be kept for 28 days.

Form 15

The Age of Partnership

The Age of Partnership

*Europeans in Asia
before Dominion*

edited by
Blair B. Kling
and M. N. Pearson

*Published with the support of
The Maurice J. Sullivan & Family Fund
in
The University of Hawaii Foundation*

The University Press of Hawaii
Honolulu

Copyright © 1979 by The University Press of Hawaii

All rights reserved. No part of this work may be reproduced or transmitted in any form or by any means, electronic or mechanical, including photocopying and recording, or by any information storage or retrieval system, without permission in writing from the publisher.

Manufactured in the United States of America

Library of Congress Cataloging in Publication Data
Main entry under title:

The Age of partnership.

Includes bibliographical references.
1. Asia—History—Addresses, essays, lectures.
2. Asia—Relations (general) with Europe—Addresses, essays, lectures. 3. Europe—Relations (general) with Asia—Addresses, essays, lectures. I. Kling, Blair B.
II. Pearson, Michael Naylor, 1941–
DS33.7.A3   1979   301.29'4'05   78–31650
ISBN 0-8248-0495-3

NOV - 6 1980

ASIA

Arabia
Deferta Tina
Median
Hagiar
Cathema
PERSIA
Tabas
Kileki
Fefd
Kosir
Karzeko
Naged Castle
Ching
Darabgerd
Baijer
Tarom
The
Persian
Gug
Gomron
Pfa
Gro
RED
Medina
Calif
Gulf
Bahara I.
Ormuz
Jambo
Jamama
Catema
Tin
Jod
dah
ARABIA
Julfar
Turva
G. of Ormus
20
Mecca

Svaken
Yemen
or Arabia Felix
Maskat
Zoar
C. Re
Dhafar
Hadramut
Hatkoa
Kanara
Makuulka
Malriaka
Arkiko
Zibit
Sanaa
I. de Curia Muria
Dhofar
Moca
Makulla
Belula
Sts
Aden
Kushem
of Babelmandel
Socotra I.
10

0

A
NEW & ACCURATE MAP
of
ASIA
Drawn from
Actual Surveys,
and otherwise Collected from
Journals;
assisted by the most approved
Modern Maps & Charts.
The whole being regulated by
Astronl Observations
By Eman. Bowen

10

40
50
Longitude
60

TIBET

Timurkand
Halak
Dshaprong
Tite
L. Puka
Lia L.
Tonker
I. Tertari
Charlong
Tamba
Delly
Gor
Tsanpu
Taguian R.
Iza
Guesjour
chatisan
ACHEM

Jeselmere
Asmer
Agra
Gualeor
Bacar
Ganges R.
Patna
BENGAL
Dianga
AVA
Arakan
Ava

MOGUL'S R.

EMPIRE

Diu
G. of Cambaya
Surat
Golco
Inda
Mitton
Ramana
Ballasor
BAY OF
IA
PEGU
Pegu
I. Bombay
Dabul
Visapour
Ciacola
Arcamoron
Negrais
Martaba
Rajapour
Vingrela
I. Goa
Carnar
Borcelore
Mangalon
Goldonde
Culour
Musulipatan
Bezoart
Riatcoula
Carnata
Arme
gon
Pellicate
Madras or Fort St. Geor.
Pondechery
Ft. St. David
Negapatan
Tanjou
Gingi
BENGAL
Tanai
Anda man
Ind.e
Tenaceri
Maduré
Cochin
Cotale
C. Comorin
Jaffanapatan
Trinquimale
Balacola F.
Canicubar
Sombrire
Nicobar I.
Quede
Colomba
Gallo
Candy
Velune
Dandera
CEYLON I.
achin

Maldivie
Islands
Male

THE INDIAN

Colomates

I. Diego Roiz

Adomatis

OR

Bas das
Chagas

Candu I.

SUNDA

Grattosa

Apalioria

EASTERN OCEA

Mintaon I
Good Fortune

Najau I.
Bencolen

70 from 80 London 90 100

Kong-chang
Si-ngan
Chonkur
Ha-nai-hoy-fong
Qui-te
Fu-ning
Heyngan SEA
Nangasa
Pau-king
Siang-yang
Pong-yang
CHINA
Nan-king
Ngan-tu
Nван-king
chi
Na-ng-chew
King-po
Shangtu
Cey-cheu
King-chen
Tenchew
Lequeas
Ching-tu
Chong-king
Kyen-kyang
Suichen
Chinche
Honan
Chang-sha
Shwi-chen
Win-chen
Yong-ing
Ching-hyang
Yong-chweng
Yang-riging
Yven-chen
Yen-ping
Fu-chew
Ton-cha
Yun-nan
Pau-king
Kan-chen
Te
Lesin-chen
Hing-n'ha
I. dos Reys Ma
Ching-wha
Chua-ch
Chou-chen
Formosa I.
Su-chew
Chau-king
Tay-wan
Barteon
Kircho
Kanton
Hey-chen
Bashee I.
Meng
TUN
QUIN
Laychew
Macao
Ava
Segovia
LUCONIA or
MANILLA
Kyongchen
Porcelone
Haynan I.
Triangles
P. of Casiguran
Cochinchira
PHIL
IPPINE
Poakingha
Thoansa
False
Quinnin
SIAM
Louvo
Siam
Praed
Shoals
Manilla
Str. of Manilla
Tegu
Hartalan
Cambadia
Mindora
Philipina o
Tandaya
Falip
Lamathan
Cianpa
Paragoa I.
I. Layta
St. John Pay
I. S L A N D S
MINDANAO
Mindanao
Tegan a I.
C. Henry
Caldero
I. disc
Ligor
Patana
Nattina
Borneo
Sanguin
Sion
Pera
anamba I.
BORNEO
MOLU
C
Malacca
Sambas
Manado
C. Roman
Lava
Toloy
CELE
Gilolo
NI
Banca I.
Dati
BE
Mahidor
Bilato
Burol
Cera
Nant
Palambom
Benger
Macasar
NDA
ISLANDS
Jan
pandan
ISLAND
Enganol.
Madura
Flores I.
Amboyna
Hig
Sunda Str.
Banton
JAVA
Datay
Malatian
Palambuan
Bally I.
T. Lumbava
Ambol
TIM
Sandelbosch
Concordia
E A N
Rotti I.
10 0
11 0
12 0
13

These Essays
Are Written in Honor of
Holden Furber
Teacher, Colleague, Friend

Contents

Acknowledgment

The editors wish to thank the South Asia Regional Studies Center at the University of Pennsylvania for funds to assist in the preparation of the manuscript.

The Age of Partnership

Introduction

M. N. Pearson

This book of essays on the Age of Partnership has been put together by friends, colleagues, and former students of Holden Furber. Blair B. Kling, coeditor of this volume and one of Furber's early students, evaluates his contribution in the last essay. Here it is necessary only to say that Furber, especially during his twenty-five years (1948–1973) at the University of Pennsylvania, was the man who pioneered the modern study of South Asian history in the United States, just as more generally the late W. Norman Brown created in this country the discipline of South Asian studies.

Despite his numerous publications, which are listed elsewhere in this volume, Furber's reputation as a scholar today rests largely on two books: *John Company at Work* and the recent *Rival Empires of Trade in the Orient, 1600–1800*. The first, as is borne out by its recent republication, has apparently achieved international status as a modern classic; it is therefore natural that the contributors to this present volume constitute an international group. Furber's most recent work, moreover, seems certain to become the standard account of its area and period. Yet the theme on which the present volume is based is only implicit in these two books and in most of Furber's other publications. It was made explicit in the address he delivered when he was elected president of the Association for Asian Studies in 1969.

In this address Furber, as a good historian, was trying to demonstrate the relevance of the past for the present and future. He saw the need for a fundamental reordering of Asian-Western relations in the present, postimperial, world, and he looked to the preimperial past for guidelines. He pointed to cooperation between Asians and Europeans in the sixteenth to early eighteenth centuries, especially in the commercial and intellectual spheres. Furber was speaking while United States involvement in Vietnam was at its height. He could well have joined the many scholars both in America and elsewhere who at this time attempted to expiate the colonial and neocolonial activities of their fellow countrymen by finding a Golden Age in the precolonial past and forecasting one for the future. It was typical of Furber's honesty and tough-mindedness that he refused to close his eyes to less pleasant contacts, such as slavery and racial discrimination in general. Nor was he entirely sanguine about the chances for a new Age of Partnership between Asia and the West, an age which would reproduce the values of the preimperial past and avoid its defects.

The essays in this book investigate in some detail various aspects of relations between Europeans and Asians before the colonial expansion which began in the late eighteenth century. This introduction is concerned with some of the problems of writing the history of this period; it also attempts to sketch in broad terms the main themes of Asian-European relations at this time. The essays in the bulk of the volume are detailed studies of some of these themes.

In writing on this period, roughly the sixteenth to eighteenth centuries, we are faced with a historiographical problem—the Europeans of whom we write became, soon after the period of our concern, colonial rulers in large parts of Asia. The temptation is thus to find the seeds of empire in all their activities.

The general historiographical problems peculiar to Asian history are addressed in my essay in this volume with the help of two case studies from the time of the Portuguese, the first Europeans in Asia. The problems are, to say the least, both complex and understudied. No one today would be so crass as to find the seeds of the British Indian empire in Hawkins' arrival in Surat in 1608 or discover the beginnings of the Dutch East Indies in the activities of J. P. Coen in Java a little later. We all know that the British in India were of minor significance for at least a century and that their Indian empire had as its two basic preconditions the collapse of the Mughal empire and certain economic and scientific developments in England in the eighteenth century. Similarly, the boundaries of the Dutch East Indies (and so of independent Indonesia) were not laid down until the Anglo-Dutch treaty of 1824, a treaty which was designed to solve European problems.

Yet to reverse the focus, to avoid the distortions of the "seeds of empire" school of imperial historiography, is not so easy as may appear. Two of the several reactions to this school hardly constitute a step forward. There is, on the one hand, the tendency to swing around and write of the Europeans rather than the Asians as the villains—to emphasize, for example, the piracy of the British and the Portuguese rather than that of the coastal inhabitants of China and western India. This viewpoint may be emotionally satisfying, but it hardly solves any historiographical problems. In particular, it still presents the early Europeans as being more important than they really were. They still have an impact, only now it is seen as a lawless and brutal one.

Another corrective which historians have used is to deny the early Europeans any importance at all. By extension this approach has even led to a tendency to denigrate the whole field of colonial history. Thus, say these iconoclasts, in the preimperial period the real frontiers of knowledge lie in the study of areas outside the cognizance of the early Europeans: the spread of Islam in Indonesia, internal developments in Japan, the rise of the Ottoman empire, and its later fall, in the Middle East. The role of the Europeans is seen as insignificant, or at best incidental, with the blundering Europeans occasionally having some impact, but not the one they expected. Thus Spanish missionary activity in Japan leads, all unexpectedly, to the closing of the country. Thus the unification and pacification of Indonesia by the Dutch foster the spread of Islam. Thus Portuguese naval attacks in the Indian Ocean inadvertently weaken the Mamluks and help the Ottoman conquest of Egypt.

The present volume is far from being an attempt to revive imperialist history. Nor indeed, we suspect, would Furber approve of such an aim. It can, however, be seen as an effort to redress the balance a little. The basic intent is neither to vilify nor to ignore the early Europeans in Asia but rather to place them, in several areas and several times, in a correct perspective and see them as operating, successfully or otherwise, in the context of this time and place—not as the progenitors of predestined imperialism. The result is a kaleidoscope of different impacts and experiences. C. R. Boxer writes on the failure of missionaries in China; Sinnappah Arasaratnam describes the mixed success of the Dutch in Malaya; I discuss the similarly varied experiences of the Portuguese in western India. Peter Marshall's essay, however, is written in the context of growing British influence in Bengal. Joseph Jerome Brennig's contribution describes the varied success of the Dutch and British in their attempt to import a European form of commercial organization into an Asian economy. Om Prakash's careful study shows exactly how the Dutch influenced trade from Bengal, while Ashin Das Gupta demonstrates how little impact the Europeans had on Gujarati trade to the Red Sea.

Many of the essays in this volume are not even concerned with success or failure in any imperial sense. Rather, they describe Europeans in Asia at particular times: Europeans who make or lose money, who are prejudiced against Asians or admire their culture, who in commercial matters work with them or try to supplant them. Here later dominion, or value judgments in general, are not important. Europeans are simply living in Asia, and working, with varying degrees of success. None of us would deny that in many, perhaps most, areas of human life at this time in Asia the Europeans had little or no impact; but by the same token none of us see any need to deny them such success and influence as they did have. In fact, historians concerned primarily with the activities of colonial powers and Europeans should be able to cooperate with the historian writing on areas of Asia and levels of Asian society where the European presence was slight. We ignore each other at our peril: the two schools should not be separate or hostile but rather symbiotic.

The problem of changes over time is closely related to these reflections. In broad terms the degree of European influence is best depicted by a curve which rises slowly (the sixteenth century), then declines a little (the seventeenth century), rises again but still slowly (the eighteenth century), and finally rises increasingly steeply (the nineteenth century). This variation apparently has contributed to faulty assessments of the European impact. It is pointless to deny that the Iberian powers were important in some areas in the sixteenth century. The Portuguese did affect Asian trade in spices, did tax most of Gujarat's external trade in the century, did convert thousands of people to Christianity, and did change decisively the balance of power on the Malabar coast. The Spanish did conquer most of the Philippines and did convert most of the Filipinos, as well as many Japanese. These are facts. Yet they need to be handled with caution. First, Iberian activities did not affect most Asians most of the time. Second, these were not unidirectional European actions taken in a vacuum. In the Philippines, let alone in Japan, Christianity was extensively modified even while it triumphed. In western India the Portuguese had to cooperate with, as well as oppress, the wealthy traders of Gujarat. In the spice trade the Portuguese, for all their efforts, succeeded only in modifying, not replacing, the patterns by which Asian spices reached Europe. In the Philippines Spanish rule did little to change authority relations; it simply added an upper level to an existing structure.

Some day these impacts may be measured, but in the meantime it is our impression that these Iberian activities, limited though they were, constituted more of a European impact than did the total of European activities in the seventeenth century in Asia. The Spanish vegetated; the Portuguese declined. Certainly their influence was less than it had been. Yet the incoming British and Dutch, and later French and Danes, had different objectives and faced different conditions. For this century in most areas they merged into existing networks, both political and commercial, and were in no way remarkable. This development seems to mark a decline in European influence. It was only as their bases back in Europe changed, especially in Britain, and as political conditions in some areas of Asia were transformed by events having little to do with Europeans, that this situation changed in the second half of the eighteenth century. From this time European influence expanded. But this influence was far from being the same in all places; nor was it equal on all levels of society; nor, even in the nineteenth century, was it unidirectional.

This curve seems to be closely related to Asian rather than European conditions: indeed it now appears almost predictable. Iberian success in the sixteenth century came in the northern Philippines, the most underdeveloped area of coastal Asia, and in the field of sea trade, a matter of no concern to most Asian rulers. Further expansion does not come until further soft areas appear: in the eighteenth century this means primarily the decline of the Mughal empire in India and growing weakness in the states of Java. But in the nineteenth century the pattern changes. Now Asian decline is not necessary. Europe is moving fast and no Asian state can advance enough to avoid being disadvantaged by this change in positions.

The essays in this volume bring out the complex nature of Asian-European contact before dominion. The spheres in which this contact took place were largely dictated by the reasons for the European presence in Asia. The two great areas were trade and religion. Under the rubric "religion" should be included intellectual contacts, for these were largely concerned with European discoveries of Asian religion. The balance between trade and religion shifted from place to place and time to time, but clearly for the Dutch and English, and usually the French, trade was the main concern. For the two Iberian powers, Europe's pioneers in Asia, the balance was more even. "Christians and spices" hardly explains why the Portuguese came to India late in the fifteenth century, yet at the least both strands were there and were important. Nor is it entirely correct to see religion as merely providing a sacral coating on the hard and fundamental economic motivation. Most Portuguese were God-fearing, did try to follow their religion as they saw it, and could be swayed by appeals from their priests. A similar blend was evident further east in the Philippines, the first and until the late eighteenth century the largest European colony in Asia. The Spanish conquest of two-thirds of the modern republic was no doubt again part religious and part economic in motivation, yet even after it became clear that the crown was not going to make money from this most distant possession, the islands were retained, partly for prestige but more because no Most Catholic ruler could abandon a Christian colony.

Two of the essays in this volume address themselves to questions of religious and intellectual contact in the eighteenth century. Rosane Rocher's study of N. B. Halhed's life and poetry concludes that "through the vicissitudes of a checkered career, two constants remained unchallenged: his interest in Hinduism and his devotion to Hastings." That Halhed's verse seems to have been almost obsessed with Hinduism is entirely typical of the late eighteenth century. Those few Europeans who were interested in Asian intellectual achievements were almost all preoccupied exclusively with Asian religion. Nor is this predilection to be wondered at. What, they thought, could Asian science, laws, and philosophy teach people reared in a culture which was producing scientific and industrial revolutions? Occasionally other areas of inquiry, notably legal systems, were studied, but solely to improve the effectiveness of European rule. Religion was the area where intellectual contact took place. Thus we have Halhed's curious poems, which in Rocher's words demonstrate his "continuing captivation with Hinduism" and are one example of a "common preoccupation" in the late eighteenth century: the "blending of Christian and Hindu myths."

Halhed was of course not a missionary, nor even an evangelical; his attitude to Hinduism was one of lively interest more than anything else. True, he condemned popular late-eighteenth-century Hinduism, but only because it deviated from the true religion of the Vedas. Strip away the grotesque accretions and one had a most admirable religion. But such was obviously not the attitude of the Roman Catholic missionaries who had come to Asia specifically to convince non-Christians of the errors of their ways and convert them to the only true religion.

Yet conversion did not always mean partnership: at times it seems that even to priests an Asian Christian was to be considered more Asian than Christian. Here in fact we meet a particularly disagreeable and dishonest form of the racism to which Furber referred and which has recently been the object of numerous studies. Those of C. R. Boxer are outstanding. His essay in the present volume describes what European missionaries in China thought of as partnership— "the horse and rider, with the white man as rider." It is clear from Boxer's essay that many pious and intelligent men were denied ordination in China simply because they were Chinese: after 150 years of missionary effort less than 5 percent of the priests serving in China were Chinese. Given the usefulness, and devotion, of those who were ordained, and of the lay catechists, it could be argued that the church really deserved to fail to convert China to Catholicism.

The European preoccupation with trade in Asia was evident throughout this period and in every part of the continent where Europeans penetrated. At the state level, we note the massive Portuguese attempt in the sixteenth century to take over all Asian trade in spices and to control and tax all other trade. This effort failed, but it demonstrates clearly the interests and intentions of the Portuguese. Not for nothing was their ruler during the period of their greatest success in Asia, Dom Manuel (1495–1521), called by his French neighbor the Grocer King. Similarly, in the Philippines the colony's economic lifeline, the celebrated Manila galleon which for over two hundred years plied between Manila and Acapulco, was a state undertaking. And again on the governmental level, the late-starting French trading activities were much more subordinate to the state than were the Dutch and English trading companies.

The English and the Dutch, whose activities in Asia were directed by trading companies, were of course even more focused on trade. Indeed, missionary activities were discounted and discouraged, for anything which might upset the natives could hinder trade. Not only religion was subordinated to trade by these two companies; politics were too. Consequently trade was protected by whatever policy seemed expedient: at times craven submission, as in Japan; at times defiance and armed attack, as in Java.

Among individual Europeans, trade continued to be

dominant. Hence the sizable, and for the companies delete-rious, private trade of both English and Dutch employees of the trading companies. Hence the extensive trading activi-ties of the missionary orders, especially the Jesuits (but here the secular and sacred were inextricably mixed, for they claimed they needed trading profits to finance their mis-sions). Hence the massive investments in the Cambay trade fleet and the Acapulco galleon by the European inhabitants of Goa and Manila.

Indeed, in this prenational period for many individuals trade was more important than one's country. While Spain and Portugal were united, from 1580 to 1640, trade be-tween their colonial possessions was prohibited. This ban, however, did little to stop trade between Spanish Manila and Portuguese Macao. As regards sixteenth-century India, my essay in this volume offers several examples of Portu-guese—officials, private individuals, even priests—engaging in trade with an enemy of the Portuguese state.

This paramount interest in trade and commerce is re-flected in several of the essays in this volume. My study is not centrally concerned with economics, but it does show the Portuguese in sixteenth-century western India engaged wholeheartedly in commercial activities. Das Gupta's study is particularly important in the context of the earlier discus-sion of European "impacts." He describes brilliantly the organization of the massive Gujarati trade to the Red Sea in the first quarter of the eighteenth century. The Dutch and British trading companies, even after a century in Surat, were unable to compete with the Gujaratis on this critical route. The Europeans could trade successfully in products the Gujaratis were not interested in, notably spices and cof-fee. But in the paramount trade, that in cotton cloth, they got nowhere in this period. Gujarati trade declined in the early eighteenth century, however, for reasons having noth-ing to do with the Europeans. Das Gupta finds the decline to be primarily a result of political instability in the Yemen and in Gujarat. In terms of our earlier analysis, this instability created a new "soft area" in an economic sense, and the Europeans were later able to move in and fill what was essentially a vacuum. Just as the British conquest of India was predicated on Mughal decline, so was a flourishing European trade to the Red Sea consequent on a decline in the effectiveness of Gujarati traders. Europeans took advantage of, but did not cause, these political and economic declines.

Prakash's detailed study investigates the impact of Dutch activities on trade from Bengal in the later seventeenth century. He shows that the Dutch and other Europeans did modify considerably the organization of trade from India. Yet in terms of volume and direction his analysis of trade between Bengal and Southeast Asia shows that the Dutch had rather little effect. Trade on this route conducted by Mughal officials declined, but for reasons which apparently had nothing to do with the Dutch. Indian merchant trade, however, remained rather stable; possibly an increase would have occurred were it not for Dutch competition and their passport policy. Overall it is difficult to see any qualitative change as a result of Dutch activities to 1720.

Arasaratnam's essay deals with the same European power, The Netherlands, but in a different area and a later period. Here we see the Dutch behaving much more forcefully: trade is now supported, in a typical late eighteenth-century fashion, by military and political activities. In Malaya in the second half of the eighteenth century the Dutch were faced with a changed situation consequent on the development of the Chinese tea trade, increased English trade between eastern India and Malaya and the rise of the Bugis in Johore. They responded with a political and military offensive which left them more involved in the peninsula, though not always successfully. Thus despite Dutch efforts, British trade and interest in the area increased greatly, culminating in the acquisition of Penang Island in 1786. In response to this partial British success the Dutch engaged in some fundamental reflecting on their trade policies, which foreshadowed changes made early in the nineteenth century after the end of their trading company. But the weakness of the Dutch East India Company in the late eighteenth century, coupled with British rivalry and the resilience of several Malay powers, blocked major Dutch territorial expansion in Malaya.

These essays by Prakash and Arasaratnam illustrate the mechanisms of European commercial policies in Asia and describe the lengths to which European powers would go to safeguard their trade. Indeed, it appears that territorial expansion was prevented not by lack of interest but by lack of means in the face of declining local strength and inter-European rivalry. In these state-level activities there is scant evidence of partnership between Asian and European quasi states. But among individual merchants, or groups of merchants, there is cooperation, accommodation, and mutual interaction. Brennig's study is a case history of the Dutch and English attempt to create joint-stock companies among the native merchants of Coromandel. His conclusions demonstrate fully the complexity of this sort of interaction. To help their own trading ventures these two European companies tried to import a new, but for them advantageous, method of commercial organization. Their success was limited, even in those sectors of the Coromandel economy where they were most influential. This limited success, however, was apparently not a result of simple lack of enterprise on the part of Coromandel's merchants. For some of them the joint-stock form involved commercial disadvantages; for all of them it clashed with certain basic values in their society. Not for the first time, and certainly not for the last, did European forms not fit precisely in an Asian environment.

Marshall's study of masters and banians in eighteenth-century Calcutta provides another, and fascinating, illustration of cooperation and mutual benefit in the economic sphere. Everyone knows that these things happened: Marshall gives us a detailed case study that tells us why, when, and how. From his essay it becomes clear that a banian engaged in personal service to a European was much more than a servant: the relationship was really a commercial one based on mutual interest and profit. A major aspect of Marshall's study is his depiction of continuity in most parts of this master-banian relation throughout the eighteenth century, a continuity which was disrupted by nineteenth-century commercial changes but not by the political conquest of Bengal by Britain in the second half of the eighteenth century.

We hope that the contribution of this volume will be to facilitate a more accurate picture of Europeans in Asia before dominion. Furber contributed greatly here, and in a sense all our essays constitute elaborations or footnotes to his work. Yet we see this preimperial period as one in which much remains to be done, for there are still problems, large and small. Prakash, for example, confesses himself unable to explain why the trading activities of Mughal officials declined late in the seventeenth century. The explanation could tell us much about the resources of these nobles in this period and thus contribute to the ongoing debate on the decline of their empire. Brennig's essay centers on an issue of major concern for economic historians. Given a sophisticated merchant community, ample capital, and some rise in demand, why did manufacturing techniques in seventeenth-century India fail to change or even, by and large, fail to take account of new methods introduced by the Europeans? Moreover, the whole problem of different European reactions to different Asians needs more work. Why, for example, were the Portuguese more brutal and more high-handed than any other European group while at the same time they had a greater cultural and social impact on Asia than their seventeenth-century supplanters? Finally, Das Gupta in this volume and elsewhere has made impressively well-documented claims concerning the deleterious influence of political instability on merchant prosperity. His claims seem to be unanswerable; what we need now are studies of political and military constraints on trade at times when Asian empires were apparently strong and stable. The seventeenth-century European travel literature makes much of the nobles' oppression of merchants and the insecurity of trade routes. Even so, merchants suffered more interference in the eighteenth century in India: there seems to be an opportunity here for a quantified comparative study. The list of topics deserving research in this period could be extended almost indefinitely.

And this field is of crucial importance. By itself it constitutes a huge and colorful arena in which were played out a vast variety of contacts between many groups of Asians and Europeans. Of equal significance, historians of colonial rule in Asia, and of indigenous responses to this rule, need a firm understanding of the immediately preceding period as a baseline for their work. We hope we have contributed to such an understanding.

Corruption and Corsairs in Sixteenth-Century Western India: A Functional Analysis

M. N. Pearson

Any historian writing about any society at any time is faced with the problem of interpreting the past in its own terms rather than through twentieth-century eyes. Western historians writing on Asia have two other difficulties to contend with. First, any Asian society is demonstrably more different from any western society than is, say, English compared with Spanish society. For a westerner writing on Asia the task of getting inside the area is thus apparently much more difficult than if one were to study another western area. Second, until recently western scholars specializing in Asia were all too often fellow citizens of colonial rulers in some part of the area. This colonial legacy, not to mention current neocolonial attitudes, simply aggravates the first problem, which is itself formidable enough.

Perhaps, however, we Asianists really have an advantage over our colleagues working on colonial America or Tudor England. For them it is all too treacherously easy to find "nationalism" and other modern phenomena, for they are dealing with societies demonstrably rather similar to those in which they live. But the first thing we learn when we start to study Asia is that it is definitely, indeed apparently totally, different. Language, people, geography, culture: everything is strange. Only the most uncouth and slipshod historian can pretend to find "democracy" in ancient India or "feudalism" in the Muslim period (though such discoveries have, regrettably, been made). Thus in theory, though lamentably not always in practice so far, it should be easier to start our studies with a clean slate and a mind uncluttered with extraneous and deceptive cultural baggage.[1]

Historians of South Asia have so far been remarkably unselfconscious about these problems.[2] They are content to write on, unconcerned to elucidate and analyze the assumptions and prejudices which must color their work.[3] The purpose of this essay is not, however, to name names but to suggest an underlying unity in the historiographical problems we face. Every historian is faced with preconceptions stemming from the basic fact that the scholar is situated in the present but writing about the past. Western historians of Asia have in addition to avoid cultural biases. But the basic necessity is to see past societies, whether more or less culturally different, in their own terms and to analyze groups and practices in terms of their functions in such societies. What follows is an attempt at such a functional analysis of a practice, "corruption," and a group, "corsairs," in sixteenth-century western India. The treatment of the first in older historical writing shows a failure to see the past in its own terms; the treatment of the second reflects both this and also cultural bias.

Everyone is against corruption today. The word itself is immediately recognized as having derogatory connotations that the official of whom it is used is not fit to hold public office. Late nineteenth-century English writers on the Portuguese empire in India all pointed to the existence of "corruption" in the Portuguese administration as one important reason for the decline of this empire. F. C. Danvers put it like this: "A laxity of Government, and a general corruption amongst the servants of the State, in which each one, regardless of the public interests, sought but his own benefit and the accumulation of wealth, only too certainly prepared the way for the downfall of Portuguese rule in India."[4] R. S. Whiteway, W. W. Hunter, and a little later Vincent A. Smith all agreed.[5] These writers did adduce other reasons for the Portuguese decline: the two favorites were mixed marriages, which produced "a languid population of half-breeds," and "the grip of religious superstition."[6] But a more recent writer, the American F. C. Lane, plumps for corruption as the sole cause of what he regards as a Portuguese decline in the later sixteenth century.[7]

Danvers, Whiteway, Smith, and Hunter were all associated with the English Indian Civil Service or its affiliates. All were oriented to what seemed to them to be its higher standards, or at least ideals, as compared to the sixteenth-century Portuguese Indian administration. This outlook is made perfectly explicit by Whiteway and Hunter. The former opined that Portugal lacked "that official class which is the backbone of efficient civil administration" and pointedly praised "Albuquerque's business habits—habits that are now, as they were then, the right ones for an administrator."[8] Hunter, in his panegyric to the British empire in India, pointed out that Portugal "represented the reactionary spirit of medievalism, as against the modern methods of the Protestant nations."[9]

These observations obviously refer to the temporal problem of historical writing. The tendency to find the roots of the present in the past—and to condemn the past if it does not live up to the ideals of the present—has, since 1931, often been known as "whiggishness." Herbert Butterfield's classic description of this tendency applies exactly to the work of these four British historians: the tendency to "emphasize certain principles of progress in the past and to produce a story which is the ratification, if not the glorification, of the present."[10]

What were the standards by which a sixteenth-century

Portuguese administrator in India felt he should regulate his conduct? He was obviously not a member of a modern bureaucracy in the Weberian sense.[11] The difference is seen particularly in the method of selection for office and the whole conception of what holding an office entailed. Appointments to high office were made by the king of Portugal; those to the lower ones were made by his governors or captains in India. They were made on strictly personal grounds, not on the basis of suitability or training. There were two main grounds. First was past meritorious service, usually in a military capacity, either by an appointee or his or her forebears. Thus the daughter of a deserving *fidalgo* ("noble"—literally "son of a somebody") would receive from the king as her dowry an office which would go to her successful suitor. Similarly, the great historian Diogo do Couto received his position as official chronicler not so much because he had demonstrated literary ability as because he had served in the Portuguese fleets in India for several years. That he emerged as a productive and skillful chronicler says little for the way in which he was selected.

The second criterion, used increasingly as the finances of the state deteriorated, was purchase: offices were put up for sale to the highest bidder. Here also the basis of selection was personal; in this case the determining factor was wealth rather than past service. Training or skill was not considered, although an informal scheme restricted those who could bid. A non-*fidalgo*, however wealthy, could not bid for the captaincy of a prestigious fort such as Diu.

Not only the selection for office, but also the conception of office, was governed by personal factors. An appointee's loyalties were not to an impersonal conception of an office in which he was to discharge certain functions guided by established rules. Rather, Portuguese officials of all grades treated their offices as a personal service to the king who had appointed them. They owed obedience and loyalty to him personally or to his deputy; so long as the king or governor was satisfied there were no other criteria to be met.

Thus what is at issue here, and what has been obscured by the whiggishness of Lane and the four earlier British writers, is not a "good" administration juxtaposed with a "corrupt" one so much as a modern bureaucracy contrasted with a premodern one. At least in aspiration, the nineteenth-century Indian Civil Service conformed to Weber's definition of a "modern officialdom" characterized essentially by the "abstract regularity of the execution of authority, which is a result of the demand for 'equality before the law' in the personal and functional sense."[12] On the other hand, the Portuguese Indian administration was, as noted, far from any ideal of abstract regularity; it was governed, both as regards appointment and performance, mainly by personal factors.

A Portuguese official was appointed to a post as a person, and the post became in effect his property during his tenure. Any distinction between public and private funds was blurred. The bulk of his salary came not in cash from the capital of Goa but in the form of various privileges and perquisites, such as the right to collect a certain tax or to trade on a particular route.[13] These rights were laid down in the official letter of appointment, but they shaded off into other customary rights—such as the privilege of being allowed to demand a gratuity before issuing a *cartaz* (a pass for a merchant ship)—which were unspecified but hallowed by tradition. These unofficial but tacitly accepted perquisites in turn merged into outright illegal exactions and abuses, notably demanding forced loans from local traders and trading in goods which were meant to be royal monopolies. The perquisites and the unofficial privileges were regarded by king and governor as unexceptional, but they did try to limit the abuses.

This system of payment was reflected in the prices paid for the various offices. The posts were seen as property from which the holder expected to make a profit, and he thus was willing to pay much more for a lucrative post than for one with few opportunities for pickings, even if the status of the latter was higher than that of the former. In a sale of 1618 more than twice as much was paid for the post of judge of the Goa customhouse as for the captaincy of the whole city; the high status attached to the captaincy could not compete with the perquisites, legal and otherwise, available to a customs official. The post of captain of Diu was worth five times and that of Hurmuz fourteen times that of Goa, for these two forts were notoriously profitable.[14]

The prevailing attitude was well expressed by the *fidalgo* who visited a religious house to say good-bye to the inmates before leaving to take up an appointment as captain of a fort. One of the clerics counseled him, "Be content with what is yours, favor the poor, and do justice." The *fidalgo* retorted that he fully intended to get all he could, as did all the others, "because I am not going to my fort for any other reason than to come back rich."[15]

The fuzzy distinction between public and private property can be illustrated by many instances in the sixteenth century. All Indian ships trading out of the Gulf of Cambay in Gujarat were meant to call at the Portuguese fort of Diu to pay customs duties and get a Portuguese pass. Sometimes, however, a Portuguese captain would supplement his salary by taking a bribe from an Indian trader, in return exempting his ship from having to call at Diu.[16] In one particularly flagrant case a Portuguese sea captain used his fleet to protect such a transgressing Indian trader not only from pirates but also from other more law-abiding Portuguese ships.[17] Yet this Portuguese was simply protecting the man who provided a presumably substantial part of his salary.

The most common means of supplementing an income was forced trade: a local merchant would be forced to buy a product he did not want, and at a high price, or sell to the captain or other officials at a low price. Thus one of the official perquisites of the captain of Diu was the right to trade on a monopolistic basis to East Africa. The main item in the return cargo was ivory. This the captain handed over to the head of the local Gujarati merchants, who in turn forced other merchants to buy it.[18] Other merchants were forced to carry goods free on their ships, sometimes to places where they did not want to go. Forced loans were also frequent, sometimes secured by means of arbitrary arrests.[19]

Complaints of these abuses in Diu date from the 1540s, but they do seem to increase in frequency late in the century and into the seventeenth century. A captain of the Portuguese fort of Hurmuz in the 1550s was proud of having made only 40,000 xerafins during his tenure. This was in fact a very substantial sum, but later captains made up to seven times more than this.[20] The apparent general increase is no doubt a consequence of better documentation for this period, but it is to be expected that abuses would increase as Portuguese power declined. Diu's revenues, for example, fell sharply in the seventeenth century thanks to Dutch and English competition. The captains of Diu were more and more driven to abuses to make the profits they felt they should gain from their position.

Dubious practices were legion. In the later years of the century captains of forts began taking artillery from the forts for use in their own ships.[21] Throughout the century there are records of Portuguese ships seizing and plundering native ships which had Portuguese passes.[22] An account of the revenues of Goa for 1545 ended by saying: "This is what Goa yielded last year, apart from what was stolen by the officials."[23] A year later an official complained that he had been trying to get opium for the king's trade but had been hindered by the fact that the Portuguese officials in charge of trade seemed more interested in sending this product to Gujarat (with which state Portugal was at war at the time) and other places than in obtaining it for the king.[24]

In 1566 another official represented various abuses to the governor and for his pains was forced to flee Goa and seek refuge "among the Hindus and lax Christians of Bardês."[25] Perhaps Diogo do Couto best summed up the state of the administration late in the century when he wrote: "For the king's property to increase it should pass through few hands, and the fewer hands of officials it has contact with the greater will be its increase."[26]

Such instances of what today would be called "corruption" can usually be explained by the confusion in most officials' minds between public and private property. Such confusion was part of every administration at this time: the distinction has been made explicit, and an attempt made to enforce it, only in the last two centuries. Why then the contemporary criticism just quoted? The explanation is that this criticism was of abuses ("abusos," not the modern "corrução") of the system. The governors and chroniclers were not complaining of corruption in the modern sense (for they were not twentieth-century men) but of people who went beyond the bounds of custom in taking perquisites. To take the cannon needed for the defense of an important fort was clearly going too far. So was the plunder of a native ship with a Portuguese pass or accepting a bribe for exemption from customs payments. Indeed, according to one contemporary the tyranny of the Portuguese captain of Diu caused a frontal attack on the fort by the neighboring state of Gujarat: "The captain of the fort caused the siege of Diu because he behaved so badly to the King of Gujarat and the local Muslims that if they had been Christians they would have had good cause to become Muslims."[27] Such abuses were regarded as bad because they could lead to Indian retaliation or increased attempts to evade Portuguese trade control. No one complained because the captaincy of Hurmuz sold for fourteen times that of Goa: the fact of greater perquisites in Hurmuz was part of the system and appears remarkable only today.[28]

There remains the question of the effectiveness of such an administrative system. "Abusos" were clearly dysfunctional, and the governors complained about them, but the whole network of perquisites and influence, of a shadowy line between public and private property, *was* the system: "corruption" was functional in sixteenth-century terms. The Portuguese Indian administration was not ideal. It was probably less efficient than a modern bureaucratic structure, or certain other sixteenth-century systems, but it is a solecism to criticize the Portuguese administration for its failure to fit an ideal nineteenth and twentieth-century model.

If "corruption" in the sixteenth century was less simple than the modern use of the word implies, so also was "piracy" in the southwestern coastal area of India called Malabar. Natives of Malabar who attempted to trade outside the Portuguese control system, and anyone else in the area who opposed them, were described by the Portuguese as "cossarios" or "Malavares"; the terms were usually interchangeable.[29] A "cossario" (in modern Portuguese "corsário") is, strictly, a corsair.

Modern Portuguese historians continue to use "corsário" to describe anyone who did not submit to Portuguese control of their trade in Malabar."[30] There is no way of knowing exactly what they mean by this term; presumably something between pirate and privateer is implied. More confusion appears when we consider the doyen of foreign scholars of the Portuguese empire (and my fellow contributor to this volume), C. R. Boxer. In a Portuguese work he used "corsário," in an early English work he called them "pirates," and in his standard history of the Portuguese colonial empire he consistently uses "corsair."[31] Again there is some ambiguity, but clearly Boxer does not regard these people as simply pirates.

Two Indian nationalist writers, K. M. Panikkar and O. K. Nambiar, reverse the coin. Nambiar, in his book on the Kunjalis, the admirals of the zamorins of Calicut (the main opponents of the Portuguese in the sixteenth century in Malabar), glorifies these guerrilla warriors and regards them as patriots, even nationalists. The title of the first edition of his work nicely sums up his revisionist aim: *Portuguese Pirates and Indian Seamen*.[32] Panikkar foreshadowed Nambiar's findings and stressed that the Kunjalis were not pirates: they were auxiliaries of the zamorins.[33]

None of these writers attempts to discriminate. One blanket term, whether "corsário," "corsair," "pirate," or "admirals of the Zamorin," is used. All these writers follow the sixteenth-century Portuguese accounts in making the Malabaris a monolithic group. All use the same sources; the differing results depend on author's bias. But these Malabaris were undefined only to their contemporary European observers. Grouping them under one (usually derogatory) label is an example of both whiggishness and cultural bias, for in their own, Indian, terms these people were not homogeneous. In functional terms some were pirates, some were corsairs, some were guerrilla warriors, and many were inoffensive traders.

What was the sixteenth-century context in which these Malabaris operated? As soon as they got to India the Portuguese tried to monopolize all trade in spices. Throughout the century and later a stream of decrees and instructions from Portugal and Goa insisted that all trade in spices was reserved entirely for the Portuguese crown and its agents. If this monopoly could be enforced, the Muslim powers in India, the Red Sea, and Egypt would lose their most profitable trade while the Portuguese could buy cheap in Asia and sell dear in Europe.

This basic policy, in effect a codification of the prohibitions of the previous twenty years, was laid down by the Portuguese king D. Manuel in 1520 and repeated with minor variations throughout the century:

We forbid and order that no captain, factor, secretary of a factory, or any other official concerned with trade or justice, or any

other person of whatever rank or status he may be, whether
Christian or Muslim or any other, trade, or cause to be traded,
or transport, pepper, cloves, ginger, cinnamon, mace, nutmeg,
lacre, silk, or borax, nor in any way buy any of these things.[34]

Any Portuguese offending was to lose all his property and
salaries; a Muslim was to be imprisoned after forfeiting all
his goods and the ship in which the forbidden article was
found.[35] Occasionally a closely regulated trade within Asia
was permitted, and puppet rulers sometimes were concili-
ated by being allowed to trade in pepper in limited quantities. Further, the crews of ships returning to Portugal were
paid partly by being allowed to take small quantities of
spices with them. Nevertheless, Portugal did try to reserve
all pepper trade within Asia to agents of the king and to
restrict the transport of pepper to Europe to Portuguese
ships sailing via the Cape of Good Hope.[36]

This policy was never completely enforced.[37] There was
much evasion of the Portuguese system, and in some cases
there was open armed opposition to their pretensions. In
this opposition the zamorins of Calicut, on the Malabar
coast, were prominent, for Calicut had been the great Indian center for the spice trade in the fifteenth century. If
Portugal could enforce its monopoly, Calicut would be
ruined while Cochin, formerly subordinate to Calicut and
in the sixteenth century a Portuguese puppet, would prosper. The zamorins thus had good economic reasons to resist,
and in any case it seems that they simply found Portuguese
demands to be unfair. In 1502 Vasco da Gama demanded
that the zamorin expel from Calicut all Muslims from Cairo
and the Red Sea. The zamorin refused—"for it was un-
thinkable that he expel 4,000 households of them, who
lived in Calicut as natives, not foreigners, and who had contributed great profits to his Kingdom."[38]

Not only the rulers of Calicut, but also her local merchants and traders, resisted the Portuguese claims. The Portuguese wanted to monopolize the trade in Malabar pepper,

but this was the main product of the area. The Portuguese forbade trade to Aden and the Red Sea, but this was the main route sailed from Calicut. The Portuguese attacked merchants from these two places, but these were the main purchasers of Malabar's products. The Portuguese forced contracts at fixed low prices on the Malabar rulers for the supply of pepper, but other merchants offered much higher prices. The Portuguese later in the sixteenth ccntury treated all ships from Calicut as pirates and sank them on sight, even ships carrying only provisions, and sometimes ships with Portuguese passes. What choice did the merchants of Calicut, and their ruler, have but to resist?[39]

Commercially, this resistance took the form of continuing to trade in pepper. The trade direct to the Red Sea from Calicut was blocked more or less effectively by the Portuguese, and the great foreign Muslim merchants of Calicut had by 1513 moved out to safer parts, such as the Red Sea, or Hurmuz, Gujarat, and Vijayanagar.[40] There the big traders sat in safety and waited for the pepper to come to them. Reports of direct trade between Calicut and the Red Sea are few, and they disappear completely during the 1530s.[41] From this time the pepper went to the Red Sea from Kanara, north of Malabar, from the Bay of Bengal, and from Achin in Sumatra.[42]

It was easy enough for the great foreign merchants to move out and let others bring the pepper to them and for the Red Sea traders to get pepper from other production areas. The local merchants of Calicut had no such alternatives, but even so they had little difficulty in acquiring pepper in Malabar. They were helped by Portugal's lack of control over the areas where pepper was grown. In Malabar the Portuguese exercised a tenuous control over the coastal area through their puppet rajas, but none at all inland. Given that the Portuguese tried to pay low prices and paid one-quarter of the price in goods (usually copper) for which the growers had little use, it is not difficult to understand how easily the "illegal" traders found their cargoes. In 1520 a Portuguese official asked an important trader why he had stopped bringing pepper to the coast and selling it to the Portuguese. He replied: "Because I find that there are many people who beg me to sell it, and pay the price I want in my own house, without troubling me to come to the coast."[43]

The Portuguese were dependent for their supplies on the petty rajas of the producing areas and the merchants who operated between the growers and the exporters. To conciliate the rajas they paid them regular pensions, but these were not always sufficient to ensure their goodwill and cooperation. In 1549 the raja of the main production area, appropriately called the "king of pepper" by the Portuguese, decided to retaliate against the insults and abuses to which he was subjected by the raja of Cochin. His method was to ally with Portugal's traditional enemy, the zamorin of Calicut. As a result the Portuguese were involved in four years of war in the area, and during this time it was very difficult for them to get pepper to send to Portugal.[44]

The growers of the pepper were mostly Hindus, but the initial purchasers were St. Thomas (Nestorian) Christians. They, however, were too afraid of the Portuguese and their Inquisition to bring the pepper to the coast, so they usually sold it to the Muslim traders who traditionally handled this trade. The Muslims sold it to the Portuguese in Cochin and other coastal forts and also to other exporters. Apparently later in the century some of the Christians were persuaded to bring the pepper themselves, but at least for the first half of the century the Portuguese were largely dependent for their pepper cargoes on their supposed inveterate enemies, the Muslims. These Muslims often rubbed salt in the wound by supplying pepper that was dirty or wet.[45]

That the Portuguese got poor-quality pepper was, however, due more to their own bad management than to the malice of Muslim traders. Ideally, the capital to buy pepper should have arrived on the ships from Portugal late in the year. Since the pepper was harvested in December or January, the Portuguese could have used their capital to make purchases at leisure throughout the next year, buying only clean dry pepper at times when the market was low. About fifteen months after the capital had arrived, the pepper would be loaded on the next year's ships and sent off to Portugal. In fact the Portuguese were never able to get this far ahead. The capital arrived late in the year, and the Portuguese had then frantically to buy whatever pepper was available, get it loaded, and dispatch the ships in time for them to round the Cape of Good Hope before the end of the monsoon. A succession of letters to the king throughout the century described this unsatisfactory arrangement and urged him to have the capital available for the whole year, but the king could never afford to do this. He had to have his capital, in the form of pepper, back in Lisbon as soon as possible. As a result, his officials were reduced to borrowing money from local Portuguese merchants, the city of Cochin, and the raja of Craganore.[46] When the capital arrived, a hard-pressed governor would often take part of it for military necessities, despite the king's frequent prohibitions of such conduct.[47]

One final factor should be mentioned which again decreased the control of the Portuguese crown over the pepper production of Malabar: the tendency of both Portuguese officials and private Portuguese merchants to indulge in the highly profitable "illegal" trade themselves. In 1519 the governor left for a cruise in the Red Sea. Seizing their chance, the remaining officials in India reportedly sent cargoes of pepper north to Cambay in ships belonging to the "pirates" of Malabar.[48] A year later a native official of the raja of Cochin told the king of Portugal that Portuguese officials bought pepper in Cochin for their own illegal private trade at prices higher than the fixed official price at which it was bought for the king. Now the local merchants wanted to sell all their pepper at this high price.[49] Other reports of Portuguese and local inhabitants of Portuguese areas trading in pepper, both north to Hurmuz and Cambay, and in southeast Asia, continue throughout the century and later.[50] In the 1630s even clerics, including one of the inquisitors, were accused of such trade.[51]

Once they had the pepper, the local traders who chose to ignore Portuguese trade restrictions had two export routes available: overland to Coromandel and north by sea to Gujarat. The former trade was safe from Portuguese interference, as they had no control over the inland areas of Malabar. Great amounts were transported either by coolie or on bullocks to Coromandel, and from there they were distributed all over eastern India and Bengal. Considerable quantities of this pepper were also taken, especially by Gujaratis, to the Red Sea.[52]

The other route, by sea to Gujarat, was considerably more risky. It was navigated in small, light-oared craft called *paroes*, which could escape up the numerous rivers of the western coast if they were seen by the Portuguese. The Portuguese ships were usually too large to follow them, and it was not always possible to land a party to pursue them or carry out reprisals on their helpers. These traders in fact in the 1520s felt themselves so secure that they would sail north to Gujarat and on the way take mocking potshots at the Portuguese coastal forts. They even sailed tantalizingly close to the cumbersome warships of the dreaded Vasco da Gama, when he was back in India as viceroy in 1524, keeping just out of range and showing complete contempt for his armada. Da Gama, who had a tendency to choler at any time, and was certainly more used to massacring Malabaris than to being laughed at by them, "was scandalized at such disrespect."[53] But the Portuguese were far from being totally ineffective. There are frequent reports of their destroying or at least blockading large numbers of Malabari pepper ships. As one example, in early 1525 they caught fifty-three such ships getting ready to sail and burnt them all.[54]

These Malabari *paroes* sailed in fleets, loaded with pepper and bound for Gujarat, of at times over one hundred sail. The pepper they carried was usually consumed locally in Gujarat and North India. Some was taken to the Red Sea, but as Portuguese patrolling the mouth of the Gulf of Cambay increased in efficiency, once Diu (1535) and Daman (1559) were taken, the Red Sea trade in pepper from Gujarat slackened. It also seems that this tighter control slightly reduced the amount of pepper brought north by the Malabaris; presumably the overland route to Coromandel was substituted. Certainly the pepper which used to go to Gujarat did not later in the century go to the Portuguese, for they took less and less to Europe as the century progressed.[55]

Other Malabaris were not traders resisting an unjust Portuguese attempt to impose a monopoly—they were pirates. Indeed, piracy had been quite widespread in western India in the fifteenth century, both in the Malabar and Gujarat areas.[56] In the next century piracy continued, and it was not confined to western India. The Persian Gulf, for example, was notoriously dangerous.[57] In the Malabar area open piracy—ships attacking on sight all merchant vessels for the purpose of robbing them—continued in the sixteenth century, though it is clear that some of this piracy was created by the Portuguese. Not only did their monopolistic policies leave little outlet for legitimate (in their eyes) trade, but they abused those trying to conform to their system.[58] The most flagrant case of this abuse was an important Cochin merchant who traded to Gujarat with two ships. Although he took Portuguese passes each time, some plunder-hungry Portuguese seized his ships. He then moved to the hostile city of Calicut and became an inveterate enemy of the Portuguese.[59] Piracy, in fact, was often resorted to in despair.

Others called "cossarios" by the Portuguese were really

guerrilla auxiliaries of the zamorins of Calicut. In the first quarter of the sixteenth century these guerrillas often worked hand in glove with the Calicut merchants whom the Portuguese were trying to displace. The merchants financed their ships in return for protection for the merchants' trade ships.[60] Battles between Portuguese ships and those commanded by members of the Kunjali Marakkar family were frequent in the sixteenth century, and this conflict surely was war, not piracy, for the Kunjalis usually worked closely with the zamorins.[61]

In these battles the Portuguese were worsted as often as not. A Jesuit in 1575 said the Malabaris were ''absolute rulers of all the seas of India because of our sins and carelessness, and their power and force is waxing while ours is waning.''[62] Portuguese ships were afraid to sail alone; another Jesuit said that because of the Malabaris the voyage from Goa to Cochin was more dangerous than that to Portugul.[63] In the early 1580s a letter noted with surprise that the Portuguese fleets had made the western Indian coastline secure against the Malabaris—''an unusual situation.''[64] This amelioration was only temporary. In the late sixteenth century all Portuguese ships, and native ships trading within their system, sailed in convoys protected by warships.

Both sides suffered in the continuing Malabar-Portugal warfare, as also did numerous noncombatants, both Portuguese and local. The Portuguese regularly cut down palm trees in enemy areas. This measure was something of a sixteenth-century ultimate weapon, for the tree provided several staple products and it took seven years for a newly planted palm to reach maturity. Most Portuguese captains disdained taking prisoners when they captured a Malabari vessel.[65] On one particularly bloody occasion in 1524 a Portuguese captain returned with his fleet to the city of Goa having captured some Malabari ships. The Portuguese fleet sailed in, ''flying as flags in their masts and spars many hanging Moors, in order to terrorize the enemy and delight the city; and in order that the Kanarese sailors of this fleet might share in the glory, they took the heads of thirty dead Malabaris and twelve Moors who still lived. They were handed over to the fury of the lads of Goa, who stoned them to death.''[66] The Malabaris appear to have responded in kind.[67] A list of Franciscan martyrs shows six killed by Malabaris in the 1550s alone.[68]

Given the large and rather clumsy ships the Portuguese used in the first half of the century, the type of warfare adopted by the zamorin's sailors was very suitable. In 1538 a Portuguese captain told the king how well armed the Malabari *paroes* were and how "150 of them leave from one port and do all the damage they can, and I go after them, and as many again leave from another port and go somewhere else, and do as much damage also, and a man doesn't know which way to turn.''[69] These *paroes* usually returned to shore each night, and they maintained close contact with the people ashore. They posted observers on hills who lit fires when a Portuguese fleet was sighted, so warning the *paroes* at sea. The *paroes* then lowered their masts and rowed up a river until the Portuguese had passed.[70] Later in the century the Portuguese finally built lighter ships called *sanguiceis*.[71] This measure improved the effectiveness of Portuguese patrolling, yet they were at times outwitted still. In 1568 a Portuguese ship closed with an enemy, and the Portuguese all gallantly boarded her. The Malabaris deserted their own ship, swam to the empty Portuguese one, and sailed happily away.[72]

Many others whom the Portuguese indiscriminately called pirates were in fact legitimate traders. To the Portuguese, anyone trading in pepper, or in anything to Calicut in time of war, was a pirate—but these traders were pirates only from the Portuguese viewpoint. The confusion is obvious in the case of those trading in pepper to Gujarat. It is present also in the following account: In 1525 a Portuguese governor attacked "more than 100 war-paroes of the Malabaris which were coming back from Gujarat, whence they had gone loaded with pepper, and they were bringing back rice and other foodstuffs.''[73]

Nevertheless, the distinction between a pirate and a guerrilla fighter or a legitimate trader *was* often blurred. The Portuguese policy of indiscriminate attacks was thus to some extent justified. At times the zamorins disclaimed all responsibility for attacks on the Portuguese, though they did so more because they were at these times threatened by the Portuguese than because the attacks were really carried out without their approval. But the Kunjali Marakkars do seem at times to have operated rather independently, notably in the 1590s.[74] Some traders were not above a little piracy if opportunity offered: in 1530–1531 ''some of the subjects of the Zamorin and others . . . set sail in a fleet of thirty grabs for Gujarat, the object of their voyage being generally trade.''[75] The operative word is ''generally,'' and the subsequent account of their activities sounds suspiciously like piracy. A fair summing up would be as variegated and perhaps as confused as the sixteenth-century situation it described. It would have to admit the existence of considerable piracy in Malabar in the sixteenth century. But it would also have to note that much of this piracy was created by the policies of the Portuguese, while many others whom the Portuguese attacked as pirates were, except in Portuguese eyes, legitimate traders or guerrilla fighters defending Calicut from Portuguese attacks.[76]

The truth, in fact, was a good deal more complex than can be revealed if all seafaring Malabaris are lumped together, whether as corsairs or patriots. Similarly, to describe as corruption all official conduct not fitting an ideal twentieth-century model is to obscure rather than elucidate. To follow the categorizations of the sixteenth-century Portuguese, whether in acceptance or rejection, is to allow oneself to be blinkered by their point of view, distorted as it was in the midst of battle. They indiscriminately saw Malabaris as hostile and outside the system they had set up to control western Indian trade. But the Malabaris did not accept Portuguese pretensions: neither should we. Portuguese officials knew nothing of twentieth-century standards of official conduct: neither should we when we write of these men. Both "corruption" and "corsairs" were complex phenomena. This is clearly revealed when they are seen functioning in their own time and culture.

NOTES

The following abbreviations are used in the notes:

ANTT   Arquivo Nacional da Torre do Tombo, Lisbon.
APOCR   J. H. da Cunha Rivara (ed.), *Archivo Português Oriental* (Nova Goa, 1857–1877), 6 vols. in 10 parts.
Barros João de Barros, *Asia* (Lisbon, 1945–1946), 4 vols.
ANTTCC Corpo Chronologico, ANTT, Lisbon.
Couto   Diogo do Couto, *Da Asia* (Lisbon, 1778–1788), 15 vols.
HAG   Historical Archives of Goa, Panaji, Goa.
LM   "Livros das Monções do Reino," HAG.

In references to the chronicles by Barros, Couto, and Fernão Lopes I have followed the usual custom of quoting década, book, and chapter numbers. Thus Couto VII, i, 8, is Couto, década VII, book i, chapter 8.

1. This paragraph was prompted by J. H. Hexter's observations in *Reappraisals in History* (New York, 1963), especially pp. 201–207.

2. This is not the case for Southeast Asian historiography. For a bibliography of the extensive debate following on from J. C. Van Leur, see David Joel Steinberg (ed.), *In Search of Southeast Asia: A Modern History* (New York, 1971), pp. 441–442. Two excellent studies of the Portuguese chronicles are J. B. Harrison, "Five Portuguese Historians," in *Historians of India, Pakistan and Ceylon*, ed. C. H. Philips (London, 1961), pp. 155–169, and C. R. Boxer, *Three Historians of Portuguese Asia: Barros, Couto and Bocarro* (Macao, 1948).

3. Three exceptions I know of are Robert I. Crane, *A History of South Asia* (Washington, 1973), especially pp. 5–27; K. W. Goonewardena, "Dutch Historical Writing on South Asia," in Philips, *Historians*, pp. 170–182 and especially pp. 180–182 (both these are rather brief in their

discussion of perspective); and B. S. Cohn's provocative "African Models and Indian Histories," in *Realm and Region in Traditional India*, ed. Richard Fox (Durham, N.C., 1977).

4. F. C. Danvers, *The Portuguese in India* (London, 1894), vol. 1, p. xxxix.

5. R. S. Whiteway, *The Rise of Portuguese Power in India* (London, 1899), pp. 174, 324–325; W. W. Hunter, *A History of British India* (London, 1899–1900), vol. 1, p. 176–185; Vincent A. Smith, *The Oxford History of India* (Oxford, 1919), p. 335.

6. Whiteway, p. 13; Danvers, vol. 1, p. xxviii; Smith, p. 335.

7. F. C. Lane, "National Wealth and Protection Costs," in *War as a Social Institution: The Historian's Perspective*, ed. Jesse D. Clarkson and Thomas C. Cochran (New York, 1941), pp. 39–41; F. C. Lane, "The Mediterranean Spice Trade: Further Evidence of Its Revival in the Sixteenth Century," *American Historical Review* 45(1940):589. Few historians today would argue with C. R. Boxer's explanation of the Portuguese decline. He sees it as being primarily a result of the arrival of the better-organized and better-financed Dutch and English in Asia from late in the sixteenth century. See *The Portuguese Seaborne Empire* (London, 1969), pp. 106–119. See also the stimulating analysis in Niels Steensgaard's important book, *Carracks, Caravans, and Companies: The Structural Crisis in the European-Asian Trade in the Early 17th Century* (Copenhagen, 1973). (Also published as *The Asian Trade Revolution of the Seventeenth Century: The East India Companies and the Decline of the Caravan Trade*, Chicago, 1974.) In his view the Portuguese had no chance of success, once they were faced with the competition of the Dutch and British companies, because of the "structural differences" between the Portuguese and the caravan traders on the one hand and the Dutch and the British trading companies on the other.

8. Whiteway, *Rise of Portuguese Power*, pp. 13, 124 fn.

9. Hunter, *History*, vol. 1, p. 317.

10. Herbert Butterfield, *The Whig Interpretation of History* (London, 1931), p. v. More recently Sylvia Thrupp has coined the rather unlovely term "temporal ethnocentrism" to describe basically the same phenomenon. J. H. Hexter reverses the coin in his amusing article "The Historian and His Day" (*Reappraisals*, pp. 1–13), for he claims to know more about early modern Europe than about present-day America and unconsciously takes the perspective of the former when looking at the latter. This is perhaps an ideal perspective for the historian, but for most of us it will remain only an ideal.

11. Max Weber saw "legal domination" as the essential element in a modern state and regarded the development of a modern bureaucracy as

necessary for legal domination to become effective. Several specific characteristics have to be found in a bureaucracy in order for there to exist "a system of legal domination in which the exercise of authority consists in the implementation of enacted norms." For these see Reinhard Bendix, *Max Weber: An Intellectual Portrait* (New York, 1962), p. 424. For a translation of Weber's own words see H. H. Gerth and C. Wright Mills, *From Max Weber: Essays in Sociology* (New York, 1958), pp. 196–204. For an important discussion of the conflict between the ideal of the modern bureaucratic state and the survival of earlier practices in modern Southeast Asia see W. F. Wertheim, "Sociological Aspects of Corruption in Southeast Asia," in *State and Society: A Reader in Comparative Political Sociology,* ed. Reinhard Bendix (Boston, 1968), pp. 561–580. Gunnar Myrdal finds a similar situation prevailing in India today: *Asian Drama* (New York, 1968), vol. 2, pp. 948–950. See also Ralph Braibanti, "Reflections on Bureaucratic Corruption," *Public Administration* 40(1962):357–372. Steensgaard is again interesting on this topic: *Carracks, Caravans and Companies,* especially pp. 19–21, 93–95.

12. Gerth and Mills, *From Max Weber,* p. 224 and generally pp. 196–244.

13. For the scope of these legal perquisites in the 1580s see British Museum Add. MS 28433, ff. 19–74v and 166–173, where are set out the various voyages and other privileges for the captains of most of the forts of India.

14. Arquivo Histórico Ultramarino, Lisbon, "India," caixa 5, account of 15 February 1618.

15. Diogo do Couto, *Dialogo do Soldado Prático* (Lisbon, 1937), p. 14.

16. For example, R. A. de Bulhão Pato (ed.), *Documentos Remettidos da India, ou Livros das Monções* (Lisbon, 1880–1935), vol. 3, pp. 167–168; LM, 12, 44v–45; LM, 28B, 378–378v.

17. Alberto Iria, *Da Navegação Portuguesa no Indico no século XVII* (Lisbon, 1963), p. 84.

18. APOCR, vol. 6, pp. 1250–1251; see also ANTT, "Colecção de São Vicente," vol. 26, ff. 93v–94v.

19. José Wicki, "Duas relações sobre a situação da India Portuguesa nos anos 1568 e 1569," *Studia* 8(1961):177–178; *Studia* 3(1959):75–76; "Provisões dos Vice Reis," HAG, vol. 2, ff. 129–129v; ANTTCC, 1-97-26; APOCR, vol. 3, pp. 105–106, 564–566; Arquivo Histórico Ultramarino, caixa 14, petitions of September to December 1642; *As Gavetas da Torre do Tombo* (Lisbon, 1960–1970), vol. 5, p. 327.

20. Couto, VIII, cap. 1.

21. APOCR, vol. 3, pp. 230, 292; "Provisões, Alvarás e Regimentos," HAG, vol. 2, ff. 276v–277; "Livro Morato," HAG, ff. 253–254.

22. Fernão Lopes de Castanheda, *História do descobrimento e conquista da India pelos Portugueses* (Coímbra, 1924–1933), VI, xxxv; Gaspar Correa, *Lendas da India* (Lisbon, 1858–1864), vol. 2, p. 508; ANTTCC, 1-92-88.

23. *As Gavetas*, vol. 3, p. 213.

24. ANTT, "Colecção de São Lourenço," vol. 4, f. 509. For similar conduct in early seventeenth-century Ceylon see P. Pieris, *Ceylon and the Portuguese, 1505–1658* (Tellippalai, Ceylon, 1920), p. 191.

25. ANTTCC, 1-108-12.

26. Couto, XII, i, 8. See his *Dialogo do Soldado Prático* for detailed and trenchant criticism of the prevailing abuses.

27. *As Gavetas*, vol. 5, p. 327.

28. As is to be expected, the situation in premodern China was similar: "In the Chinese empire the term 'corruption' must be understood in a special sense as the carrying to excess of practices that, when not excessive, were a normal and recognized part of government." J. K. Fairbank, E. O. Reischauer, and A. M. Craig, *East Asia: The Modern Transformation* (Boston, 1965), p. 108. Similarly, in Iran until very recently "the derivation of the largest possible personal profit from government office was not only expected but was regarded as his official right. . . . The practice was no secret, nor did any stigma attach to it. It was only later that the Western attitude toward peculation by public officials came under discussion and ostensibly won public approval." Joseph M. Upton, *The History of Modern Iran: An Interpretation* (Cambridge, 1968), pp. 23–24.

29. See Couto, VIII, cap. 19; LM, vol. 12, f. 261; ANTT, "Colecção de São Lourenço," vol. 1, ff. 338–338v; António Bocarro, *Década 13 da História da India* (Lisbon, 1876), p. 213; Diogo do Couto, *Vida de D. Paulo de Lima Pereira* (Lisbon, 1903), pp. 23, 47, 54, 72, 76–77; Ludovico di Varthema, *The Itinerary of Ludovico di Varthema* (London, 1928), p. 63; ANTT, "Colecção de São Vicente," vol. 14, f. iv; A. de S. S. Costa Lobo (ed.), *Memórias de um soldado da India*, by F. R. Silveira (Lisbon, 1877), pp. 83–84.

30. For example, A. Botelho de Sousa, *Subsídios para a história militar marítima da India* (Lisbon, 1930–1956), vol. 1, pp. 108–124, 353–357; vol. 2, pp. 16–17, 243, 357.

31. Respectively, in C. R. Boxer and Frazão de Vasconcelos, *André Furtado de Mendonça* (Lisbon, 1955), pp. 11, 21; "The Portuguese in the East (1500–1800)," in *Portugal and Brazil: An Introduction,* ed. H. V. Livermore (Oxford, 1953), p. 233; *The Portuguese Seaborne Empire* (London, 1968), pp. 58, 298, 299.

32. O. K. Nambiar, *Portuguese Pirates and Indian Seamen* (Bombay, 1955); *The Kunjalis: Admirals of Calicut* (London, 1963).

33. K. M. Panikkar, *Malabar and the Portuguese* (Bombay, 1929), p. 143.

34. *Boletim do Conselho Ultramarino: Legislação Antiga* (Lisbon, 1867), vol. 1, p. 59. Similar prohibitions throughout the century and later are given in APOCR, vol. 5, p. 292; vol. 3, pp. 6–7, 567–568, 650–652; "Livro Morato," HAG, ff. 61–62; "Livro Verde," HAG, vol. 1, ff. 101v–103v; LM, vol. 19D, f. 1200v.

35. *Boletim do Conselho Ultramarino*, vol. 1, p. 59.

36. *Annaes Marítimos e Coloniaes* (Lisbon, 1840–1846), vol. 4, p. 120; ANTTCC, 1-27-78; ANTT, "Colecção de São Vicente," vol. 14, f. 161; ANTT, "Documentos Remetidos da India," vol. 8, f. 183.

37. Recent discussions of this important topic include: Jan Kieniewicz, "The Portuguese Factory and Trade in Pepper in Malabar during the 16th Century," *Indian Economic and Social History Review* 6(March 1969):61–84; Vitorino Magalhães-Godinho, *L'Economie de l'Empire Portugais aux XVᵉ et XVIᵉ Siècles* (Paris, 1969), pp. 537–828; M. N. Pearson, "Commerce and Compulsion: Gujarati Merchants and the Portuguese System in Western India, 1500–1600," Ph.D. dissertation, University of Michigan, 1971, pp. 106–129.

38. Barros, I, vi, 5.

39. Couto, *Vida de D. Paulo de Lima Pereira*, pp. 76–77; Zain-al-Din, *Tohfut-ul-Mujahideen*, trans. M. J. Rowlandson (London, 1833), pp. 153–154; Francisco de Andrade, *Chrônica do muyto alto e muyto poderoso Rey destes Reinos de Portugal Dom João o III deste nome* (Coímbra, 1796), vol. 4, pp. 499–500; Barros, I, vi, 3; Couto, VII, x, 17.

40. *Cartas de Affonso de Albuquerque* (Lisbon, 1884–1935), vol. 1, p. 126.

41. Fernão Lopes de Castanheda, *História*, VI, lvii; VIII, xii, xliii; *O Oriente Português* (Goa), vol. 2, p. 286.

42. See, for example, ANTT, "Colecção de São Lourenço," vol. 3, ff. 34, 305v; ANTTCC, 1-107-9; Couto, VII, x, 3; José Wicki (ed.), *Documenta Indica* (Rome, 1948), vol. 7, pp. 88–89, 530; R. A. de Bulhão Pato, *Documentos Remettidos*, vol. 4, p. 312.

43. *Cartas de Affonso de Albuquerque*, vol. 4, pp. 174–175. This source on pp. 175–176 estimates the total production of the Malabar area at about 16,000 bares. Some 2,000 to 2,500 bares were used locally, 3,000 escaped inland, and 500 to 600 went to Diu by sea. Of the remaining 9,000 bares, the Portuguese got some, but a large amount also went to Hurmuz, Diu, the Red Sea, and Coromandel. See also *Documentação Ultramarina Portuguesa* (Lisbon, 1960–1967), vol. 3, pp. 373–375. A report of 1533 explained to the king why he got so little pepper. Other merchants paid "all in money and at the requested price, and Your

Highness pays in copper and money and at a fixed price" (ANTTCC, 1-50-65). See also José Wicki (ed.), "Duas Relações sobre a situação da India Portuguesa nos anos 1568 e 1569," *Studia* 8(1961):216–217, and *Cartas de Affonso de Albuquerque*, vol. 1, pp. 329–330.

44. Couto, VI, viii, 2, 3, 4, 8, 9; VI, ix, 18, 19; VI, x, 15, 17. For the pensions see P. S. S. Pissurlencar (ed.), *Regimentos das Fortalezas da India* (Bastorá, Goa, 1951), pp. 217–219; "Alvarás e Provisões de Sua Magestade," HAG, vol. 1, f. 77; *Documentação Ultramarina Portuguesa*, vol. 1, pp. 261–262.

45. "Cartas de Vice Reis," ANTT, 95; António da Silva Rego, *História das Missões do Padroado Português do Oriente*(Lisbon, 1949), p. 390; António da Silva Rego (ed.), *Documentação para a história das missões do Padroado Português do Oriente: India* (Lisbon, 1947), vol. 2, pp. 353–354, vol. 4, pp. 479–480; Fernão Lopes de Castanheda, VI, lxxiii.

46. A. da Silva Rego, *História*, p. 139; A. da Silva Rego (ed.), *Documentação*, vol. 4, p. 495; Barros, III, iv, 7: Artur Basilio de Sá (ed.), *Documentação para a história das missões do padroado Português do Oriente: Insulíndia* (Lisbon, 1954), vol. 1, pp. 333–334; LM, vol. 21A, p. 222; ANTTCC, 1–30–36, 1–52–32, 1–82–2, 1–86–89, 1–94–73, 1–107–86.

47. For example, "Alvarás e Provisões de Sua Magestade," HAG, vol. 1, ff. 78–78v, 110, 202v.

48. ANTTCC, 1–25–108.

49. ANTTCC, 1–27–69.

50. ANTTCC, 1–83–74, 1–94–54; Archivo Histórico Ultramarino, caixa 3, no. 4; *As Gavetas da Torre do Tombo*, vol. 3, p. 215.

51. LM, vol. 13A, ff. 220–220v; vol. 17, f. 68.

52. *Cartas de Affonso de Albuquerque*, vol. 4, p. 175; ANTTCC, 1–30–36, 1–105–90; R. A. de Bulhão Pato (ed.), vol. 2, p. 156.

53. Barros, III, ix, 2; ANTTCC, 1–30–36.

54. Barros, III, ix, 5.

55. ANTT, "Colecção de São Vicente," vol. 11, f. 37; *Documentação Ultramarina Portuguesa*, vol. 1, p. 418; Barros, III, ix, 2–3; III, ix, 5–6; III, x, 9; IV, iv, 17; J. Wicki (ed.), "Duas relações," pp. 210–211.

56. S. D. Goitein, *Studies in Islamic History and Institutions*(Leiden, 1966), p. 348; ANTT, "Colecção de São Vicente," vol. 14, f. iv; "Ma'athir-i Mahmud Shahi," corrected copy in Department of History, M.S. University of Baroda, ff. 21–23; S. C. Misra and M. L. Rahman (eds.), *The Mirat-i Sikandari* (Baroda, 1961), pp. 131, 145–146; John Briggs (trans.), *The Rise of the Muhammadan Power in India* (Calcutta, 1908–1910), vol. 4, p. 65 for pirates off Gujarat; for Malabar, Abd-er

40 • Corruption and Corsairs in Western India

Razzak's account in R. H. Major (ed.), *India in the Fifteenth Century* (London, 1857), p. 18; *The Itinerary of Ludovico di Varthema*, p. 63.

57. Bibliotheca Nacional de Lisboa, "Descrição das terras da India Oriental," MS 9163, f. 23; ANTTCC, 1-86-120; Couto, X, v, 7; for the Persian Gulf see ANTTCC, 1-35-52; ANTT, "Colecção de São Lourenço," vol. 2, f. 30; vol. 4, p. 459v; ANTT, "Livro de Leis de D. Manuel," f. 137.

58. Gaspar Correa, *Lendas da India*, vol. 2, p. 519; Fernão Lopes de Castanheda, VI, xlviii; Zain-al-Din, pp. 157-158.

59. Barros, IV, viii, 12.

60. Correa, vol. 2, p. 777; Barros, III, ix, 3.

61. Barros, IV, iv, 25; IV, viii, 12; ANTTCC, 1-77-36; Boxer and Vasconcelos, *André Furtado de Mendonça*, pp. 11, 21; ANTT, "Colecção de São Vicente," vol. 5, f. 132v; R. S. Whiteway, *The Rise of Portuguese Power in India*, p. 47; *Documentação Ultramarina Portuguesa*, vol. 1, p. 422; Correa, vol. 2, pp. 777, 810; APOCR, vol. 3, p. 284.

62. *Documenta Indica*, vol. 10, p. 3.

63. Ibid., vol. 8, pp. 120-121.

64. A. da Silva Rego, *Documentação*, vol. 12, p. 783.

65. Diogo do Couto, *Vida de D. Paulo de Lima Pereira*, pp. 76, 77; Couto, VII, x, 17; *Documentação Ultramarina Portuguesa*, vol. 1, p. 418.

66. *Documentação Ultramarina Portuguesa*, vol. 1, p. 422.

67. For example, Couto, VIII, cap. 19; APOCR, vol. 3, p. 928; *Documenta Indica*, vol. 6, p. 278.

68. *O Oriente Português*, vol. 8, pp. 22-26.

69. ANTT, "Colecção de São Lourenço," vol. 1, f. 338v.

70. J. Wicki (ed.), "Duas relações," p. 211; A. de S. S. Costa Lobo (ed.), *Memórias*, pp. 83-84.

71. APOCR, vol. 3, p. 929; Couto, XII, ii, 2. On the etymology of this word see Couto, X, v, 7, and J. H. van Linschoten, *The Voyage of John Huyghen van Linschoten to the East Indies* (London, 1885), vol. 2, pp. 169-170.

72. Couto, VIII, cap. 28.

73. Fernão Lopes de Castanheda, VI, lxxxiii.

74. Couto, VII, x, 17; Linschoten, vol. 2, pp. 169-170; F. Mendes da Luz, *O Conselho da India* (Lisbon, 1952), pp. 440-441.

75. Zain-al-Din, p. 126.

76. O. K. Nambiar, *The Kunjalis*, p. 97; *The Travels of Pietro Della Valle* (London, 1892), vol. 2, pp. 201, 356; S. N. Sen (ed.), *Indian Travels of Thevenot and Careri* (New Delhi, 1949), pp. 18-19; LM, vol.

14, pp. 214–215. To at least some extent R. S. Whiteway did try to discriminate: "Some of the so-called pirate leaders were, however, commanders under the Samuri, carrying on a guerilla warfare" (p. 47). For interesting parallels with the situation in nineteenth-century Malaya see Nicholas Tarling, *Piracy and Politics in the Malay World* (Melbourne, 1963).

Asian Trade and European Impact: A Study of the Trade from Bengal, 1630–1720

Om Prakash

It is generally accepted that the discovery by the Portuguese of an all-sea route to the East Indies ushered in a new era in the history of Euro-Asian trade. The direct procurement by the Europeans of Asian goods at source and the resultant involvement of the European trading bodies and individual merchants in trade within Asia had important consequences for the organization, and the volume, composition, and direction, of intra-Asian trade carried on by the Asian merchants. In section I of this essay, we will analyze the ways in which the organization of this trade from India was modified by the arrival of the European merchants on the Asian scene. In section II, we will discuss the changes in the trade carried on by Asian merchants between Bengal[1] and Southeast Asia during this period and evaluate the policies followed by the Dutch East India Company vis-à-vis Asian traders. In section III, we will examine some conclusions.[2]

Among the sources of evidence used in this essay are the *Dagh-Register,* a daily record of important transactions maintained at the chief eastern establishment of the Dutch

East India Company at Batavia (present Jakarta); the *Corpus-Diplomaticum Neerlando Indicum*, a collection of treaties and agreements between the company and the Asian governments; and the unpublished records of the company preserved at the Algemeen Rijksarchief in The Hague. The evidence in the records consists of the correspondence among the various factories of the company and, starting in 1671, lists of ships to and from the ports of Balasore and Hughli compiled by the Dutch factors from the local customhouse registers, hereafter referred to as shipping lists.

I

The sixteenth and seventeenth centuries were characterized by an intense rivalry and hostility among the European nations engaged in the eastern trade. In fact, European trading vessels were equipped with artillery and other weaponry. For example, there was the galleon, ''a boat formidable in armament and swift in manoeuvring that could serve at the same time as a deadly warship and as an efficient merchantman.''[3] On the other hand, the bulk of the Asian vessels engaged in intra-Asian trade were either unarmed or armed very inadequately.[4] When attacked by a European vessel, the Asian vessel could ordinarily do little but surrender. Thus in 1612 an English fleet under the command of Sir Henry Middleton seized a dozen or so Gujarati ships off the entrance to the Red Sea.[5] Even more typical of the situation was the capture in 1695 by the notorious English pirate Avery (alias Bridgman) of one of Emperor Aurangzeb's large pilgrim-cum-trading ships, the *Ganj-i-Sawai*, even though it was armed and provided with nearly five hundred soldiers in addition to the regular crew.[6]

Most Asian governments were in no position to intercede on behalf of their nationals because of the limitations of their own naval strength. In the case of India, this was true equally of the zamorins of Calicut, the sultans of Gujarat, and the Mughal emperors. Admittedly, the Mughals had an imperial department of admiralty and maintained regular flotillas at Gujarat on the west coast and at Bengal on the east coast. But the vessels that constituted these flotillas and the artillery available to them strictly limited their capacity to take the offensive. Probably the most revealing evidence of the gross inadequacy of the naval arm of the Mughal defense forces and of the consequent high price they were willing to pay for naval assistance from others is provided by the Mughals' request to the Dutch governor-general in council at Batavia for ten to twenty warships for the Chittagong campaign in the 1660s. In return for this assistance, the Mughals were prepared to exempt the company in perpetuity from the payment of customs duties throughout the empire and give it one-fourth of the territory that might be conquered (or make cash payment in lieu thereof at the option of the company). In addition, the costs incurred were to be reimbursed.[7]

A major consequence of the Europeans' naval superiority was a conscious attempt by the companies to control the volume, composition, and direction of the Asian merchants' trade with a view to protect and enlarge their own interests in the Euro-Asian and intra-Asian trade. This attempt at control was made through the instrument of the *cartaz*—the pass which every Indian vessel, for example, was, in principle, obliged to obtain from a company prior to sailing.[8] The request for a pass might or might not be acceded to; if granted, the document specified, among other things, the items the vessel was permitted to carry and the ports it was allowed to call at. Vessels not in possession of the document as well as those violating its provisions were liable to be seized and confiscated along with the cargo carried. Thus, by the pass system, Indian traders engaged in the intra-Asian trade lost the complete freedom of navigation on the high seas which they had enjoyed before the advent of the Europeans. Admittedly, freedom of navigation had even earlier been subject to interference by Asian pirates but that was more in the nature of a nuisance—albeit a costly one—rather than an arbitrary and institutionalized check on the very principle of freedom of navigation.

The superior fighting capability of their ships encouraged a number of European—mainly English—adventurers to start out from Europe with the intention of engaging in piracy in the Indian Ocean.[9] The considerable increase in the incidence of piracy in the Arabian Sea made the European companies trading in the Mughal empire recognize the incipient danger. For in the absence of a strong navy, the only course available to the Indians was to require these companies to counter the menace of European piracy.[10] An alarming increase in the 1690s in the activities of European pirates operating in the Arabian Sea brought matters to a head. The seizure in 1695 of the pilgrim vessel *Ganj-i-Sawai*[11] belonging to Emperor Aurangzeb and of the *Fath Muhammadi*[12] belonging to the merchant-prince of Surat, Abdul Ghafur—both of which were on their way back from the Red Sea—led to a demand being made on the European companies to provide armed vessels as round-trip escorts to Indian ships going from Surat to the Red Sea.[13] The agreement with the Dutch stipulated the provision, for each trip, of two armed vessels of 1,000 lasts[14] each with the necessary crew as round-trip escorts to all Indian ships on the Surat–Mocha–Jeddah voyage. In the event of an attack by ships other than those operated by the English or the French East India Company, the Dutch escort vessels were to provide full protection to the Indian ships. As compensation for this service, the company was to be paid 40,000 rupees per trip for each vessel it provided. Half of this sum was to be provided by the *mutasaddi* (port official) of Surat out of the customs duties collected there; the other half was to be jointly subscribed by the merchants whose ships were to be escorted. The company was free to carry its own cargo or freight goods on the escort vessels it made available.[15]

The piracy, however, continued.[16] The merchants of Surat under the leadership of Abdul Ghafur, decided to suspend all trade until compensation was obtained from the European companies.[17] The administration was forced to take action, and early in 1699 the companies were obliged to provide full compensation for losses suffered at the hands of European pirates by Indian merchants operating from Surat. The Dutch were made responsible for ships plying between Surat and the Red Sea ports, the English for those operating between Surat and the Malay peninsula, the Indonesian archipelago, and the Philippines as well as those going to South Indian ports. The French were made answerable for vessels operating between Surat and the Persian gulf.[18] In the face of the superior naval strength of the European companies, however, the demand for compensation turned out to be unenforceable.[19] The Indians agreed to a compromise, and in March 1704 the obligation of the companies was again restricted to the provision of escort vessels to Indian ships operating between Surat and the Red Sea ports of Mocha and Jeddah.[20] Needless to emphasize, this arrangement introduced an altogether new element in the pattern of Indian foreign trade in this period.

Another manifestation of the superiority of European vessels and navigational expertise and equipment was requests by Indian merchants for freighting goods in these vessels, occasionally for chartering whole ships, and for the loan of crew and equipment. While individual European merchants did accept freight cargo,[21] the bulk of the freight traffic was handled by the European companies. By far the most important Asian route along which both the Dutch and the English companies carried on a substantial amount of freight traffic was that between India and Persia. Soon after the conclusion of the 1652 agreement with Shah Abbas II, the Dutch factors at Gombroon estimated that the company could hope to earn 20,000 florins[22] per annum by carrying Indian merchants' freight cargo to and from Persia.[23] English participation in the Indo-Persian freight service went up rather rapidly from about 1680 onward. From the beginning of the eighteenth century, the English even began chartering whole ships to Indian merchants. Striking instances of this practice are the chartering of the *Colchester* in 1702 to one of the leading Armenian merchants of Calcutta, Sarhad Israeli, for Gombroon and Basra[24] and the chartering of the *Hester* to the company's Hindu broker, Janardhan Seth, in 1707 for Persia.[25] As English participation in the freight traffic between India and Persia developed, the freight charges appear to have declined.[26]

There was considerable demand by Indian merchants for European captains, steersmen, and sailors.[27] While some of these personnel were deserters from the European companies, the majority of them came on loan from the companies for specific voyages on mutually agreed terms. Given a general shortage of these functionaries, particularly because of desertion, the companies agreed to their loan only sparingly. Ordinarily it was only the senior state officials whose displeasure the companies wished to avoid that were provided with the loan of these personnel.[28] The same applied to the loan or sale of navigational equipment such as anchors.[29]

Individual European and Indian merchants also cooperated with each other in a variety of ways. For one thing, these traders collaborated in financing voyages to and from various Asian ports. In 1661, for example, the Dutch factors reported the arrival at Balasore from Ceylon of a vessel financed jointly by a Muslim merchant and a Dutchman named Jacob.[30] Twenty years later, a Frenchman, Jean de St. Jacqy, is recorded as having financed the *Nossenboor* jointly with a Bengali merchant, Hari Shah, on a voyage from Balasore to Achin.[31] Occasionally, the European merchants used the services of Indian agents for equipping and dispatching ships on their behalf.[32] Finally, the Dutch East India Company provided Indian merchants engaged in intra-Asian trade with bills of exchange on Dutch factors in different parts of Asia.[33] Of course this facility, as well as the loans of equipment and personnel, was offered in an attempt to influence the Indian merchants' trade to suit the company's interests.[34]

II

During this period, the Dutch East India Company's participation in intra-Asian trade was significant and growing.[35] Between Bengal and the Malay-Indonesian archipelago[36] the company's trade constituted an important segment of its intra-Asian trade. The principal items of export from Bengal to this region were opium and coarse cotton textiles. The amount of opium exported by the company increased from 1.7 metric tons in 1660–1661 to 25.8 metric tons in 1688–1689 and 73 metric tons in 1717–1718. The figures in the case of coarse cotton textiles were less than 3,000 pieces in 1666–1667, over 10,000 pieces in 1690–1691, and nearly 50,000 pieces in 1711–1712. The value of the company's total exports from Bengal to this region went up from 326,000 florins in 1693–1694 (the first year information was available) to 576,000 florins in 1713–1714.[37] Among the items imported, the amount of cloves the company sold in Bengal went up (in metric tons) from 0.91 in 1673–1674 to 2.24 in 1683–1684 and 3.51 in 1716–1717. The figures for nutmeg and mace respectively were 0.81 and 0.13 metric tons in 1673–1674, 1.41 and 0.18 in 1683–1684, and 2.34 and 0.09 in 1716–1717.[38]

It is against this background of the Dutch East India Company's significant and growing interest in the trade between Bengal and the Malay-Indonesian archipelago that we will investigate changes in the Asian merchants' eastward trade from Bengal. Among the Asian merchants, those based in Bengal[39] dominated this branch of trade,[40] providing us a link between the movements in this trade and developments in the Bengal region.

The Asian merchants' eastward trade from Bengal consisted of four subbranches: (1) the trade with Arakan and Pegu; (2) the trade with Siam with Tenasserim as the principal port; (3) the trade with Sumatra and the Malay peninsula with the ports in the area being Achin, Malacca, Perak, Junk-Ceylon, and Kedah; and (4) the trade with Manila in the Philippines.[41] The eastward trade was carried on from both the Hughli and the Balasore ports, though the latter was considerably more important.[42]

The evidence regarding movements in Asian merchants' trade from Bengal has been drawn until 1671 from the *Dagh-Register* and from correspondence between Hughli and Batavia and thereafter from shipping lists. The evidence prior to 1671 is rather fragmentary and consists only of number of ships operated or intended for operation along a given route by year. The information in the shipping lists of outgoing and incoming vessels at Balasore and Hughli is somewhat more detailed insofar as these lists, compiled by Dutch factors from the local customhouse registers at the behest of their superiors at Batavia, do contain, for each vessel listed, the name of the merchant, the port of destination/origin, the cargo carried, and, occasionally, the place of domicile of the merchant, the name of the captain *(nakhuda)*, the name of the agent, if any, who had equipped the vessel, and the name and type of the vessel. But the information pertaining to cargo is largely unusable because of wide variety of units of measure that cannot always be translated into a common unit. Thus one has to rely simply on the number of vessels operated to ascertain movements in trade. Insofar as there is no evidence to suggest a change in the size and composition of the Asian vessels engaged in trade between Bengal and Southeast Asia during this period, this procedure would not seriously bias the results in either direction, even in the absence of information on tonnage.[43] For this analysis I have ignored ships operated by European companies, by factors of these companies engaged in intra-Asian trade on their own, and by private European merchants. However, ships operated by Armenian merchants have been included in these calculations. It might be pointed out that similar shipping lists are not available for the other two ports in the Bengal region: Pipli in Orissa and Calcutta in Bengal. This shortcoming should not significantly affect the broad conclusions drawn from the shipping lists for Balasore and Hughli alone, however. In the case of Pipli, the port itself went out of operation around 1670 when the river on which it was situated silted up. In the case of Calcutta, the port began to be used only after the founding of the town in 1690 and the transfer there of the English East India Company's chief factory in Bengal. Calcutta does not seem to have been used by Asian merchants to any significant extent for trade between Bengal and Southeast Asia during this period.[44]

In the Asian merchants' eastward trade from Bengal, the Arakan-Pegu and the Philippines subbranches were comparatively insignificant. The trade with Tenasserim in Siam, on the other hand, was very important. It was reported in 1636 that the amount of textiles imported into Tenasserim that year by four Muslim ships—two of which had come from Bengal—was large enough to cause a glut in the local textile market.[45] In 1642, the Dutch factors ascribed the poor sale of textiles in Siam by the company to the large imports by Indian merchants from the Coromandel coast and Bengal.[46] We find a similar suggestion made once again nearly twenty years later.[47] In 1672, as many as twelve Asian vessels were getting ready at the port of Balasore for a voyage to Tenasserim.[48] But soon thereafter trade along this subbranch seems to have declined rather rapidly. Thus, from the shipping lists, one finds that the number of Asian vessels that left Balasore for the port of Tenasserim was only four each in 1680–1681, 1681–1682, and 1682–1683. In the five seasons between 1697–1698 and 1701–1702 for which comparable information is available, not a single Asian ship left Balasore for Tenasserim. According to the lists of ships that came into Balasore, the number from Tenasserim diminished from eight in 1682 to four in 1683 and one in 1699, the last year for which information is available.[49] Taking individual items of trade, one finds that the amount of tin imported by Asian merchants from Tenasserim into Balasore declined from 1551 maunds[50] in 1683 to 370 maunds in 1699. Copper imports declined from 1,135 maunds in 1682 to 325 maunds in 1699, while the number of elephants imported came down from 122 in 1682 to 10 in 1699.[51] As far as the port of Hughli is concerned, the information in the shipping lists becomes available only from 1696–1697 onwards. By that time the decline in this trade had perhaps taken place already.[52]

Another major eastern port of call for Asian ships from Bengal was Achin on the northern tip of Sumatra. The number of these ships was stated to be at least six in 1643–1644 and at least four in 1664–1665.[53] As in the case of the trade with Tenasserim, the trade with Achin also declined perceptibly over the last two decades of the seventeenth century. Thus, according to the shipping lists, the number of ships that left Balasore for Achin came down from an average of two per annum between 1680–1681 and 1683–1684 to one in 1698–1699 and none at all between 1699–1700 and 1701–1702. Similarly, according to the lists of ships arriving at Balasore, three vessels came in from Achin in 1682 and two in 1683; there are no entries whatever for Achin in 1698 and 1699. As for the port of Hughli, over the twelve seasons for which information is available between 1696–1697 and 1717–1718, the number of ships that left this port for Achin was two in two of these seasons, one in another two, and none in the other eight. Similarly, over the ten seasons between 1700 and 1718 for which information is available regarding Asian ships coming into Hughli, only two ships arrived from Achin—one in 1704 and one in 1717.[54]

Finally, as far as the Malay peninsula is concerned, at least four ships from Bengal were reported to have called at Malacca in 1641–1642.[55] In October 1642, the authorities at Batavia noted that merchants from Bengal and Achin had imported into Perak quantities of textiles large enough to halt the company's sale of textiles there.[56] In November 1653, Prince Shah Shuja, Faujdar Nawazish Khan of Raj-mahal, and Diwan Malik Beg of Orissa were reported to be getting ready a ship each to be sent to Kedah.[57] But by the time we reach the period for which information is available in the shipping lists, trade along this route had already declined considerably. Of the Asian vessels leaving Balasore, only one is reported to have gone to Kedah in 1697–1698; of those arriving at Balasore, one finds only one vessel from Malacca in 1683. As for the port of Hughli, only one ship is reported to have left for Malacca in 1715–1716 and another as having arrived from Malacca in 1706. Regarding the other ports in the peninsula, only one ship is recorded as having left Hughli for Kedah in 1715–1716. No vessel arrived at Hughli from these ports during the years for which information is available.[58]

Considering all the ports in the eastward trade together—including those in Arakan-Pegu and the Philippines—we find that the number of vessels leaving Balasore for these ports came down from an annual average of seven in the early 1680s to three in 1697–1698, to two in 1698–1699, to one each in 1699–1700 and 1700–1701, and to zero in 1701–1702, the last year for which information is available to us. As for the ships coming into Balasore, these totaled twenty in 1682 and 1683 together; in the 1690s, there was only one in the years 1698 and 1699. As far as the port of Hughli is concerned, over the twelve comparable seasons between 1696–1697 and 1717–1718, the number of vessels that left this port for the region was four in one season, three in another, two in yet another, one in another five, and none in the remaining four.[59] Similarly, over the ten seasons between 1700 and 1718 for which comparable information is available to us, the number of vessels that came into Hughli from this region was three in one of the seasons, two in another, one in another four, and none in the remaining four.[60] Taking into account the totality of the available data for both Balasore and Hughli, it appears that the Asian merchants' eastward trade from the ports of Bengal registered a fairly marked decline in the last years of the seventeenth and the early years of the eighteenth centuries.

The outstanding feature of this decline was the changing participation of Mughal state officials—the *mansabdars* of whom those with a rank of 1,000 *(zat)* and above constituted the Mughal nobility.[61] The members of this group usually possessed significant liquid capital, and foreign trade was a profitable channel of investment. Besides, given the limitations of the system of checks and balances in the Mughal administrative structure, they could generally count upon an extensive misuse of their positions of authority for private gain, in the process significantly augmenting their profit from trade. The most obvious misuse of authority in this context was to force producers and merchants under their jurisdiction to supply goods that these officials exported at prices considerably below the ruling market prices.[62]

There is evidence to suggest that among the merchants based in Bengal it was the state officials who dominated the Bengal-eastward trade through the greater part of the seventeenth century. All six of the Asian vessels reported in November 1653 to be getting ready to leave Bengal for the eastward ports belonged to these officials. Two of these vessels belonged to Prince Shah Shuja, subahdar of Bengal (one vessel was scheduled to go to Tenasserim and the other to Kedah), another two to Diwan Malik Beg of Orissa (one bound for Achin and the other for Kedah), and one each to

Faujdar Nawazish Khan of Rajmahal (scheduled for Kedah) and Nawab Inoriya Muhammad of Orissa (scheduled for Tenasserim). In fact, even the seventh vessel recorded as being equipped at Balasore (for a voyage to Masulipatam) was also operated by an official: Faujdar Ahmed Beg of Hughli.[63] According to the shipping lists for the early 1680s, the domination of these officials in the Bengal-eastward trade was continuing. But from the late 1690s onward, when the information in the shipping lists is resumed, if not earlier, state officials virtually disappeared from this trade. Thus, of the total of twenty-six eastward-bound ships—including those to Arakan-Pegu and the Philippines—that left Balasore in the four seasons between 1680–1681 and 1683–1684, thirteen were accounted for by merchants based in Bengal. Of these thirteen vessels, as many as eight were on the account of state officials. In the five seasons between 1697–1698 and 1701–1702, of the seven vessels that left Balasore for the eastward ports on the account of Bengal-based merchants, only three were operated by officials. Similarly, of the twenty vessels that arrived at Balasore from the eastern ports during 1682 and 1683, eleven were operated by merchants based in Bengal. Of these eleven vessels, seven were on the account of state officials. The sole vessel that came into Balasore from this region in 1699 was operated by an ordinary merchant. As far as Hughli is concerned, only two incomplete lists of outgoing vessels are available for the 1680s. These lists contain a total of seven eastward-bound vessels, all of them on the account of merchants based in Bengal. Six of these vessels were operated by officials. No information regarding ships that came into Hughli is available for the 1680s. As for the 1690s, 1700s, and 1710s, it is remarkable that the Hughli shipping lists for the period do not contain the name of a single Bengal-based official of the Mughal empire.[64] Thus, after 1690 there was a virtual pullout of officials from participation in the eastward trade. On the other hand, the trade of ordinary Bengal-based merchants showed no decline in volume and only a relative decline in proportion to the total Bengal-eastward trade.

To evaluate the role of the Dutch East India Company in bringing about this decline in the Bengal-eastward trade, we must examine the company's pass policy for the eastward region.[65] Soon after its arrival in the archipelago at the beginning of the seventeenth century, the company acquired, through a series of treaties between 1605 and 1621 with a number of petty rulers in the region, significant trade privileges including monopsonistic rights in all three major spices—clove, nutmeg, and mace—grown in the spice islands.[66] To benefit from these privileges and others that might be obtained later,[67] it was considered essential to regulate the trade of the rival merchants in the Malay-Indonesian archipelago. Nothing very much, however, seems to have been done in the direction of evolving a long-term pass policy for Asian shipping in the region until after the conquest, from the Portuguese in 1641, of Malacca, the principal seaport in the area. This conquest made the company an important power in the archipelago. The pass policy announced by the company in 1641 for Asian vessels trading with the Malay peninsula was meant to restrict direct access for these vessels to the "tin ports" north of Malacca and get them to carry out all their trade at Malacca itself.[68]

The restrictions imposed on Asian shipping in the Malay peninsula, however, proved largely ineffective while these vessels had continuing free access to the port of Achin. Since the Achinese and Malay merchants conducted a good deal of trade between the peninsula—particularly Perak, a vassal state of Achin—and Achin, Asian merchants could get at Achin practically everything they wanted from the peninsula.[69] It was against this background that the Batavia council adopted a resolution in July 1647 imposing an embargo on all Asian shipping in the "tin ports" and Achin.

Asian vessels infringing the embargo were to be seized and confiscated.[70] Factors all over Asia were provided with the necessary instructions about the issue of passes in the new context. In 1653 the embargo on Achin was lifted,[71] and after 1660 passes seem to have been issued for both Achin and Malacca on a fairly liberal basis.[72] But the company's policy of refusing to grant passes for the Malay ports of Perak, Kedah, Junk-Ceylon, and Bangery continued.[73] As far as the port of Tenasserim was concerned, passes appear to have been issued throughout the period.[74]

Was it the company's pass policy and its growing trade between Bengal and the Malay-Indonesian archipelago that brought about a decline in the total Asian merchants' eastward trade from Bengal? We have seen that trade conducted by ordinary merchants registered no particular decline. If ordinary merchants could survive the Dutch competition, it seems unlikely that the officials would have been forced to move out—particularly when they had available to them extensive powers to enhance their profit from trade. As regards the company's pass policy, we have seen that by the 1660s the only ports in the region for which the company refused to issue passes were those in the Malay peninsula excepting Malacca. While the company undoubtedly had the power to refuse passes for the banned ports to state officials engaged in trade,[75] in practice the possibility of retaliatory action by these officials-cum-traders on the company's factors under their territorial jurisdiction[76] made the company hesitant in vigorously enforcing its pass policy vis-à-vis this group. Indeed, the company even had to tolerate their violation of its policies. In 1656, for example, a vessel sent out by Prince Shah Shuja to Kedah—one of the formally banned peninsular ports—refused to pay the Malacca toll on its way back. In lieu thereof, the Dutch factors at Malacca forcibly took out from the vessel tin worth 1,631 rupees. This incident, coupled with the Hughli factors' refusal to provide naval assistance to the government for the proposed campaign against Arakan, caused the prince to threaten to raise the customs duty payable by the Dutch at Hughli from the usual 4 percent to 20 percent except on imported bullion. Intervention by officials friendly to the company persuaded the prince to offer to settle the affair for 7,521 rupees, which the prince claimed was the local value of the confiscated tin. The final settlement was for 4,339 rupees.[77] In view of this situation, the company's pass policy is unlikely to have imposed any significant hardship on state officials engaging in trade between Bengal and the eastward ports.

Our conclusion must be that the significant growth in the company's trade between Bengal and the Malay-Indonesian archipelago and its pass policies were not responsible for the near-withdrawal of state officials of the Mughal empire from participation in the Bengal–Southeast Asia trade. This conclusion finds strong support in the history of the Asian merchants' trade between Bengal and the Maldive Islands. This trade was dominated by merchants based in Bengal and, unlike the Bengal-eastward trade, it continued to grow until the close of the period. According to the shipping lists, the number of ships from Balasore to the Maldives increased from an annual average of three in the early 1680s to seven between 1697–1698 and 1701–1702. Moreover, one finds that the amount of rice exported to the Maldives from Balasore went up from 27,000 maunds in 1680–1681 to 50,500 maunds in 1697–1698; the amount of coarse cotton textiles increased from 1,200 pieces in 1680–1681 to 2,600 pieces in 1699–1700; the amount of opium increased from 2.5 maunds in 1682–1683 to 4.5 maunds in 1697–1698.[78] The number of ships from Hughli to the Maldives was three in 1699–1700 and four in 1704–1705; between 1706–1707 and 1717–1718, this number in any one year was two or less.[79] Considering the ports of Balasore and Hughli together, there is little doubt that the trade between Bengal and the Maldives increased during the closing years of the seventeenth and the early years of the eighteenth centuries.

But while the Bengal-Maldives trade grew during this period, the participation of state officials declined markedly. Of the twelve vessels that left Balasore for the Maldives in the four seasons between 1680–1681 and 1683–1684, as many as eight were on the account of state officials. By way of contrast, in the five seasons between 1697–1698 and 1701–1702, of the thirty-seven vessels that left Balasore for the Maldives, only one was on the account of an official. As for the port of Hughli, the only information we have for the 1680s is in two incomplete shipping lists: state officials accounted for three of the six vessels recorded as having left for Maldives. In the 1690s, 1700s, and 1710s, on the other hand, none of the vessels that left Hughli for the Maldives was on the account of a state official.[80] Thus the state officials practically withdrew from a *growing* trade which, in addition, was characterized by the lack of company competition and the absence of a restrictive pass policy (the company had no trade relations whatever with these islands). The Dutch East India Company, therefore, had little to do with the officials' near-withdrawal from trade.

The rapidity of that withdrawal is rather intriguing. It is well known that the period after 1679 witnessed a large increase in the number of *mansabdar*s (officials)—chiefly because of the great influx of the Deccanis into the ranks of Mughal *mansabdar*s[81] with no corresponding increase in the land area available for allotment of *jagir*s (land holdings) for their support. This development led to a crisis in the mansabdari-jagirdari system involving a decline in the flow of incomes of the *mansabdar*s. But insofar as continuing participation in foreign trade was dependent on the stock of capital available with the officials engaged in trade which, in turn, was unlikely to have depleted at a rate commensurate with the pace of their withdrawal from trade, the cessation of their foreign trading activities could not be a consequence merely of the crisis in the mansabdari-jagirdari system. A definitive analysis of the factors responsible for the near-withdrawal of the state officials from participation in Bengal's foreign trade must await further research.

The company's pass policy may have been more effective in the case of ordinary merchants engaged in foreign trade from Bengal since they were not in a position to retaliate. In fact, however, these policies did not lead to any discernible decline in the volume of trade carried on by these merchants. While the precise circumstances leading to this situation are not clear, it is possible that these merchants operated on the basis of English passes[82] or no passes at all and the Dutch chose to ignore the same. It is, however, important to note that while the trade carried on by these merchants along this route did not decline perceptibly, neither did it grow—implying a decline in the *relative* share of these merchants in the growing total trade.[83] It is this decline that might be ascribed to the company's generally restrictive pass policies coupled with the commercial privileges it enjoyed in the Malay-Indonesian archipelago.

III

To conclude, the coming of the Europeans had a wide-ranging impact on the organization of the Asian merchants' trade from India in the seventeenth century. The great disparity in naval power led to the Indians' loss of freedom of navigation on the high seas. Besides, it gravely intensified the problem of piracy in the Arabian Sea. The piracy, in turn, prompted a major innovation in the organization of Indian foreign trade in the form of a European escort service for Indian vessels operating between Surat and the Red Sea ports. There was, of course, also a considerable amount of collaboration among European and Indian merchants in the conduct of trade stemming partly from European superiority in navigational experience and equipment.

Over the period covered by this study, the Asian merchants' trade between Bengal and Southeast Asia declined— a decline composed of a virtual withdrawal from foreign trade by the officials of the Mughal empire and a lack of growth in the trade carried on by ordinary merchants. This near-withdrawal from the trade by state officials was independent of the Dutch East India Company's pass policies and trading privileges. These policies and privileges might, however, have restrained the *growth* of the trade of ordinary merchants.

NOTES

I am indebted to K. Sundaram for useful discussions on this study. I have also benefited from comments on an earlier draft by Arun Das Gupta, Ashin Das Gupta, Dharma Kumar, and Tapan Raychaudhuri.

1. In this study, "Bengal" or "Bengal region" denotes the territory now covered by Bangladesh (excluding the district of Chittagong) and the Indian states of West Bengal, Bihar, and Orissa.

2. For a preliminary analysis of some of the issues discussed here, see my "European Trading Companies and the Merchants of Bengal, 1650–1725," *Indian Economic and Social History Review* 1(3) (1964): 37–63.

3. Carlo M. Cipolla, *Guns and Sails in the Early Phase of European Expansion: 1400–1700* (London, 1965), p. 83.

4. In his description of the Indian trading vessels, Dutchman Van den Broecke stated that the guns they carried were of little use because they were mounted in the wrong place and were, therefore, completely without shelter. Besides, the Indians did not know how to handle them. Quoted in M. A. P. Meilink-Roelofsz, *Asian Trade and European Influence in the Indonesian Archipelago between 1500 and about 1630* (The Hague, 1962), p. 376, n. 97.

5. Meilink-Roelofsz, *Asian Trade,* p. 187.

6. This vessel was captured between Bombay and Daman while on its way back from Jeddah carrying a cargo worth approximately 2 million rupees. See F. W. Stapel (ed.), *Corpus-Diplomaticum Neerlando Indicum, Bijdragen tot de Taal-, Land-, en Volkenkunde Van Nederlandsch Indie,* no. 93, p. 124 (editor's introduction); Alan Villiers, *The Indian Ocean* (London, 1952), p. 184.

7. Letter from the Dutch factory at Hughli to the council at Batavia (hereafter H.B.), 6. 1. 1665, Koloniaal Archief (hereafter K.A.) 1143, ff. 47–50; resolution adopted by the Batavia council on 27 July 1665, K.A. 580, ff. 194–204; *Dagh-Register gehouden in't Casteel Batavia,*18 August 1665, p. 226, and 29 March 1666, pp. 38–42.

8. While in theory the pass issued by a company rendered the Asian vessel immune from attack by the ships of that company alone, the companies generally honored each others' passes.

9. For a description of the European pirates' activities in the Indian Ocean, see Sir William Foster, *The Embassy of Sir Thomas Roe to India 1615-19* (London, 1926), p. 388, n. 1; J. N. Sarkar, *The History of Aurangzeb* (Calcutta, 1924), vol. 5, pp. 342–358; F. W. Stapel (ed.), *Corpus,* 93, pp. 124–127, 144–146; J. N. Sarkar, "The Affairs of the English Factory at Surat, 1694–1700," *Indian Historical Records Commission Proceedings,* vol. 5, January 1923, pp. 6–13; Villiers, *Indian Ocean,*pp. 182–192; and S. C. Hill, "Episodes of Piracy in the Eastern Seas, 1519–1851," *Indian Antiquary* 49(1920): 1–21.

10. In his letter dated 14 February 1618 to the Court of Directors of the English East India Company, Thomas Roe wrote: "I have only two poynts to touch. That these seas begin to bee full of rovers, for whose faults wee may bee engaged . . . and must tell yow, if yow bee not round in some course with these men [the pirates], yow will have the seas full and your trade in India is utterly lost and our lives exposed to pledge in the hands of Moores. I am loath to lie in irons for any mans faults but myne own." Foster, *Embassy of Sir Thomas Roe,* p. 451.

11. See note 6.

12. J. N. Sarkar, *The History of Aurangzeb* (Calcutta, 1924), vol. 5, p. 343.

13. The English company agreed to this arrangement on 6 January 1696; the Dutch did so on 26 September 1696. Sarkar, *History of Aurangzeb,* vol. 5, p. 351; Stapel, *Corpus,* 93, pp. 124–127.

14. A last represented about 120 cubic feet.

15. Stapel, *Corpus,* 93, pp. 124–127.

16. In 1698, the ship of a Turkish merchant resident in Surat, Hassan Hamidan (or Hamid Khan), was captured by a Dutch pirate between Bombay and Surat. See Stapel, *Corpus,* 93, pp. 144–146, 150–152; H. B. 10.3.1699, K.A. 1516, ff. 39–40; enclosure to H.B. 6.4.1699, K.A. 1516.

17. Ashin Das Gupta, "The Maritime Merchant, 1500–1800," presidential address to the Medieval India section of the Indian History Congress, Jadavpur University, Calcutta, 1974, p. 12.

18. Stapel, *Corpus,* 93, pp. 144–146, 150–152; H.B. 10.3.1699, K.A.

1516, ff. 39–40; enclosure to H.B. 6.4.1699, K.A. 1516; Littleton and council to the directors of the New English Company, 6.3.1702, O.C. 7892, ff. 21–28, vol. 57, India Office Library.

19. In August 1703, following the seizure by a European pirate of a Surat ship while on its way back from Mocha, the Dutch were asked to provide compensation of the order of 600,000 rupees. When the factors refused to meet this demand, the Dutch trade at Surat was banned and the factors were put under house arrest. The governor-general in council at Batavia recognized the need for decisive action and rushed a fleet of seven ships to Surat. The fleet arrived off Surat in October 1703, captured five Indian ships in the area, and blockaded the port. See Stapel, *Corpus,* 93, pp. 221–222; Littleton and council to the directors of the New English Company, 6.3.1702, O.C. 7892, ff. 21–28, vol. 57; H.B. 22.3.1702; H.B. 12.3.1703, K.A. 1570, f. 3.

20. Stapel, *Corpus,* 93, pp. 221–222; H.B. 22.3.1704, K.A. 1584, ff. 10–15.

21. The *Don Juan,* operated by a Portuguese merchant, was reported to have carried, in addition to the merchant's own cargo, substantial freight belonging to the "Moors" on a voyage from Balasore to Malacca in 1688. See list of ships that left Balasore in 1687–1688, K.A.1343, ff. 714–715.

22. During this period the usual rupee-florin exchange rate was 1:1.2.

23. Estimate dated 25 May 1652, K.A. 1079, ff. 349v–350.

24. Diary of the Old English Company kept at Calcutta, 29 December 1702. F.R. Calcutta, vol. 4, ff. 20–22.

25. Letter from the Court of Managers to the United English Company in Calcutta dated 17 April 1708, Letter Book 13, ff. 255–256. Of course, on the other hand, when the companies were short of vessels along particular routes, they too made use of Indian vessels for freighting cargo. In 1665, the Dutch East India Company transported cargo worth 89,715 florins from Bengal to Coromandel on an Indian vessel (letter from the Dutch factory at Pipli to the council at Batavia [hereafter P.B.]10.3.1655, K.A. 1100, ff. 374–375). At times whole ships were chartered by the companies. Thus in 1661 an Indian ship, chartered by the English arrived at Surat from Achin (*Dagh-Register,* 18 October 1661, p. 327). In the same year, the Dutch East India Company chartered four Indian vessels for the transportation of rice from Bengal to Ceylon (H.B. 20.10.1661, K.A. 1226, f. 723).

26. In 1685, for example, the Dutch entered into a contract with a number of Bengal merchants for the transportation of passengers and freight to Persia on the *Walenberg* at a cost of 10,000 rupees. But soon thereafter the English offered substantially better terms. The Dutch

answered by reducing their price to as low as 3,570 rupees. The documents are silent regarding the eventual outcome of the price war, but we do know that the price offered by the English in the second round was even lower. Letter from the council at Batavia to the Dutch factory at Hughli (hereafter B.H.) dated 27.5.1686, K.A. 816, f. 213.

27. In 1663, for example, the *Surat*, owned by Mondas Naen and captained by a Dutchman, Dirik van de Velde, arrived in Siam from Surat (*Dagh-Register*, 9 December 1663, pp. 659–660).

28. The Dutch company provided in 1654 three steersmen to Prince Shah Shuja, in 1660 one steersman to Emperor Aurangzeb for a voyage to Ceylon, and in 1666 one steersman to Nawab Amin Khan for a voyage to Tenasserim and another to the faujdar of Hughli, Syyad Jalal (P.B. 12.3.1654, K.A. 1094, ff. 625v; H.B. 29.11.1660, K.A. 1126, f. 49; H.B. 1.4.1666, K.A. 1149, ff. 2240–2241). Similarly, the English company was reported to have loaned several steersmen to Nawab Khan Dauran in 1665 (H.B. 26.3.1665, K.A. 1143, ff. 563–565).

29. In 1666, for example, the Dutch company sold some navigational equipment to Nawab Amin Khan (H.B. 1.4.1666, K.A. 1149, ff. 2240–2241). Three years earlier, the English factors at Surat had asked the Court of Directors for "ten or fifteen anchors for the supply of the King's jounks" (William Foster, *The English Factories in India, 1661-64*, p. 211; quoted in Satish Chandra's "Commercial Activities of the Mughal Emperors during the Seventeenth Century," *Bengal Past & Present* 78(146) (July–December 1959): 92–97.

30. *Dagh-Register*, 29 November 1661, p. 399.

31. List of ships that left Balasore in 1680–1681. Enclosure to H.B. 9.4.1681, K.A. 1258, ff. 1285–1291.

32. Thus the *Fateh Shahi* is recorded as having arrived at Hughli on the account—ostensibly personal—of the director of the French East India Company in Bengal in 1716 from Surat and the following year from Persia. On both these occasions, the vessel had been equipped by one Sheikh Nasir, who is reported to have himself accompanied it on the latter of these two trips. See list of ships that came to Hughli in 1716, K.A. 1769, ff. 210–212; list of ships that came to Hughli in 1717, K.A. 1783, ff. 91–92.

33. Thus in 1663 the Dutch factors in Hughli issued bills of exchange on the factors in Ceylon of the order of 5,000 rupees to the *nakhuda* of the ship of the Emperor Aurangzeb and 1,000 rupees to the *nakhuda* of the ship of the governor of Hughli (*Dagh-Register*, 8 April 1663, p. 142).

34. To take an example, in the 1660s, given the insufficiency of the domestic output of rice in Ceylon, the company was interested in ensur-

ing a regular supply of Bengal rice to this island through the agency of the Indian merchants. The offer of assistance in various ways was, therefore, used to promote trade along this branch. Thus in 1667 the factors in Bengal told Nawab Naurullah Khan that his request for a loan of two sailors could be acceded to if he agreed to send his ship to Ceylon rather than Pegu as he had planned (H.B. 15.11.1667, K.A. 1152, ff. 720v–721.

For a fascinating account of the extensive cooperation during this period between Europeans and Asians in the world of business and other fields, see Holden Furber, "Asia and the West as Partners Before Empire and After," *Journal of Asian Studies*, 28(4)(August 1969): 711–721.

35. For details, see my "Dutch East India Company and the Economy of Bengal, 1650–1717," Ph.D. dissertation, University of Delhi, 1967.

36. This region includes the Malay peninsula and the Indonesian archipelago.

37. Calculated from the export invoices in the letters from the factory at Hughli to the council at Batavia.

38. Though these figures relate to sales in Bengal, they could be used as a proxy for imports from the archipelago since these spices were imported exclusively from this region. (Calculated from the "statements of goods sold in Bengal" in the enclosures to the letters from the factory at Hughli to the council at Batavia.)

39. Other Asian merchants participating in the eastward trade from Bengal were based in other parts of India or in the Malay-Indonesian archipelago.

40. This observation is based on a detailed analysis of the information pertaining to the place of domicile of the Asian merchants available in the shipping lists.

41. The principal items of export to and import from the eastward region were as follows (arranged in a descending order of importance):

Subbranch	Exports	Imports
(1) Arakan and Pegu	Textiles, rice, oil, butter, opium	Cash, elephants, ivory, tin
(2) Siam	Textiles, rice, butter, opium	Elephants, spelter, bell metal
(3) Sumatra and Malay peninsula	Textiles, rice, opium, butter, saltpeter, raw silk	Tin, gold, pepper, spelter, copper, bell metal
(4) Philippines	Textiles, rice, butter	Tin, ivory, copper

This information is based on shipping lists and the correspondence between the Dutch factors at Hughli and Batavia.

42. This pattern emerges from an analysis of shipping lists.

43. For the period 1671 to 1718, the available lists of Asian ships that left Balasore for various destinations and those that came into Balasore numbered thirteen each. For Hughli, the corresponding numbers were eighteen and twenty-two. Since not all these lists pertain to the same period of each sailing season, they are not always fully comparable with one another. Our interest lies primarily in establishing trends in the volume of the eastward trade from Bengal. An analysis of the available lists suggests that the bulk of the outward movement of ships from Balasore to the ports of interest took place between January and March and that from Hughli between December and the following March. On this basis, I have selected the lists of outgoing vessels for the following seasons, which are broadly comparable:

Balasore: 1680–1681 to 1683–1684, 1697–1698 to 1701–1702

Hughli: 1696–1697, 1699–1700, 1704–1705, 1706–1707 to
1709–1710, 1711–1712 to 1713–1714, 1715–1716,
1717–1718

For purposes of illustration, however, two incomplete lists pertaining to vessels that left the port of Hughli in two seasons in the 1680s have also been used. As far as the incoming vessels are concerned, the construction of a comparable series of lists posed certain problems. For example, for the 1698 season, there are two lists of ships coming into Balasore covering the periods 28 February 1698 to 20 August 1698 and 1 September 1698 to 20 February 1699; the beginning and end dates of actual sailings were 10 March 1698 to 18 August 1698 and 16 October 1698 to 4 December 1698 respectively. The other lists available for Balasore pertain roughly to the period covered by the first of these two lists; none pertaining to October–December in other seasons is available. I have, therefore, ignored the list pertaining to October–December 1698. Based on the comparable lists for Balasore, my conclusion is that there was a distinct decline in the volume of Asian merchants' trade between Balasore and Southeast Asia between the early 1680s and late 1690s. If this conclusion is to be negated by reference to the possible pattern of shipments in the months of October to December in each season, it would be necessary to presume a contrary and offsetting movement over these two decades in the volume of trade conducted during these months. Since the list for October–December 1698 contains no shipment from Southeast Asia, it appears reasonable to reject such a presumption. For this analysis, I have selected the lists of the incoming ships for the following seasons, which are broadly comparable.

Balasore: 1682, 1683, 1698 (first list only), 1699

Hughli: 1700–1702, 1704, 1706, 1708–1710, 1717, 1718

44. The available evidence suggests that at the beginning of the eighteenth century the port of Hughli was still the focal point of the trade from the province of Bengal (as distinct from the Bengal region which included Bihar and Orissa). Thus Alexander Hamilton, who visited Bengal in 1705–1706 wrote of Hughli: "This Town of *Hughly* drives a great Trade, because all foreign Goods are brought thither for Import, and all Goods of the Product of *Bengal* are brought hither for Exportation. . . . It affords rich Cargoes for fifty or sixty Ships yearly, besides what is carried to neighbouring Countries in small Vessels" (Alexander Hamilton, *A New Account of the East Indies*, ed. William Foster, London, 1930, vol. 2, p. 12).

45. Letter from the council at Batavia to the Board of Directors in Amsterdam (hereafter B.XVII) 28.12.1636, K.A. 1029, f. 186.

46. *Dagh-Register*, February 1642, p. 122.

47. *Dagh-Register*, 17 November 1661, p. 364.

48. H.B. 28.3.1672, K.A. 1178, f. 117.

49. The lack of correspondence in the shipping lists between the number of outgoing vessels in a given season and those arriving in the immediately following season is partly explained by the fact that a vessel sent out, for example, from Balasore to Tenasserim might have been directed to come back to Surat rather than Balasore. The possibility of this happening frequently was increased by the fact that even in branches of trade dominated by merchants based in Bengal, there were other Asian merchants participating who were not based at the port of destination either. Thus the chances of the example given above being applicable in the case of a vessel operated by a merchant based at Surat are quite good.

50. A maund is approximately 82 pounds.

51. Calculated from the shipping lists.

52. The number of Asian ships that left Hughli for Tenasserim was one in 1696–1697, two in 1704–1705, one each in 1706–1707 and 1708–1709, and none in the remaining seasons for which comparable information is available. The number of ships arriving from Tenasserim at Hughli was one in 1701, three in 1710, one in 1718, and none in the remaining seasons (shipping lists).

53. *Dagh-Register*, December 1644, pp. 43–44; *Dagh-Register*, 8–9 March 1665, p. 48.

54. Shipping lists.

55. *Dagh-Register*, May 1642, p. 160.

56. *Dagh-Register*, October 1642, pp. 178–179.

57. P.B. 10.11.1653, K.A. 1091, ff. 468v–469.

58. Shipping lists.

59. According to shipping lists, the number of ships in each season
was as follows:

1696–1697	3	1709–1710	1
1699–1700	1	1711–1712	0
1704–1705	4	1712–1713	0
1706–1707	1	1713–1714	0
1707–1708	0	1715–1716	2
1708–1709	1	1717–1718	1

60. According to shipping lists, the number of ships in each season
was as follows:

1700	0	1708	0
1701	1	1709	0
1702	0	1710	3
1704	1	1717	1
1706	1	1718	2

61. The few merchants whose names are prefixed by titles such as
Nawab have been included in this category even when the office is not
identified in the relevant shipping list.

62. For details of the cases of such misuse of authority and an analysis
thereof, see my "Dutch East India Company in Bengal: Trade Privileges
and Problems, 1633–1712," *Indian Economic and Social History Review*
9(3)(September 1972): 283–285; and "Some Implications of the *Man-
sabdari* System for Economic Growth in Mughal India," *Delhi School of
Economics Working Paper No. 58,* 1969, mimeographed.

63. P.B. 10.11.1653, K.A. 1091, ff. 468v–469. In 1664–1665, fifteen
Asian ships are recorded as having left Balasore for various destinations.
Information regarding ownership is available for ten of these vessels.
Seven belonged to state officials—two each to Nawab Khan Dauran of
Orissa, Diwan Malik Beg of Orissa, and Shahbandar Nasib Khan of
Balasore and one to Nawab Amin Muhammad (H.B. 26.3.1665, K.A.
1143, f. 565). It might be noted that in the example pertaining to 1653
and possibly also in that pertaining to 1664–1665, the information does
not cover the full sailing season.

64. Shipping lists.

65. Part of the Bengal-eastward trade was carried on by merchants
operating from ports such as Tenasserim and Achin. Of the four ships
that left Balasore for Tenasserim in 1681–1682, one was on the account
of the king of Siam. In the preceding season of 1680–1681, the king had
accounted for two of the four vessels that had gone from Balasore to
Tenasserim. Similarly, in 1680–1681, of the three ships that had left
Balasore for Achin, one was on the account of an Achinese merchant. In
the absence of domicile information about the merchants engaged in

trade in respect of all the lists, it is not possible to isolate such cases on a systematic basis. For the merchants based in Southeast Asia, the trip from Bengal to their respective ports would be a return trip and, as such, the company's policy would pertain to passes for Bengal. The fact that the company by no means neglected this aspect is borne out by its refusal, in 1664, to accede to the request by merchants in Malacca for permission to trade with Bengal (*Dagh-Register,* 1 April 1664, p. 110).

66. J. E. Heeres (ed.), *Corpus,* 57, pp. 31–33, 36–41, 48–50, 50–53, 66–69, 160–161. It should, of course, be realized that since these spices were grown over an extensive area which the company found difficult to police effectively, a contraband trade conducted by Asian merchants survived until late in the seventeenth century (Meilink-Roelofsz, *Asian Trade,* p. 219).

67. In the 1640s and later, for example, the company obtained monopoly rights in pepper in Palembang, Indragiri, and Jambi and in tin in Kedah, Bangery, and Perak. Over the same period, monopoly rights were obtained in textiles and opium in Mataram, Cheribon, and Palembang. See J. E. Heeres (ed.), *Corpus,* 57, pp. 365–367, 380–386, 438–439, 528–531, 538–541; 87, pp. 151–155, 209–212, 280–282, 285–287, 291–297; 91, pp. 74–79, 136–142, 233–240, 267–270.

68. A significant contribution dealing with this and related issues is S. Arasaratnam's "Some Notes on the Dutch in Malacca and the Indo-Malayan Trade, 1641–1670," *Journal of Southeast Asian History* 10(3)(December 1969): 480–490.

69. The seriousness of the situation, from the company's point of view, would be apparent from the fact that in 1646, for example, the company found that practically all the tin produced in the peninsula had been bought up by Asian merchants. Similar was the case with pepper produced in Sumatra. See Heeres, *Corpus,* 57, p. 520.

70. Heeres, *Corpus,* 57, pp. 520–521.

71. Letter from the Batavia council to the factory at Pipli (hereafter B.P.), 21.10.1653, K.A. 780, f. 436.

72. S. Arasaratnam, "Notes on Dutch in Malacca," p. 489.

73. B.P. 21.10.1653, K.A. 780, f. 436; S. Arasaratnam, "Notes on Dutch in Malacca," p. 489.

74. This is suggested by the virtual absence of instructions from the Batavia council to the factors at Hughli to restrict the issue of passes to Asian merchants for Tenasserim, whereas the correspondence contains numerous instances of such instructions regarding Malay ports such as Kedah, Perak, Junk-Ceylon, and Bangery. However, we do have one instance where the board of directors, fearing that Bengal silk and silk piece goods imported into Siam by Asian merchants might possibly find

their way to Japan through the Chinese merchants and there compete with the company, wrote to the Batavia council to instruct the factors at Hughli not to issue passes for Tenasserim, among other ports. Letter from the board of directors in Amsterdam to the Batavia council, 8.10.1685, K.A. 459, ff. 277v–278.

75. In 1653, for example, the company refused to grant passes to the vessels of the faujdar of Hughli, Mirza Jafar, and of Diwan Malik Beg of Orissa. Letter from the factory at Kasimbazar to the Batavia council (hereafter K.B.), 3.2.1653, K.A. 1091, f. 394v; P.B. 10.11.1653, K.A. 1091, f. 448v.

76. For example, in both the cases of refusal of passes mentioned in note 75, the company had to face unpleasant consequences. Mirza Jafar placed various hurdles before the company's trade in the area under his jurisdiction (K.B. 3.2.1653, K.A. 1091, f. 394v). Diwan Malik Beg ordered the faujdar of Pipli and Balasore to have the Dutch factory in Pipli burnt down. The order was carried out. The ostensible reason given for the outrage was a clash earlier in the year between some Dutch factors and a number of Muslims carrying out the Muharram procession in the town of Pipli in which one Dutchman and several Muslims had been killed (P.B. 2.4.1653, K.A. 1091, ff. 415v; P.B. 10.11.1653, K.A. 1091, f. 448v; P.B. 15.12.1653, K.A. 1094, ff. 612–613; B.P. 28.8.1654, K.A. 781, ff. 359–363; letter from Johan Verpoorten to Nawab Shamsudaulla of Orissa, enclosure to P.B. 15.11.1654, K.A. 1094, ff. 675– 677v; H.B. 6.3.1660, K.A. 1123, f. 736v).

77. B.H. 19.7.1657, K.A. 784, f. 311; letter from the factory at Hughli to the board directors in Amsterdam, 4.12.1657, K.A. 1111, ff. 760–761; B.XVII. 17.12.1657, K.A. 1110, ff. 108v–110.

78. Calculated from the shipping lists.

79. Over the nine seasons for which information is available between 1706–1707 and 1717–1718, the number of these vessels was two in three of the seasons, one in another four, and zero in the remaining two.

80. Shipping lists.

81. M. Athar Ali, *Mughal Nobility under Aurangzeb* (Bombay, 1966), p. 11.

82. For details, see my "European Trading Companies and the Merchants of Bengal," pp. 52–53.

83. The growth in the overall volume of trade is clearly suggested by the significant increase in the company's trade along this route during this period.

Joint-Stock Companies of Coromandel

Joseph Jerome Brennig

The records of the Dutch and English East India Companies in the second half of the seventeenth century refer repeatedly to associations of local merchants of the Coromandel coast in which capital was raised through the sale of shares to members. They were, like the European companies which sponsored them, based on the principle of joint-stock partnership. These associations were not indigenous but European, a result of Dutch and English efforts to improve their trade positions through systematic reorganization of local merchant associations. The Coromandel joint-stock company was thus an early instance of the attempted transfer of a basically European commercial institution to a non-Western economic environment.

Various interpretations of the joint-stock company, both of its character and its importance to the Coromandel merchants, have appeared in recent times. One historian has suggested that the joint-stock companies represented a major opportunity for the Coromandel merchant to develop more efficient forms of merchant capitalism, an opportunity ultimately missed because of his failure to act with sufficient enterprise.[1] Another historian, noting the failure of the English to interest merchants of Bengal in forming a joint-stock company, suggests that the joint-stock company in Coromandel reflects the greater submissiveness of the Coromandel merchant to the power of European trade.[2] A third sees the joint-stock companies as providing important lessons for the local merchants, again stressing the potential in the communication of European commercial ideas to the merchants of the Coromandel coast.[3] These interpretations either exaggerate the contribution of the Coromandel joint-stock companies, ignoring the restrictions of the local commercial environment, or fail to recognize just what it was in the joint-stock companies which attracted the local merchants to European-sponsored initiatives.

This essay examines the early development of the Coromandel joint-stock companies in order to understand the manner in which this European idea of commercial organization was first applied in Coromandel. It seeks to establish several points. First, that the Dutch and English, with differing requirements in the Coromandel trade, approached the employment of a joint-stock mode of organization differently. Second, that the Dutch did not immediately ask all the merchants connected with their trade on the Coromandel coast to join in joint-stock companies; rather they moved cautiously in this direction. Third, that there were certain elements in the local merchant community that opposed the introduction of joint-stocks companies because such an institution interfered substantially with their earnings. But fourth, the general body of merchants trading with the Europeans responded favorably to the new mode of organization, not because of its utility in mobilizing capital so much as a variety of other reasons, most of them relating to the advantages of monopoly status in a particular factory's trade.

△ ˙

THE BEGINNINGS: PRE–JOINT-STOCK
ASSOCIATIONS

The arrival of the joint-stock company among local merchants in Cormandel did not occur suddenly, but rather deliberately through what appears to have been a process of trial and error. The first steps took place in the Dutch factory at Pulicat, a small port located about 20 miles north of Madras. In 1659 the merchant community of Pulicat lost one of its oldest and most important members with the departure of Chinnana for Tanjore.[4] Chinnana was the younger brother of perhaps the Coromandel coast's greatest merchant, Malaya, who at his death in 1634 had wide commercial and political influence in South India and overseas. Chinnana had spent much of his time pursuing political ambitions, but through all he remained the leading merchant of Pulicat. His departure meant that the Dutch had to deal more closely with numerous lesser merchants, many of whom they knew little about and could not trust.

The Dutch governor Laurens Pit faced not only the departure of Chinnana but other problems. Local merchants increasingly failed to pay their debts to the Dutch. Cloth did not arrive in the quantity or quality ordered, and indeed low-quality cloth was being offered at high prices.[5] Pit's analysis of the situation led him to conclude that local merchants frequently competed with one another for the labor of the weaver-producer, allowing the weaver to control price levels, much to the disadvantage of the local merchant and also the Dutch.[6] To solve this problem Pit decided to influence the manner in which local merchants conducted their trade. Beginning with a small group of merchants engaged in the trade of a fine muslin sold in the Moluccas known as "ternate cloth," he asked them to band together into an association with an understanding that they would no longer compete among themselves. Apparently as the Dutch East India Company's (VOC's) suppliers of ternate cloth these merchants had in return a monopoly of Dutch trade. Pit found that the quality of the association's cloth improved dramatically, and he proceeded to ask a second group of merchants, twelve in number, to organize an association of merchants specializing in "moree cloth," a fine white variety.[7] Pit had clearly changed existing modes of commercial organization among Pulicat's local merchants, but how far had he gone? Had he succeeded in persuading these merchants to organize joint-stock companies?

A joint-stock company, both in the European model and in the form it later took on the Coromandel coast, involved the subscription by members of capital by the purchase of shares and the joint participation in trade by members using the capital so raised. Moreover, the joint-stock company, being a complex form of partnership, required a legal or semilegal authority embodied in a charter, permitting membership to change without dissolution of the company. Nothing in Pit's brief description of the association formed during his governorship indicates that they were joint-stock companies of this description.

But while these associations lacked the structured character of joint-stock companies, they did inaugurate greater employment of capital by local merchants. Previously, capital needed to finance production came largely from the Europeans. In some cases the great merchants such as members of the Malaya family provided short-term credit, but most merchants did not wish to invest or lacked the means. Pit reported to his successor that this situation had changed during his term in office. When the Dutch informed the merchants that scarcity of resources prohibited advance payments in association, members provided short-term credit approaching 70,000 to 80,000 guilders or about 15,000 pagodas.[8] Thus while the associations which Pit had encouraged may not have been the chartered joint-stock companies of a few years later, they did permit a crucial shift in the flow of credit in Dutch Coromandel trade.[9]

Pit's associations, not quite joint-stock companies in form, offered advantages to both the Dutch and the local merchant. The Dutch, as Pit reported, gained increased reliability. Cloth was delivered in the quantities and qualities expected. Moreover, the Dutch found, perhaps unexpectedly, that the merchants in these associations were more willing to trade without immediate advances—that is, they would extend short-term credit, covering the costs of production themselves. The local merchant in his turn could regard Dutch trade as a monopoly of sufficient value to justify his investment. Furthermore, he no longer competed with other merchants for the labor of the weaver-producers. To move from this early form of association to the joint-stock company did not improve trade conditions for the local merchant as much as it formalized the contribution of local capital, an advantage of increasingly vital importance to the Dutch, whose supplies of capital were beginning to fall seriously short of requirements.

A merchant association which did not require contributions of capital appeared elsewhere in Coromandel. Such an association was established in the English factory in Masulipatnam in 1679. The English were undoubtedly familiar with the measures Laurens Pit had taken some years before, but they apparently had not applied them in their own factories. Local merchants came to the English in groups, one group specializing in fine cloth, another in coarse. Contracts were negotiated with the group as a whole but signed with each merchant.[10]

In 1679 the Masulipatnam factory was being visited by the English governor of Fort St. George (Madras), Streynsham Master (1675–1680), a man both intelligent and vigorous in action. During the negotiations for the contract the merchants of Masulipatnam refused, stubbornly Master thought, to lower their prices. Master decided to break their bargaining position by opening negotiations with merchants from the nearby port of Petapoli, then in Masulipatnam seeking English trade. For Master to consider trading with merchants outside the group customarily trading in Masulipatnam was a sharp break with trade practice. The local merchants of Masulipatnam, probably shaken by the prospect of losing their entire trade, quickly came to terms.[11] Recognizing their uncertainty, Master chose this moment to offer the Masulipatnam merchants a new contract, one which obligated parties to more than the coming year.

The new contract, while not calling on local merchants to purchase shares, did divide the total investment into equal parts, thus giving each local merchant equal access to English trade, a step ending competition. It also set forth the prices for cloth, the English here attempting to stabilize prices over a period of time. For the benefit of the local merchants, however, the contract included a specific reference to the merchants named in the contract as the "Honble Company's Merchants" and promised that no merchant could be removed except on orders from the council in Madras or the directors in London.[12]

The value of this new contract was perceived immediately by merchants of the nearby factory of Madapollem. Soon after the merchants of Masulipatnam signed their contract, the merchants of Madapollem informed Master that they desired a similar agreement. Significantly, however, they insisted on one condition: that no other merchants other than those they nominated could be included in the contract.[13] The Madapollem merchants believed that the new contract established a valuable monopoly. Moreover, a written instrument insured them against arbitrary actions by the English.

Both Pit and Master encountered favorable responses to their efforts. But a hint of opposition appears in the report of Cornelis Speelman, who succeeded Laurens Pit as the Dutch governor in 1663. Speelman in his report to his successor mentions that a broker in the Dutch factory—a figure of minor importance and not to be compared with

Chinnana—had tried to subvert Dutch efforts to organize merchants of painted cloth into an association.[14] Speelman did not believe these rumors and the broker protested his innocence, but it might be noted that a joint-stock company could interfere with a broker's source of income by enabling easier communication between the Dutch and their local merchants.

THE DUTCH JOINT-STOCK COMPANIES: 1665–1683

Once local merchants had indicated their willingness to eliminate competition and also provide credit to the Dutch, the next step in forming joint-stock companies out of these associations was not difficult. Whether Laurens Pit actually took this step is not clear, but during Cornelis Speelman's terms as governor of the Dutch factories in Coromandel the associations of Pulicat merchants almost certainly became joint-stock companies. Speelman, writing for his successor, stated that the moree cloth merchants consented to supply the full range of plain cloth, a significant increase in their trade. Moreover, they put up *("aangelegt")* 70,000 pagodas in capital.[15] Speelman here does not suggest a further extension of credit—the language Pit had used—but implies that the moree merchants had advanced this sum in cash before the trading season, a strong indication that they had formed a joint-stock company.

The Dutch introduced the joint-stock concept in factories outside of Pulicat slowly. Thus despite the importance of the factories in northern Coromandel to Dutch trade, the first joint-stock companies appear there following the inspection tour of the Dutch governor, Jacob Jorisz Pits, in 1682. His report contains charters for the joint-stock companies in the factories of Masulipatnam, Palikollu, Draksharama, and "Nagalwance."[16] The language of every charter was approximately the same. Each set out the value of shares in the company, the names of those merchants purchasing shares against the amount of each merchant's in-

TABLE 1. Joint-Stock Companies of Northern Coromandel, 1682

Factory	Number of Merchants	Cost per share (pagodas)	Total Investment (pagodas)	Average Investment (pagodas)
Masulipatnam[a]	58	300	21,300	367
Palikollu	26	250	13,250	509
Draksharama[b]	27	250	10,000	370
Nagalwance	18	200	4,600	255

Source: K.A. (Koloniaal Archief, The Hague) 1267, 25 April 1682, ff. 2006b–2010b; 27 March 1682, f. 1897; 23 March 1682, f. 1871–1871b; 14 April 1682, f. 1935–1935b.

[a]Masulipatnam's four joint-stock companies are here treated as one. The number of merchants in Masulipatnam's companies includes groups of two or three merchants who had joined in purchases of a share or portion of a share. Each such group has been treated as equivalent to a single merchant.

[b]In 1683 the Draksharama merchants were organized into five separate joint-stock companies. Here they have been treated as a single group for comparative purposes.

vestment, and various obligations imposed by membership. Each company had several merchants who acted as managers and were responsible for the proper administration of trade.[17] Unlike the document which Streynsham Master offered the merchants of Masulipatnam two years earlier, these Dutch charters contained no references to cloth prices or varieties, suggesting more strongly their long-term validity.

Variations in the charters do occur, however. Each joint-stock company could be distinguished by the amount of capital invested; and each merchant invested a different amount. These differences have been summarized in Table 1.

The contrast between Masulipatnam and the factories in the Godaveri delta, Palikollu and Draksharama, is perhaps most striking. Masulipatnam was the central market and main urban center in northern Coromandel, yet the investments of its merchants in the Dutch factory's joint-stock company were significantly less, on the average, than the investments of the merchants of the rural factories of the Godaveri delta. One explanation for the difference is the smaller volume of the textile trade in Masulipatnam in the 1680s. By this time Dutch exports in northern Coromandel were centered on plain cloth—guinees, parcalles, and salempores—which was produced primarily in the Godaveri delta.[18] The lower average investment may reflect lower Dutch demand in Masulipatnam for capital.

But if this explanation might explain differences between Masulipatnam and other factories, it does not explain the difference between Palikollu and Draksharama. Both these factories exported a similar quantity of textiles.[19] Yet the average investment of the merchants in these factories differed significantly. Here the general situation of the factory in northern Coromandel might have played a role. When he was recommending that the Dutch encourage local investment in the textile trade, Laurens Pit had warned that in southern Coromandel, the region below Pulicat, political insecurity made merchants wary of publicizing their wealth.[20] Northern Coromandel, firmly under the rule of the Kingdom of Golconda, had a fair degree of general political stability, but nevertheless the local administrators of the kingdom were not above extortion. In such circumstances the merchants of Palikollu may have felt more secure than the merchants of Draksharama, for Palikollu and not Draksharama had been under Dutch administration since 1636.

The total capital invested in these joint-stock companies was less than what was required to finance production. Palikollu's case serves as an example. According to Streynsham Master's *Diaries,* the Dutch factory in Palikollu purchased cloth in a year valued between 70,000 and 80,000 pagodas.[21] The proportion of this total required in advance varied, but the maximum was about half and the minimum a third of the total investment.[22] On this basis the operating capital required in Palikollu ranged from 20,000 to about 40,000 pagodas. Clearly the investment of 13,250 pagodas of the Palikollu joint-stock company fell short of the factory's minimum needs. Although it is not explicitly stated, the difference between the amount of local capital available and the requirements of trade was met through Dutch capital as before.

A final point worth stressing about the figures shown in Table 1 is the distribution of capital available for investment in northern Coromandel. Despite the importance of Masulipatnam as the central marketplace of this part of the coast, the merchants connected with the Dutch factory there did not invest most of the necessary capital. The merchants of the factories located in the Godaveri delta, however, had a major share of the total capital invested. The minor investments of the merchants of Nagalwance, a factory which dealt in a relatively small volume of cloth for the Dutch, provides further variation in the distribution pattern. Capital available for the textile trade was not concentrated in an urban center but distributed in rural areas where textile production and agrarian output were high.

Further development of the Draksharama joint-stock company following the departure of Jacob Jorisz Pits from northern Coromandel provides additional understanding of merchant response to its introduction. The original organization of the Draksharama merchants into five small joint-stock companies, each with a capitalization of 2,000 pagodas, reflects Dutch efforts to adjust the joint-stock company to existing modes of merchant organization. Prior to 1682 most merchants of the Draksharama factory were members of six small groups, evidently partnerships, containing two to six persons each. A few merchants traded independently. The groups appear to have reflected caste distinctions—all the merchants of weaver castes belonged to a single large partnership group while the others were composed of merchant-caste members.[23] Dutch records do not indicate how these partnerships came into being, but possibly they were the associations formed following Governor Laurens Pit's efforts in Pulicat in the 1660s. Perhaps they were associations formed quite independently of Dutch influence. Whatever the basis of their establishment, the Dutch regarded them as being of some importance, for when they called for a joint-stock company in Draksharama they established not the unified company of merchants found in Palikollu but five small joint-stock companies, the members of which reflected the pattern of the earlier partnerships.

This multiple form of organization did not last, however; in 1683 the merchants of Draksharama requested that they be permitted to reform into a single joint-stock company on the Palikollu company pattern. Concurrently they increased their level of investment from 10,000 to 13,250 pagodas, the same total investment made by the Palikollu company.[24] This new capital came in equal parts from the addition of new members and the increased participation of old ones.

The value of the joint-stock company, or indeed of any monopoly company trading with the Europeans, was revealed two years later in the reaction of local weavers to the formation of a single merchant company in Draksharama. Complaining against what they regarded as a break with custom, the weavers presented the local official of the Kingdom of Golconda (the havaldar of Draksharama) a gift *(peshkash)* of 1,000 pagodas, probably a sizable sum for weavers to raise, to force the merchants to break up their combination. The official made no effort to help the weavers, but only sought Dutch bribes not to act. Nevertheless, the incident reveals the extent to which the coordination of merchant trade had influenced merchant-weaver relations.[25] As in Pulicat years earlier, the new association had reduced the power of the producer to dictate prices and quality to the merchant because of shortages in labor.

If the local merchant recognized advantages in the reorganization being encouraged by the Dutch, the particular form of a new manner of organization, whether joint-stock enterprise or any other, may have been less important. To accede to the wishes of the Dutch meant only that the local merchant admitted the practical wisdom of pleasing those who controlled such a profitable trade. Thus a group of merchants of the city of Rajamundry, located at the head of the Godaveri delta, a city in which the Dutch had never established a factory, formed a joint-stock company on their own initiative and approached the Dutch for trade.[26] They had quickly recognized the pattern of association which the Dutch favored in the preceding year and imitated it in the hopes of attracting new trade. It was not their interest which encouraged the introduction of a joint-stock company but a perception of Dutch interest. And in fact the regulated contribution of local operating capital, the primary contribution of the joint-stock company, favored the exporter more than the local merchant by releasing him from the burden of capitalizing trade. But if questions may be raised as to whether the joint-stock company was an institution fully understood and recognized by local merchants in the same manner as perceived by the Europeans, its spread among the Dutch, and later the English, factories permits us to estimate the quantity of capital which local merchants were willing to invest in trade under relatively favorable and secure conditions.

Perhaps the strongest contrast between the appearance of merchant cooperation as members of a joint-stock company and the reality of the Coromandel merchant community occurred at the English factory in Madras. As a case study, the Madras joint-stock companies reveal some important reasons why the imposition of institutions from without failed to have a long-lasting effect.

△ THE MADRAS JOINT-STOCK COMPANIES

Chinnana's departure from Pulicat opened the way for Laurens Pit to change the Dutch relationship with local merchants through the organization of merchant associations. In Madras, the center of the English operations in

Coromandel, events took a different course. Since establishing a factory there in 1640, the English had employed an important merchant as broker. But these chief merchants continued to remain powerful in the Madras market into the second half of the century. Their hold over trade was such that the directors of the English India Company in London complained to the council 'in Madras that the broker, known as the chief merchant, had what was in effect a monopoly of English trade, for all prices were established through negotiations with the chief merchant and not the general body of the merchant community.[27] Dominating the 1660s and 1670s were Kasi Viranna and Beri Timmanna, partners in trade. Kasi Viranna, following the death of Beri Timanna, became the most powerful individual in the city. When Kasi Viranna died in 1680, the younger brother of his former partner, Pedda Vencatadry, assumed the position of chief merchant.

The chief merchant's sources of income were several. First, and perhaps most important, he paid lesser merchants less for cloth than what he was paid by the English. In addition he received a commission on trade from the English as part of the payment for his service as broker. Finally, he earned a profit on the quarter of the Madras trade which he held in his own hands.[28] It was the first of these, involving complex relations with the lesser merchants of Madras, that created a conflict in the first months of Pedda Vencatadry's term as chief merchant.

Kasi Viranna at the time of his death left important matters unsettled. The accounts for the relationship between the chief merchant and broker on the one side and the lesser merchants on the other had not been adjusted for the previous five years, and the lesser merchants claimed they were owed a considerable sum. Pedda Vencatadry, as the new chief merchant, was considered liable for this debt of his predecessor. Thus when Streynsham Master, then recently returned from reorganizing the affairs of the English factories in northern Coromandel, called the local merchants together for the coming year's investment in June 1680, the lesser merchants stated firmly that there would be no investment before a settlement of their claims on the chief merchant. On 30 June, Pedda Vencatadry and his partner, Allingal Pallai, informed Master and the council that an agreement had been reached and the investment could now proceed. But Master apparently believed that the time was opportune to enforce a change in the organization of the local merchant's affairs; sloppy management and bookkeeping of the sort displayed in the recent dispute were particularly distasteful to the agent. Thus after a debate in the council, the English merchants informed the chief merchant that they were resolved "to put it into the way used at Pulicat, that is to make Joynt Stock of the Marchants to provide the whole investment . . . and to apoint Seaven or more of the principal Men amongst them to manadge the trade and to adjust their Accotts: every yeare."[29]

It must have been quickly apparent to the chief merchant that the proposed joint-stock company would end his utility as a broker, for with a reorganization of the merchant community the English could conveniently negotiate with the bulk of the lesser merchants without great inconvenience. Furthermore, Vencatadry was probably well aware that since the days when Beri Timmanna and Kasi Viranna controlled English trade together, the directors of the English East India Company in London had protested the monopolistic position of the chief merchant in Madras. Master conceivably was using the establishment of a joint-stock association in response to these demands. Thus it is not surprising that the lesser merchants sought to delay, perhaps in the hope of an indefinite postponement, Master's desired reorganization. The day following his announcement of the council's intentions, the lesser merchants informed Master that "they had long [sic] time been under Verona and now had agreed their Acc^tts: with Pedda Yenkatadry and therefore desired

that the business for this year might goe on as it did formerly and afterward they would doe as the Governor desired
and ordered."[30]

Master remained firm in his purpose, however. He informed the merchants that if they refused to enter a joint-
stock company immediately, he would find other merchants
more agreeable. But the merchants still hoped to gain a
delay, returning a few days later and claiming that their
capital was distributed among the weavers and was unavail-
able for investment in a joint-stock enterprise. Master offered to put up the capital until the merchants had their
own available, but by this time he realized that their pro-
crastination reflected the efforts of the chief merchant, who
since the mention of a joint-stock company had remained
closeted with his partners and family.[31] Master decided,
therefore, to offer Vencatadry both a carrot and a stick—he
could have membership in the joint-stock company with a
quarter of the total trade still under his control, but if he
refused he would be barred from English trade. Realizing
that further resistance was useless, Vencatadry sent word to
Master that "he wholly submitted himself to the Agent and
Councell and would com to the ffort."[32]

The council and the local merchants met in Fort St.
George to organize a joint-stock company the following
day. Master set the capital requirements of the enterprise at
50,000 pagodas, a sum nearly sufficient to provide the entire Madras investment without advance payment by the
English, one of the original purposes of the joint-stock company as Master had stated. Despite the size of this amount,
the merchants offered 75,000 pagodas to purchase 150
shares at 500 pagodas per share.[33] After further deliberation
sixty-seven merchants were permitted to join and the
number of shares was limited to one hundred. The average
investment for each merchant at 645 pagodas was considerably higher than previous examples of merchant investment in northern Coromandel. Apart from Pedda Ven-

catadry and his partners, who held twenty-five shares, thirty-six of the merchants held one or more shares. The initial oversubscription of the joint stock company and the final investment of substantial amounts by the majority of the merchants in the Madras enterprise indicate that capital resources were ample in Madras. Clearly such enthusiasm does not reflect a simple desire to please the agent and council; the local merchants sensed something of value in the joint-stock company. Perhaps it was the prospect of trade without the burden of dealing through a chief merchant, paying him a commission and receiving low prices for their cloth.

But if Master was determined to end bad management and the broker's monopoly, Vencatadry was equally determined to undermine the joint-stock company and regain his old position. Avoiding an open confrontation with Master, Vencatadry complained to Podula Lingapa, tarafdar of Poonamalee, the representative of the king of Golconda immediately responsible for relations with the English in Madras. Lingapa ordered a blockade of Madras, cutting off food supplies and trade, in September 1680.[34] On inquiring into the cause of this apparently unprovoked attack on the English, Master learned that Lingapa resented the loss of certain favors which the chief merchant in the past had usually offered him, such as interest-free loans. Pedda Vencatadry had informed him that without the profits earned through brokerage, these favors had to cease. Thus Lingapa had acted to force his return as chief broker in Madras.

Master, however, was not to be bullied. A month following Lingapa's initiation of a blockade he charged the chief merchant with a consistent effort to undermine the joint-stock company and placed him and his associates, Chinnana Vencatadry, his brother, and Allingal Pallai, his partner, in prison. He then announced that the earlier agreement which the chief merchant had made with the lesser merchants prior to the formation of a joint-stock company was void—the lesser merchants, with the support of the agent and council, could now renew their claims against the Vencatadrys.[35] The amount the lesser merchants determined as outstanding was considerable: a total of 60,000 pagodas. Allingal Pallai paid about 11,000 pagodas and gained his freedom, but the Vencatadry brothers refused to pay the 49,000 pagodas claimed of them. Master then announced that payment would be extracted through a sale of the imprisoned merchants' trade and personal goods; clearly Master threatened the ruin of the chief merchant.[36]

The night following Master's declaration of intention, supporters of the Vencatadry brothers began to leave the city, beginning a significant revolt against the English which lasted six months and at its peak involved five thousand persons. Pedda Vencatadry could call upon the loyalty of the members of right-hand castes; but, fortunately for the English, he could not influence members of merchant and artisan castes who belonged to an opposed group, the left-hand castes.[37] These remained in Madras, permitting English trade to continue. Not being able to interfere seriously with English trade, Vencatadry also found that Podula Lingapa was not willing to encourage the revolt. Without sufficient support in the city and from the local governor, Vencatadry's "mutiny" (Master's term) eventually lost momentum and collapsed. Master, confident of his control over the situation, proceeded to sell Pedda Vencatadry's trade goods for 41,000 pagodas and his family jewelry for 8,000 pagodas.[38] By the end of 1680, with the revolt over, Master released the merchants from confinement while at the same time removing them from their positions in the joint-stock company and depriving them of the earnings they had gained from the previous year's investment. Those earnings, he declared, should be shared by other members of the joint-stock company who had suffered delays and disruption of trade because of the right-hand castes' revolt.[39]

Master's effort to destroy the power of the chief merchant

seems to have succeeded, but appearances are deceiving. Early in 1681 Master was replaced as governor and agent by William Gifford. Gifford disagreed with Master's handling of the crisis of the preceding year and his harsh treatment of the Vencatadry family. Soon after his arrival the Vencatadry brothers approached him for a return of their positions in trade. Gifford after brief discussion agreed.[40] Thus differences in the English community, apparently understood and exploited by Pedda Vencatadry, had permitted the undoing of policies which Master had worked vigorously to maintain. Pedda Vencatadry pressed his advantage further and charged that Master had personally benefited from the sale of the Vencatadry family belongings. When the council inquired formally from Master as to the truth or falsity of these allegations, Master could only reply that his memory of the events was poor.[41] When Streynsham Master thus departed from Madras in 1682, he left behind him conditions little different than they stood in early 1680. Pedda Vencatadry still dominated trade and, indeed, still controlled the merchant community. Moreover, the merchant community could easily draw the conclusion that the suggestions of malfeasance brought by the council had disgraced the formerly powerful agent and added to the chief merchant's power.

The joint-stock company established in 1680, once Pedda Vencatadry assumed authority, had little chance of success. According to discussions of the joint-stock company which took place in 1688, the lesser merchants and chief merchant had been unable to reconcile their accounts for the previous five years—since 1683, that is, not long after Pedda Vencatadry returned to power.[42] These continuing disputes, similar in character to those which preceded the formation of the joint-stock company, finally caused its dissolution and reformation in August 1688. The new company, headed by Chinna Vencatadry, who had succeeded his brother on the latter's death, had only 20,000 pagodas in capital, less than half the capital of its predecessor.[43] Chinna Vencatadry died a year later and the position of chief merchant fell to one Veri Timappa or Timanna, possibly related to the late Beri Timmanna, the partner of Kasi Viranna in the 1660s and the elder brother of Pedda Vencatadry.[44]

The joint-stock company formed in 1688 had no more stability or longevity than that of 1680. By 1696 disputes between the merchants of the company involving the chief merchant's debts forced still another reorganization.[45] Chacka Serappa, a merchant lately from Pondicherry who earlier had assisted as dubash (Hindustani *do bashi,* translator or interpreter) in organizing the first joint-stock company, became chief merchant on the request of several members of the local merchant community.[46] The joint-stock company under Serappa, formed in 1697 or thereabouts, required only 10,000 pagodas, a further reduction of the company's capitalization. Following what had become established pattern, this joint-stock enterprise lasted no more than a few years. In 1703 Chacka Serappa and other merchants in the company disputed the payment of an outstanding debt to the English, despite English lectures on there being "no proportion in a joint-stock." Ultimately Serappa had to pay the debt incurred by the failure of other merchants in the company.[47]

The Madras joint-stock company had serious weaknesses. The disunity of the merchant community, the hostility toward the chief merchant by some members of the community, and the chief merchant's penchant for exploiting lesser merchants all contributed to the repeated collapse of what the English with difficulty sought to establish. Moreover, the English themselves contributed to the decline of the joint-stock company by changing their view of its usefulness for English trade. Master had originally intended that the capital provided by the joint-stock enterprise would substitute for English payment of advances, following the principle Pit had established at Pulicat years before. His successors, however, abandoned this interpretation. During discussions of the joint-stock company's problems in 1688, the council referred to the resources of the joint-stock company as insurance against bad debts, a much lower aspiration for the utility of local capital. No longer linked to the level of trade, the joint-stock company's institutional function for the English declined, contributing over the long run to the lack of interest in its continuation by all parties.

The reasons for the repeated conflicts between members of the joint-stock company are not always spelled out in the English records; much remained remote from the perceptions of the English merchant. Nevertheless, one consistent explanation for division among the merchants was the relationship between the chief merchant and other merchants in the company. The chief merchant had supposedly lost the right to contract for cloth with lesser merchants at prices lower than the English set forth in their contracts with the establishment of the joint-stock company. Master intended all merchants to receive the price which the English were willing to pay. Nevertheless, the chief merchant retained his control over prices and, just as in the dispute between Pedda Vencatadry and the lesser merchants in 1680, the conflicts of later times centered on claims by lesser merchants of underpayment. If originally the lesser merchants of Madras had shown some enthusiasm for Master's joint-stock idea, it was probably the promise of receiving full prices for their cloth. The failure of the joint-stock company to fulfill its original promise must have reduced the Madras merchant's interest in its continuation.

Beyond the differences between merchant groups within the joint-stock company lay the broad differences dividing the Madras community—the conflict between the right-hand and left-hand castes. The precise role differences between right-hand and left-hand caste groups had in the daily trade and activity of the local inhabitants of Madras varied. At times merchants belonging to one group were evidently competing with merchants in the other; at other times they cooperated.[48] But serious opposition to the chief merchant, leader of the right-hand castes, probably could only be maintained by members of the left-hand castes, merchants outside his influence. The disputes between the right-hand and left-hand castes were occasionally violent in Madras, as in 1654–1655 and in 1680, widening the division between them. Some evidence suggests that toward the end of the seventeenth century the right-hand castes, dominant in Madras for the preceding half century at least, began to lose influence to the left-hand castes. Prerogatives which the right-hand castes considered vital to their position were challenged by the left-hand group in 1707, leading to a particularly violent confrontation.[49] Under these circumstances, a joint-stock company of merchants united for a common commercial purpose in Madras was probably an impossible goal.

If not with the same severity, similar problems of instability could be found in joint-stock companies outside Madras. The joint-stock enterprise in Madapollem shortly after its organization fell victim to disagreements between groups in the merchant community.[50] But Dutch concern for the uninterrupted functioning of the joint-stock companies attached to factories apparently forestalled such difficulties. In Tegenepatnam, south of Madras, the Dutch reacted quickly when they noticed that the dominant caste of merchants (Beri Chettis) had consolidated their hold over the company through a family and marriage network—the Dutch prohibited membership in the company to relations of members.[51] It would seem that largely through such precautions the Dutch joint-stock associations remained viable well into the eighteenth century.

CONCLUSION

The Coromandel joint-stock companies clearly illustrate the complex interactions involved in the attempt to transmit European ideas and institutions into an alien environment. On the European side, the mode of introducing these companies varied considerably. The Dutch were generally quite cautious, establishing joint-stock companies only where and when they were fairly sure of the concept's acceptability. The English, however, showed little concern for local sensibilities, brushing away the protest of challenged vested interests. The Asian merchant responded in a variety of ways also. Some found profit in the greater cohesion of the merchant groups trading with one or the other of the great European trading companies as they sought a monopoly of a branch of the textile trade. They also valued the greater control the joint-stock company gave over local weaver-producers. Other merchants—those in Madras—sought freedom from subordination to a powerful chief merchant.

How should we evaluate the Dutch and English efforts to change intermerchant relationships in Coromandel? The introduction of joint-stock companies had mixed results. The Dutch, seeking additional supplies of capital from reliable local sources, apparently succeeded. The joint-stock companies they sponsored survived without evident conflict into the eighteenth century. The English did not fare so well. In Madras, their main center of trade, the joint-stock company did not succeed in undermining the power of the chief merchant—an important reason for its introduction—and it could guarantee only minor supplies of capital.

As for the significance of the joint-stock principle for local Asian merchants, the Coromandel merchant never gave the concept an independent existence. In no other sector of the economy does the joint-stock company appear to have taken hold as a mechanism for raising capital. But it would be ill-considered to suggest that the continued alienness of the joint-stock concept despite years of operation under European sponsorship reflects badly on the enterprise of the Coromandel merchant. The large-scale joint-stock company of the type established in Madras did not and could not take into account serious differences between families, castes, and intercaste alliances. Nor could it manage the conflicts between leading merchants and lesser merchants. Moreover, the value system implied in a partnership in which standing depended solely on the amount invested conflicted with the local value system tied to ascriptive loyalties. Finally, to ask why local merchants did not seek to apply the joint-stock concept elsewhere implies that the large-scale mobilization of capital was an evident necessity outside the textile trade. This assumption is not proven. The textile trade in the seventeenth century was by far the most prominent branch of commerce which required significant capital. The social and economic environment of seventeenth and eighteenth-century Coromandel thus limited the range of responses which could reasonably be expected from the local merchants. That they did respond favorably in most cases, finding real advantages in the European-sponsored associations, indicates that within those limits the Coromandel merchant displayed both acumen and enterprise.

NOTES

1. Tapan Raychaudhuri, *Jan Company in Coromandel; 1605–1690: A Study in the Interrelations of European Commerce and Traditional Economies.* Verhandelingen van het Koninklijk Instituut voor Taal-, Lande-, en Volkenkunde, Deel 38 (The Hague, 1962), pp. 147–148.

2. S. Chaudhuri, "Bengal Merchants and Commercial Organization in the 2nd Half of the 17th Century," *Bengal Past and Present* 90(2) (1970): 201.

3. S. Arasaratnam, "Aspects of the Role and Activities of South Indian Merchants, c. 1650–1750," *Proceedings of the First International Conference-Seminar of Tamil Studies* (Kuala Lumpur, 1968), vol. 1, p. 591.

4. W. P. Coolhaas (ed.), *Generale Missiven van Gouverneurs-General en Raden aan Heren XVII der Verenigde Oostindische Compagnie.* Rijks Geschiedkundige Publicatien, 125 ('s-Gravenhage, 1960–1971), vol. 3, 16 December 1659, p. 261.

5. *India Office. Mackenzie Collection (Private),* vol. 55, pp. 14–16.

6. A few years later the English experienced similar difficulties in Madras, but rather than seek out new means of organizing the local mer-

chant, they left the problem to their head merchant, a figure comparable to Chinnana in Pulicat before 1659, to solve. He did so by apportioning weaving areas to each merchant. See *Records of Fort St. George, Diary and Consultation Book, 1672–1678*, 28 September 1675, p. 73.

7. *Mackenzie Collection (Private)*, vol. 55, p. 15.

8. According to the manuscript in the Mackenzie Collection, the amount of capital invested by local merchants was between 70,000 and 80,000 guilders or about 15,000 to 16,000 pagodas; ibid. Ararsaratnam, in his "Aspects," p. 588, refers to rupees rather than guilders.

9. A similar shift in credit occurred in northern Coromandel. Christopher Hatton, an experienced English merchant in Masulipatnam, reported in 1676 that the Dutch were "indebted to the natives, the Marchants with whome they deale, and have not the wherewith to pay them." R. C. Temple (ed.), *The Dairies of Streynsham Master, 1675–1680* (London, 1911), vol. 2, p. 115. Pit's report also mentions the northern Coromandel merchants offering credit.

10. Ibid., vol. 1.

11. Ibid., vol. 2, p. 141f.

12. Ibid., vol. 2, p. 149f.

13. Ibid., vol. 2, pp. 163–164.

14. *Mackenzie Collection (Private)*, vol. 55, p. 112.

15. Ibid.

16. Pit's report, a major source of information concerning Dutch and local trade in the 1680s, can be found in K.A. (Koloniaal Archief, The Hague) 1267, 27 April 1682, ff. 1852–1046b. The village of Draksharama (transcribed variously as Daatseron and Dacherom in Dutch records) is in the center of the eastern Godaveri delta; Palikollu is in the western Godaveri delta not far from the English factory site of Madapollem; and Nagalwance (probably the village of Naugeelaconda) is on the old road from Masulipatnam and Golconda and not far from the modern district town of Khammam. Bimilipatnam, also the site of a Dutch factory, apparently did not gain a joint-stock company at this time, for no charter for the Bimilipatnam merchants appears in Pit's report.

17. For further details of the structure of the joint-stock company as organized under Dutch supervision see Arasaratnam, "Aspects," pp. 588–589. It should be noted, however, that Arasaratnam draws his examples from joint-stock companies in existence in the eighteenth century.

18. Compare the lists of textile varieties brought to Masulipatnam and the factories in the Godaveri delta in K.A. 1262, 1682, ff. 635b–636; and K.A. 1267, 21 April 1682, ff. 2053b, 2066b.

19. Ibid.

20. *Mackenzie Collection (Private)*, vol. 55, p. 16.

21. Temple, *Diaries*, vol. 2, p. 115.

22. Ibid., vol. 2, p. 143.

23. K.A. 1267, 30 September 1682, ff. 1814–1814b. This lists the Draksharama merchants under the heading "Debiteuren" (accounts receivable) and brackets those merchants trading together and the Dutch owing a common debt. The debts owed by these merchants indicate that despite their employment of their own capital they still depended on Dutch credit.

24. K.A. 1276, 13 August 1683, f. 1422b.

25. Raychaudhuri, *Jan Company*, p. 147.

26. Ibid.

27. C. Fawcett (ed.), *The English Factories in India, 1670–1676* (New Series) (Oxford, 1952), vol. 2, pp. 124–125, 146.

28. Ibid., p. 146.

29. *Records of Fort St. George, Diary and Consultation Book, 1680–1681*, 30 June 1680, p. 43.

30. Ibid., 1 July 1680, p. 43.

31. Ibid., 4 July 1680, pp. 44–45.

32. Ibid., p. 45.

33. Ibid., 5 July 1680, p. 45.

34. Ibid., 7 September 1680, p. 65. Lingapa's blockade was not simply a response to Vencatadry's appeals but part of a larger effort to bring the Dutch in Pulicat and the English in Madras under closer control.

35. Ibid., 6 October 1680, pp. 71–72.

36. Fawcett, *English Factories in India*, vol. 3, p. 32.

37. Ibid., p. 27. Many, but not all, of the castes of southern Coromandel since about the eleventh century were members of two distinct caste clusters known as followers of the right hand or left hand. These two groups had evidently gained in importance in the seventeenth century, especially in such market cities as Madras, and in 1651–1652 Madras had witnessed a severe riot between them. The chief merchant in Madras had almost consistently been the leader of the dominant right-hand castes, the chief of these being the Telugu merchant communities of Balijas and Komaties.

38. Ibid., p. 12.

39. *Records of Fort St. George, Diary and Consultation Book, 1681*, 24 February 1681, p. 7.

40. Ibid., 14 July 1681, p. 35.

41. Ibid., 17 October 1681, p. 60.

42. *Records of Fort St. George, Diary and Consultation Book, 1688*, 26 July 1688, p. 116.

43. Ibid., 19 August 1688, p. 130.

44. Beri Timmanna's name appears at the head of the signatures to the contract of 1692, the place usually taken by the chief merchant. *Records of Fort St. George, Dairy and Consultation Book, 1692*, 31 July 1692, pp. 33–34.

45. By 1694 Timmanna's associates, Allingal Pillai and Modu Viranna, were dead. A year later he himself slipped out of Madras leaving various debts unpaid, the English without a chief merchant, and thorough confusion in the Madras merchant community. *Records of Fort St. George, Public Dispatches to England, 1694–1696;* letter dated 31 January 1695, p. 40; and letter dated 30 September 1696, p. 58.

46. For the earlier mention of Chacka Serappa in 1680 see *Records of Fort St. George, Diary, 1680*, 2 September 1680, p. 64.

47. *Records of Fort St. George, Diary and Consultation Book, 1703*, pp. 24, 25, 33, passim. I disagree with Arasaratnam's interpretation ("Aspects," p. 591) in which he sees the joint-stock company functioning to instruct Serappa and the other merchants of Madras in the virtues of mutual cooperation. In a proper context the events of 1703 suggest rather that the joint-stock company was ineffective in communicating such lessons.

48. For an instance of cooperation see *Records of Fort St. George, Diary and Consultation Book, 1703*, 25 December 1703, p. 87, where merchants of both right and left-hand castes (Colloway Chittee and Pedde Tombe Chittee are explicitly identified as members of the left-hand castes; *Records of Fort St. George, Diary and Consultation Book, 1707*, 29 August 1707, p. 57) offer surety for the debts of Chacka Serappa.

49. *Records of Fort St. George, Diary and Consultation Book, 1707*, 22 August 1707, p. 54 and passim.

50. *Records of Fort St. George, Letters to Fort St. George, 1684–1685*, 16 April 1685, p. 81.

51. K.A. 1249, 2 February 1680, f. 1503b ff. Appare the Dutch organized the merchants of Tegenepatnam into a joint-stock company before introducing the concept into northern Coromandel.

European Missionaries and Chinese Clergy, 1654–1810

C. R. Boxer

This subject is one which contains many instances of both cooperation and conflict. If there was partnership, as there was, it was often (though not invariably) apt to take the form of what a premier of Rhodesia styled black and white partnership in that country—the horse and rider, with the white man as rider. I have briefly surveyed this problem in the old Portuguese colonial empire, and Fr. Horacio de la Costa, S.J., has done a deeper study of the parallel problem in the Philippines.[1] Some attention has also been devoted to certain aspects of this topic in the history of the Roman Catholic church in Japan.[2] The present essay therefore concentrates on the situation in China, where the native clergy did not become more numerous than the European until the last quarter of the eighteenth century.[3]

Although there had been converts to Christianity among the Chinese who lived in the Sino-Portuguese (or Luso-Chinese) settlement of Macao from the time of its early days, these were not, apparently, very numerous for some decades.[4] Nor could Matteo Ricci's slow, steady, but unspectacular development of the Jesuit mission in mainland China be compared with the remarkable growth of the Jesuit mission in Japan during the last quarter of the sixteenth century. These facts may help to explain why the Jesuits were even slower to set about establishing an indigenous clergy in China than they had been in Japan, where only four native priests had been ordained by 1604. The question was, of course, considered, but nothing much was done about it.

Indigenous catechists and (later) lay brothers existed in increasing numbers, but none of them obtained more than minor orders, even after long and faithful service. Father Lazaro Cattaneo, S.J., writing to the Jesuit General at Rome (on 12 October 1599) from Macao, asked him to give orders that two local Chinese brothers, Fernandez and Martinez, who had been members of the Society of Jesus for ten years, should study some aspects of moral theology so they could later be ordained, "because they have served the Company very well and they have suffered to an extent which cannot be easily expressed . . . , both for their own consolation as to further encourage others to come out to these parts to serve God." He added that although the Japanese aspirants for the priesthood had recently received minor orders at Macao and were virtuous enough, "yet they are not so Portugueseified as are these Chinese Brothers" ("não são porem tão aportuguesados como estes Irmãos Chinezes"). Cattaneo's advice was not taken at Rome; and seven years later the Jesuit General, Acquaviva, writing to the visitor, Alexandro Valignano, observed that as regards the latter's proposal to ordain some Chinese and Japanese brothers as priests, "it seems to us that the Chinese should not yet be promoted to this degree, since they are very modern in the Faith ["muy modernos na Fee"], and it is necessary to gain a better experience of them in Seminaries, etc."[5]

The first Chinese to be ordained a priest in the Society of Jesus (and the second Chinese to be ordained anywhere) was a Macao born and bred Chinese whose biography has been eruditely rescued from oblivion by Fr. Francis Rouleau, S.J.[6] Taken to Rome when a schoolboy by the celebrated Fr. Alexandre de Rhodes, S.J., the lad became separated from his mentor on the overland leg of the journey in Armenia but was able to reach the Eternal City early in 1650. After studying at Rome and (more briefly) elsewhere in Italy, he was ordained at the Jesuit College of Coimbra in Portugal, apparently in the first semester of 1664. This was ten years after the Dominicans had ordained their first Chinese priest, Gregório López (Lo Wen-tsao, originally a Franciscan protégé), at Manila in 1654.[7] There was, however, a big difference between the two men. Whereas the elderly Gregório Lo or López was a "late vocation" with a very rudimentary knowledge of Latin, Emmanuel de Sequeira had received an excellent scholastic and theological education in the west but had forgotten nearly all his Chinese by the time he reached Macao again in August 1668. After a year's intensive study, he was able to slip into China, where he did excellent work on behalf of the mission before his premature death from consumption at Peking in May 1673. Gregório López, on the other hand, with his strong countryman's constitution, was able to become the first Chinese bishop and remained active in the ministry until his death at the age of about eighty in 1691.

Despite the good work done by both these Chinese priests in mainland China during the closing stages of the persecution that had begun in 1664, during which time they were the only missionaries who could circulate freely without disguise, many of the European missionaries were still very hesitant about the advisability of an indigenous Chinese clergy at this stage. The problem came up for discussion at the so-called Canton conferences of 1666–1668, when the missionaries of the three orders (Jesuits, Franciscans, Dominicans), who were detained rather than imprisoned at Canton, had plenty of leisure to discuss matters of mission policy and communicate with their superiors and colleagues at Macao. Views were divided then, and they remained so for the rest of the period with which we are concerned. Some were for ordaining Chinese, but only those with a good knowledge of Latin (Sequeira was the sole individual with this qualification at that time); others were in favor of ordaining elderly Chinese catechists of proved virtue, even if they had no knowledge of Latin, provided that Rome allowed the use of the liturgy in Chinese; yet others, including the majority of the Jesuits at Macao, were against ordaining any Chinese. The spokesman of this group of intransigents was the elderly Portuguese Jesuit António de Gouveia, who considered the Chinese to be "full of vices, irresolute, and inconstant." These critics considered that native Chinese priests, through their (alleged) immorality and greed, would ruin themselves and the European missionaries as well.[8]

The three Jesuits at the court of Peking (the Belgian Verbiest, the Portuguese Magalhães, and the Italian Buglio) were all ardent advocates of an indigenous Chinese clergy in a memorandum which they submitted jointly at some time between August 1666 and August 1667. The Padres da Corte, as they were commonly called, emphasized that Christianity in China could only be maintained with great difficulty and could not be extended at all without the aid of Chinese catechists and priests. Such catechists and clergy could be recruited from among the mainland Chinese and from the Chinese resident at Macao and Manila. These Chinese should not be expected to know Latin, owing to the great difficulty they had in learning it, but they should be recruited preferably from among the Chinese scholar-gentry or literati (automatically excluding the Chinese communities at Macao and Manila). The missionaries should be asked to indicate the most suitable candidates, and Rome should be asked for authority to ordain them as soon as possible. Rome should also be asked to authorize a Chinese version of the missal, some principal masses, and selected portions of the Roman breviary. This would suffice as a Chinese liturgy if the pope would sanction the saying of Mass in Chinese and the ordination of elderly candidates who possessed the foregoing qualifications. If possible, a seminary should be established at Manila for training young candidates.

This representation of the Padres da Corte was supplemented by an even more strongly worded one drafted by a Belgian Jesuit, François de Rougemont, early in December 1667. He argued that in the future the Chinese government would either actively favor, merely tolerate, or actively oppose the propagation of Christianity. In the first and second eventualities, evangelization would proceed so far and so fast that the European missionaries could not possibly cope with the harvest of souls. At least 1,500 men would be needed. But even if thousands of missionaries came (a most unlikely contingency), the Chinese government would never let them roam through the empire like a potential fifth column. Indigenous priests would be absolutely essential, and equally so in case of opposition and persecution, since they alone could circulate freely under such adverse conditions. If the Japanese, who were not such a cultured and civilized race, had been allowed to have a clergy of their own—too little and too late, he might well have added—why not the Chinese after eighty years of evangelization?

Obviously with António de Gouveia, S.J., and his colleagues in mind, Rougemont admitted that some missionaries claimed the Chinese were unfit to be ordained, ''since they are corrupt, feeble, and inconstant.'' Maybe some of them are, he retorted, but were the Cretans little saints?— an echo of St. Paul's denunciation of those islanders as liars and slow bellies. Were the Ethiopians and the Indians so firm? Were there not proud and corrupt people in Europe? The Anglians were regarded as barbarians, but priests and bishops were recruited from them—an echo of Pope

Gregory's *"non Angli sed Angeli."* Nor was it an adequate
excuse to say that the work of conversion could not succeed
until the emperor of China became a Christian and the secular arm could be employed to support the ecclesiastical.
For three centuries the early church could not rely on the
secular arm, but it ordained indigenous priests in Europe
nonetheless. The Church should now do the same in China,
while awaiting the appearance of a Chinese Constantine.

Rougemont further observed, truly enough, that the experience of eighty years had shown that many catechists and
converts remained steadfast under persecution. If there had
been some apostates, there was also a Judas among the
Apostles. Touching on a more tender point, he observed
that one objection to the formation of an indigenous clergy
was that the European missionaries would lose the authority
they now held. Though he did not say so, similar objections
had been made to the formation of an indigenous clergy in
Japan but had been overruled by the visitor Alexandro
Valignano. "Are we, then," Rougemont asked rhetorically
and reproachfully, "more engaged with maintaining our
authority than with maintaining and spreading the Faith?"
In any event, he argued, this danger could be avoided by
ordaining only those whom long experience had shown were
fit for the society—that is, elderly catechists and lay brothers
who had given faithful service. If the Apostles had waited
eighty years before ordaining their converts, the priesthood
would have died with them. Must we wait, he asked, until
the oldest and best-qualified men are dead and gone or until the other religious orders, less experienced and less
qualified than the Jesuits, start to ordain native priests?

Turning to the language question, Rougemont categori-
cally advocated the use of Chinese rather than Latin by the
native clergy, but only the Mandarin form used by the official classes. There were precedents for this position in the
Roman Catholic church; moreover the Chinese, xenophobic
as they were, would never allow the widespread use of a for-

eign language which could not be understood by the magistrates, but only by those people who followed a foreign religion and consorted with foreigners. Furthermore, if Chinese priests were taught to read Latin fluently, they would be able to read anti–Roman Catholic works written in that language. They might even have access to the works of Calvin and other heretics, or they might read books which criticized the colonial claims of Spain and Portugal in America, the Philippines, and Asia.[9] If, on the contrary, the Chinese priests use only their own language, "so noble and so estimable," they will learn only those portions of the Old and New Testaments which can be taught them without fear of misunderstanding or scandal.[10]

Even if these dangers were regarded as fanciful, Rougemont added, the use of Latin by Chinese priests was impractical for various reasons: the impossibility of teaching Latin to Chinese boys of good family because their parents would not allow it; the impracticality of teaching Latin to boys of slaves or bondsmen because of the universal contempt with which they would be regarded by their compatriots on account of their origin. Finally, Rougemont recommended the ordination of elderly Chinese of good family and conduct. Distinguished by their virtue and learning, they would have prestige in pagan eyes and the confidence of the converts. Among the thousands of Chinese Christians, there were undoubtedly some pious old literati widowers who were worthy of exercising the sacerdotal functions. By ordaining them, all difficulties would be surmounted and the dangers inherent in ordaining young men would be avoided. The present persecution should be taken as a dire warning to act before it was too late. If this opportunity was missed, the outbreak of another persecution would find the missionaries lamenting that there were no indigenous priests to take their places.

Discussion of the interconnected problems of the Chinese native clergy and liturgy continued in December 1667 and

January 1668 among the missionaries of the three orders detained at Canton. The mendicants and a majority of the
Jesuits finally agreed that Chinese should be ordained as
priests, but there were profound differences of opinion
about how this should be done. Most of the Jesuits were
partisans of the Chinese liturgy. The friars, on the other
hand, headed by Fr. Domingo Fernández Navarrete, O.P.,
opposed the use of the Chinese liturgy and insisted on
Latin. Navarrete argued strongly that in China, as elsewhere, seminaries should be opened for training Chinese
boys for the priesthood; there they would have no special
difficulty in keeping sexual continence and learning Latin.
He dismissed the use of literary Chinese for a liturgical
language as impracticable. It was too equivocal and it would
be next to impossible to translate the sacred books and
Roman liturgy correctly. That it had been done in Ethiopia
was not a precedent for doing it in China. Navarrete also
claimed that only Chinese priests, trained from boyhood,
would be capable of refuting the multiple pagan sects
which pullulated in China. He argued that old men were
not naturally more continent than young ones, unless they
were so old as to be decrepit and virtually useless. "Why
condemn Chinese youth before we have tried it out to see
whether it will be found wanting?" he concluded.[11] This
frank and full discussion among the three religious orders at
Canton in 1666–1668 led to no tangible results. The differing viewpoints could not be reconciled. There was no mention of the problem of the native clergy in the final forty
resolutions which were adopted. But I have summarized the
arguments at some length, since they represented various
schools of thought which continued to attract adherents
among the European missionaries for the remainder of the
colonial period.

The Jesuit missionaries detained at Canton were able to
send one of their number, the Sicilian Prospero Intorcetta,
to Rome as their procurator. Traveling via Macao and Goa,

he did not reach the Eternal City until 1672. Intorcetta was a convinced advocate of the speedy formation of an indigenous Chinese clergy, his own preference being for the induction into the society of carefully selected adults (over forty years old) of proved virtue. They would be drawn from the scholar-gentry or literati class among the converts, not from the existing catechists, who were men of humbler birth.[12] The Jesuit General, Gian Paolo Oliva, was impressed by these arguments to the extent that he ruled (in June 1672) that Chinese candidates for the priesthood could be admitted to the society provided that they were mature (over forty) men of unblemished reputation and that the visitor of the Vice-Province of China and two-thirds of the Jesuit missionaries voted in favor of admitting them. But only a small number should be admitted in any event. A seminary for training Chinese priests could be opened at Macao if the visitor and the provincial of Japan (whose mission field was then restricted to Indochina) agreed. A clear distinction was thus drawn between candidates for the priesthood and those who already were, or wished to become, lay brothers *(irmãos)* in the Society of Jesus.

If the general was cooperative to a considerable extent, the Congregation of the Propaganda Fide, which had the most influential voice in the final papal decision, was much less so. The Propaganda, after long debates, finally authorized the nomination in principle of twelve indigenous bishops in the Far East (six for Vietnam and six for China); but this concession was nullified in practice, since the Propaganda specified that such bishops should know Latin (July 1678), which none of those men did who were otherwise eligible to be raised to the episcopacy. François Pallu, vicar apostolic of Tongking and titular bishop of Heliopolis, was the leading advocate of an indigenous Far Eastern clergy at this period. He asked that the first elderly bishops to be consecrated be excused from knowing Latin, since in due course they would be succeeded by younger men who were

now being trained for the priesthood in a seminary established in 1664 at Ayuthia in Siam, where Latin was taught
to the students. The Propaganda refused to make this concession and the project collapsed, save for the belated consecration of Gregory Lo as titular bishop of Basilea in April
1685, although his own Latin, as everyone knew, was anything but fluent. The Propaganda also showed itself to be
then and later hostile to the use of the Chinese missal and
liturgy, although this use had been conditionally sanctioned
by Pope Paul V in 1615–1616. The Belgian Bollandist,
Daniel Papebroeck S.J., argued strongly in favor of the
Chinese liturgy seventy years later, and the Italian Jesuit
Luigi Buglio compiled a whole series of liturgical works in
Chinese at Peking between 1670 and 1678.[13]

Father Francis Rouleau, in his well-documented work on
Emmanuel de Sequeira, S.J., gently chides the latter for
warmly urging the Jesuit General to take immediate and active steps for the recruiting of "sacerdoti naturali" in December 1668. Writes Fr. Rouleau: "The problem was much
more complex than the inexperienced de Sequeira realized.
All agreed *in principle* on the need of a native clergy for the
permanent foundation of the Church. But finding candidates who gave guarantees of moral probity and stability, in
a Christian community that was still relatively small and
submerged in a massive society non-Christian in its ideas
and customs, possessing no Christian schools in the modern
sense and with only a handful of overburdened pastors to
instruct them—this was the practical stumbling-block that
worried even those most sympathetic to the progress of
indigenation." This observation is largely true, but two
comments are in order. In the first place, not all the missionaries *were* agreed in principle about the desirability of
forming a strong, viable, and self-perpetuating native clergy
and episcopacy. Secondly, some of the obstacles might well
have been surmounted if the use of the Chinese missal and
liturgy had been fully implemented, as its supporters—

many of them experienced men—constantly averred. This, of course, cannot be proved, for it was never done; but the failure of the missionaries to agree on a common line of action among themselves, though natural and perhaps inevitable, did not help Rome choose the best options available to the cardinals of the Propaganda Fide.

The painfully slow progress of the development of the Chinese indigenous clergy is evinced by a few facts and figures. After the death of Emmanuel de Sequeira (Cheng Ma-no Wei-hsin) in May 1673, the next Chinese Jesuits to be raised to the priesthood were three elderly catechists, all of them over fifty years old: Wan Chi-yüan (Paul Bañes or Banhes), Wu Li (Simão Xavier da Cunha), and Liu Yün-te (Blaise Verbiest). They were ordained by Bishop Gregory Lo at Nanking on 1 August 1688 and had just enough Latin memorized phonetically to get through a tortuous reading of the Mass.[14] The next Chinese Jesuit to be ordained was Ho K'i-wen (Francisco Xavier do Rosario), born of Christian Chinese parents at Macao in 1667 and fluent in Latin.[15] He was ordained by Bernardino Della Chiesa, the Franciscan vicar apostolic and titular bishop of Argolis, at the end of 1690.[16] Four years later, another two Chinese Jesuits were ordained as priests: Kung Kuan-jo (Thomas à Cruce or Thomas da Cruz), born at Hangchow in 1668 but educated at Macao where he had entered the society in 1686, and Kuo T'ien-pang (João Pacheco), born and bred at Macao.[17] Although the Roman Catholic church was now entering its golden age in Imperial China, when the K'ang-hsi emperor's favor to the scientist-missionaries at Peking facilitated the evangelical work of those in the provinces between 1692 and 1709, progress in forming a native clergy continued to be fitful and slow. It has been calculated that there may have been as many as 300,000 Chinese Christians in 1700–1701 (though 200,000, the number given by Fr. Antoine Thomas in November 1700, seems more likely to me). These were served by over a hundred priests belonging to the various orders and institutions, but only four or five of them were Chinese, the remainder being Europeans.

The proscription of Christianity decreed by the Yung-cheng emperor in 1724, although enforced with different degrees of seriousness in the provinces, once again emphasized the need to expand the indigenous clergy and revived the problem of the Chinese liturgy. The French Jesuit mission (independent of the Portuguese since 1687) had no Chinese priests; the Portuguese vice-province had three; the Missions Étrangères of Paris had but one. The French Jesuit Superior, Julien Placide Hervieu, who had been in China since 1701, warmly pressed for ordaining elderly Chinese literati and using a Chinese liturgy. He added that many missionaries would rather not have an indigenous clergy at all than ordain young Chinese, even if the papacy forbade the ordination of elderly literati. A small majority of the Jesuits in the French mission were in favor of ordaining young Chinese, but they were (at that point) unaminous that such aspirants to the priesthood should not be trained in China itself but outside.[18] The missionaries in China—and elsewhere for that matter—also remained divided over whether to ordain only men of good family (scholar-gentry or literati) or whether to accept those of peasant and artisan stock. Advocates of the latter procedure could point to the precedent of the Twelve Apostles.[19] Meanwhile, the Propaganda had ordered that five young Chinese of good family, character, and intelligence, between the ages of ten and fifteen, should be sent to Rome, accompanied by a European missionary who knew Chinese well, in order to be educated at the Urban College of the Propaganda. The Missions Étrangères de Paris seminary in Siam was also educating adolescents from China and Indochina for the priesthood, teaching them Latin and everything else they would learn in a European seminary. The secretary of the Propaganda, in reporting Hervieu's request to the cardinals, argued that there would be no point in ordaining elderly Chinese who were ignorant of Latin, since they could only celebrate Mass and could not perform any other sacerdotal function, owing to their ignorance of moral theology. They could not, he averred, even be trusted to hear confession without grave danger of frequent misunderstanding. After consulting with several veteran missionaries then in Rome, the secretary advised strongly against allowing the use of a Chinese liturgy. He pointed out that up to now "there has not been a single European missionary who can translate into Chinese a book or even a brochure without the help of Chinese literati."[20] With the possible exception of Matteo Ricci, S.J., this statement was, I think, perfectly true; and we may return to this point later, after examining the development of the indigenous Chinese clergy for the rest of the eighteenth century.

Ehrenbert Xavier Frideli, the Austrian Rector of the Portuguese Jesuit College at Peking, wrote to the Jesuit General on 26 November 1726: "It is absolutely necessary either to found seminaries in which young Chinese can be trained, or to allow the Chinese [priests] to administer the sacraments in their own language, or to do both these things, otherwise the mission will not be able to maintain itself, let alone expand, without a miracle."[21] But his equally experienced colleague, the Alsatian Jesuit Roman Hinderer, opposed the training and ordaining of young Chinese candidates, and Hervieu continued to press for the ordination of elderly Chinese. Three such were ordained at the end of 1730, but this action was widely criticized by many of the non-French missionaries. Hervieu's successor, Joseph Labbe, reversed his policy and sent five young Chinese to be educated at the Parisian College of La Flèche in 1740. Yet another reversal occurred when Hervieu became Jesuit Superior again and obtained a ruling from the Jesuit General that Chinese should *not* be sent to France. After his death in 1746, this ban was revoked three years later at the request of the French Jesuits at Peking, and three young Chinese were sent to Paris in 1751. Two of them returned in 1766 and were criticized by Michel Benoist, S.J., for having become completely Europeanized and forgotten their own language and culture—as had happened to a lesser extent with the pioneer Emmanuel de Sequeira in the Seventeenth century. After the suppression of the Society of Jesus in 1773, the surviving French ex-Jesuits at Peking continued to form a few indigenous priests. They taught young boys Latin and ecclesiastical functions, made them catechists, and if they proved their worth by many years' service, ordained them when they had reached about forty years of age.[22]

Meanwhile, the Portuguese Vice-Province of China, which included Austrian, German, and Italian missionaries, likewise varied in its approach to this problem over the years. In 1730–1731, it had only three Chinese priests: Francisco Xavier do Rosario (ordained 1690), Thomas à Cruce (ordained 1694), and Aloysius Fan (ordained 1709), all of whom knew Latin well. However, the Padres da Corte and the Jesuits at Macao differed in their approach. The former wanted to send Chinese students to Europe for more thorough training; the latter wanted to educate them in the College of St. Joseph at Macao. This they started to do in November 1731 on the following lines: students would keep their lay dress but be taught Portuguese and educated and treated like European novices; after their novitiate, they would learn Latin and moral theology. The courses would take from eight to ten years, during which time it would become clear whether they had a genuine vocation. If so, they would be ordained and become missionary priests. If less worthy, but adequate, they would become *irmãos coadjutores,* or coadjutor-brothers. If they had no aptitude or vocation, they would be dismissed. This scheme was put into practice, but the suppression of the Jesuits in the Portuguese dominions by the (later) Marquis of Pombal in 1759–1762 resulted in the closure of the college and the collapse of the scheme before it had time to turn out many native priests.[23]

As for the Dominicans, they, too, had chopped and changed their position. Two years after their ordination of Gregory Lo, the Chapter-General of the order at Manila decided that henceforth no Chinese should be admitted as a novice or ordained as a priest. They maintained this negative attitude despite Gregory Lo's own plea for a native clergy after he had become titular bishop of Basilea. They only reversed this stand in 1730–1732, when their own missionaries working in Fukien province asked leave to send some Christian boys to Manila to be educated for the priesthood. Three were admitted straightaway, and the Castilian crown later approved this project and gave the Dominican Convent of Santo Thomas at Manila a grant for the maintenance of six Chinese students.[24] The Franciscans did not try to ordain any Chinese priests, either then or later.

Perhaps the most successful of the institutions for training Chinese clergy was the "collegio dei Cinesi" at Naples, which had been founded by an Italian former missionary to China, Matteo Rippa. This institution opened its doors in July 1732. It functioned, with considerable ups and downs, until 1888, and during the eighteenth century it produced an impressive number of Chinese priests, as compared with those formed by the Jesuits and by the Missions Étrangres de Paris in France. Pope Benedict XIV, who, like most of his predecessors, showed no enthusiasm for the use of Chinese as a liturgical language, expressed himself as delighted with the progress in Latin and theology made by eight Chinese students from Naples, whom he personally interviewed in 1751.[25]

One of the outstanding native priests produced in the eighteenth century was André Ly, whose role in keeping the mission going in times of persecution was in some ways comparable to that of Gregory Lo in the seventeenth century. He had been educated for fifteen years at the General College of Siam, maintained by the Société des Missions Étrangères as a seminary for the training of indigenous Asian clergy, principally Indochinese and Chinese from 1664 to 1769. He was ordained in 1725, and he worked thereafter in China (mostly in Fukien and Szechwan) for over forty years until his death in 1774. Adrien Launay has published the journal he kept in Latin, covering the period 1747–1763. It is much to be wished that an English translation was available, as it is an unrivaled source for indicating what the Chinese priests thought of their European colleagues and superiors. It is interesting, but not surprising in view of his educational background, to note that André Ly was opposed to the use of Chinese as a liturgical language; and he urged that the indigenous clergy should know Latin. Apart from anything else, he doubtless realized that their European colleagues would respect them more if they did.[26]

From the preceding sketch, it will be seen that the formation of an indigenous Chinese clergy was truly a thing of shreds and patches—or "painful *tâtonnements*" as Fr. Francis Rouleau, S.J., has characterized it. There were never enough of them to go round, and their education varied between Macao, Manila, Peking, Ayuthia, Paris, and Naples, as well as in a few of the inland towns and cities of China. For many years their number was far less than that of the European missionaries in China, although they, together with the catechists, bore the brunt of the daily missionary work, especially in times of persecution when the Europeans were more or less continually "on the run." In 1739, there were still only eighteen Chinese priests working in mainland China, as compared to a total of seventy-six European missionaries, thirty of whom were at Peking and eleven at Macao. Of the eighteen Chinese priests, eleven were Jesuits, three were Propagandists, and four were from the Missions Étrangères.[27]

As a result of the persecution of 1746–1748, conditions

became still more critical, but the proportion of Chinese clergy rose. Of forty-four European missionaries working in the provinces, only sixteen remained. Only one Chinese priest was caught, although most of them had to move elsewhere than in their usual districts for a time. The Chinese priest who was caught, a Jesuit named Diogo (Jacobus) Madeira Pao, apostatized under torture, recanted his apostacy, but relapsed a second time under renewed torture. The examining magistrate did not realize that Madeira Pao was a priest but thought he was merely the servant of the Portuguese Jesuit missionary, Antonio José Henriques, who had been in China since 1726 and was arrested at the same time and subsequently killed in prison. Diogo Madeira Pao was released after a short imprisonment. Having with some difficulty been absolved by a German Jesuit at Peking for his double apostacy (as the Portuguese refused to do so), he seems to have ended his life as a model sower of the Gospel seed on the island of Hainan.[28]

Much more serious for the missionaries, both European and Chinese, was the persecution of 1784–1785, which has been admirably described and analyzed by Fr. Bernard H. Willeke, O.F.M.[29] He makes the point that this was the first time the Chinese officials realized there were Chinese priests who knew western languages and who were appointed and paid by the papacy. The wording of the imperial decree of 31 December 1784 banning the native clergy (*shên-fu*) may imply this, but it is hard to believe that such was really the case.[30] Even though Diogo Madeira Pao never admitted his priestly status while apostatizing twice under torture, there were a fair number of voluntary apostates embittered against the missionaries throughout the seventeenth and eighteenth centuries. These apostates (one would think) probably told all they knew without being prompted. They must have known of the existence and the ecclesiastical status of such active and long-lived indigenous priests as Gregory Lo, Thomas à Cruce, Paul Su, and Adrien Chu, to mention only some of the best known.[31] There were also two Chinese Jesuits deported from Macao to Goa and Lisbon together with their European colleagues in 1762, but the local Chinese officials made no attempt to rescue them, as they easily could have done, perhaps because they chose to regard them as Europeans. In any event, the Chinese priests caught in the persecution of 1784–1785 were treated much more severely than their European coprisoners, several of whom were speedily pardoned by the Chien-lung emperor and others subsequently.

As invariably happened during these periodic bursts of active persecution, the advocates of developing an indigenous clergy raised their voices more loudly and were listened to with greater attention at Rome. But, as also invariably happened, no sooner had the storm blown over than the advocates of "gradualness" made their voices heard. Their opinions prevailed. In 1785, the secretary of the Propaganda at Rome, Msgr. Stefano Borgia, argued that the consecration of Chinese bishops as soon as possible was the only effective way to save Christianity in China from extinction. But later reports indicate that the storm had abated and the future looked brighter. Moreover many, perhaps a majority, of the surviving European missionaries felt that the Chinese clergy were not yet ready to assume episcopal responsibilities and that the leadership of the Chinese church must be retained in foreign hands. The Propaganda therefore decided (5 March 1797) to consecrate more foreign bishops, but no Chinese.[32] Still, at long last the Chinese priests were more numerous than their European coworkers, despite the severe losses both categories had suffered in 1784–1785. The Roman Catholic mission in China counted 113 priests in 1810, of whom 35 were foreigners, thus leaving the indigenous clergy with a substantial majority.[33]

Readers who have persevered thus far will realize that the Roman Catholic church in China never had enough priests, whether foreign or indigenous, to serve a widely scattered

Christian community which may have numbered as many as 300,000 in 1700, when there were about 100 foreign missionaries, and which still numbered about 120,000 in 1740. In other words, the church in China depended on the Chinese catechists even more than it did on the Chinese priests. Many Christian communities in remote rural districts could only be visited by a priest once every few years and sometimes not for many years on end. When the golden days of the mission in the reign of the K'ang-hsi emperor were over, the missionaries could only circulate in the provinces with the greatest circumspection, usually at night. In times of persecution they did not live in houses but on boats which frequently changed their anchorage along the rivers and canals or else in caves in the mountains or in miserable wooden shacks.[34]

Under such circumstances, despite the prodigies of endurance and self-denial frequently displayed by the fugitive, concealed, or incarcerated European missionaries, it was only the Chinese priests and catechists who could circulate freely. The maintenance of the church in China depended on their loyalty and devotion. Nor did they fail in the testing times of trial and tribulation. The European missionaries were apt to complain that their converts were timid and irresolute under persecution, contrasting them unfavorably with what they had read about the admirable steadfastness of the Japanese converts in 1614–1640.[35] Yet their own voluminous and detailed reports from the mission field often contradict this allegation of Chinese cowardice. Apostates and backsliders, of course, there were, as was only to be expected among communities which included many half-instructed or long-neglected individuals; but most of the actual apostacies were made under savage torture, or the dire threat of it, and many apostates subsequently returned as penitents to the fold.

During the persecution of 1664–1668—not a very severe one, it is true—most of the adult baptisms administered by

Gregory Lo during his circuit of the provinces were of catechumens who had been converted and prepared for the sacrament by individual catechists or by those who acted as heads of their local Christian community when no priest was available. It was also trusted catechists who acted as couriers between the Chinese Christian communities and the imprisoned European missionaries.[36] The same happened in later persecutions, and it was the courier-catechists who were entrusted with the task of smuggling into the interior the newly arrived priests at Macao—a task which they accomplished often at very considerable risk to themselves and which they ran for twenty, thirty, or more years on end. As typical examples, we may cite Mark Yuan, Bishop Laimbeckhoven's faithful courier-catechist, and the Dominican catechist Raimundo, who always brought from Canton the annual *socorro* of chocolate and pieces of eight for the Spanish missionaries in Fukien, as well as recruits for the mission.[37] In the course of the eighteenth century, women were frequently employed as catechists, and they often proved to be even more zealous and effective than the men.[38]

It should also be noted that even when converts and catechists gave way under torture—and Chinese judicial torture was very severe indeed—they usually managed to frame their admissions in such a way as to avoid involving the missionaries directly. Father Bernard Willeke correctly notes of the persecution of 1784–1785: "Though the Manchu government usually succeeded to a remarkable degree in finding out the facts, the Christians often enough did find plausible, yet evasive, answers which satisfied the questioning officials."[39] True enough, and the same applied to all the previous persecutions. These evasive tactics help to explain why foreign missionaries in hiding were so rarely caught, and why the persecutors were so often diverted from their quarry like hounds on a false scent.

One other point should be mentioned in conclusion, although church historians, in their understandable inclination to extoll the merits of their persecuted coreligionists, seldom mention and never stress it. Christianity could have been stamped out in China, or driven underground as it was in Tokugawa Japan, if the anti-Christian edicts had been ruthlessly and systematically enforced over a long period of time, or if the Buddhist and Taoist neighbors of the Christians had consistently denounced their presence to the local authorities. Neither of these two things occurred. Even in the great persecution of 1784–1785, the most serious and systematic to date, some provinces were hardly affected at all, and the Christian community at Peking remained undisturbed, as did those in Fukien. Local mandarins often dissimulated about the presence of missionaries in their districts, either out of toleration or else because they did not want to admit that missionaries were active in the regions under their jurisdiction, or both. Even when direct and categorical orders came from the Dragon Throne to intensify the search for hidden missionaries, these orders were by no means always implemented.

The Chinese have often been taxed—not least by many of the missionaries—with being basically xenophobic. Yet time and again we find that the presence of a passing foreign missionary in a Chinese village merely drew curious crowds to peep at him and his outlandish face (his clothes, of course, were Chinese), but they did not give him away.[40] Thousands of "heathen Chinese" must have known of the activities of Chinese priests and catechists, yet informers were rare, as the whole history of the mission shows to any impartial reader. While amply acknowledging, therefore, the steadfastness and courage of European missionaries and Chinese clergy and catechists alike, we should not forget that the mass of the people, especially in rural districts, must have tolerated the propagandists and the adherents of the foreign religion, even if they never joined it. As for the attitude of the Manchu emperors during the eighteenth century, however stern the wording of their anti-Christian edicts, the fact remained, as Père Antoine Gaubil, S.J., wrote in 1750 to one of his correspondents in France: "Ici on a liberté pour la capitale, en Europe on ne l'a pas à Londres, Amsterdam, Stockholm."[41]

NOTES

1. C. R. Boxer, *The Portuguese Seaborne Empire, 1415–1825* (London, 1969), pp. 250–261; idem, "The Problem of the Native Clergy in the Portuguese and Spanish Empires from the Sixteenth to the Eighteenth Centuries," in *The Mission of the Church and the Propagation of the Faith (Studies in Church History*, vol. 6), ed. C. J. Cuming (Cambridge, 1970), pp. 85–105; Horacio de la Costa, S.J., "The Development of the Native Clergy in the Philippines," in *Studies in Philippine Church History*, ed. Gerald H. Anderson (Ithaca, 1969), pp. 65–104, a revised and enlarged version of an article first published in *Theological Studies* 8 (June 1947).

2. Hubert Cieslik, S.J., "The Training of a Japanese Clergy in the Seventeenth Century," in *Studies in Japanese Culture*, ed. J. Ruggendorf, S.J. (Tokyo, 1963), pp. 41 et seq.; Jesús López Gay, S.J., "Las Organizaciones de laicos en el apostolado de la primitiva misión del Japón," in reprint from *Archivum Historicum Societatis Iesu*, vol. 36 (Rome, 1967), pp. 1–31; C. R. Boxer, *The Christian Century in Japan, 1549–1650* (Berkeley, 1951), pp. 72–90, 218–226, 326, 395.

3. Two very useful articles on the indigenous Chinese clergy in the seventeenth and eighteenth centuries, but which do not claim to exhaust this subject, will be found in Johannes Beckmann, S.M.B. (ed.), *Der Einheimsche Klerus in Geschichte und Gegenwart* (Schöneck-Beckenried, 1950)—by Xavier Bürkler, S.M.B., "Die Bewährungsgeschichte des Chinesischen Klerus im 17 und 18 Jahrhundert," pp. 119–142, and by Johannes Beckmann, S.M.B., "Die Lateinsche Bildung des Chinesischen Klerus im 17 und 18 Jahrhundert," pp. 163–187. I have avoided repetition of these articles and approached the problem from another angle.

4. The Spanish Franciscan lay brother, Fray Juan Pobre, was, however, clearly exaggerating when he claimed in 1597 that the Jesuits had never converted more than five local Chinese to Christianity. See C. R. Boxer, "Friar Juan Pobre of Zamora and His Lost and Found 'Ystoria' of 1598–1603 (Lilly MS. BM 617)," in *Indiana University Bookman* 10 (1969):25–46, esp. p. 39.

5. Pasquale M. D'Elia, S.J., *Fonti Ricciane. Documenti originali concernenti Matteo Ricci e la storia delle prime relazione tra l'Europa e la*

Cina, 1579-1615 (Rome, 1942-1949), vol. 1, pp. *cxxx* n, 292 n. Valignano was already dead when Acquaviva wrote this letter on 12 December 1606.

6. Francis A. Rouleau, S.J., "The First Chinese Priest of the Society of Jesus, Emmanuel de Siqueira (Cheng Ma-no Wei-hsin), 1633-1673," 50-page reprint from *Archivum Historicum Societatis Iesu,* vol. 28 (Rome, 1959).

7. Rouleau, "The First Chinese Priest," p. 20 n; José M. González, O.P., *Biografia del primer Obispo Chino* (Manila, 1946).

8. François Bontinck, C.I.E.M., *La Lutte autour de la liturgie chinoise aux 17ᵉ et 18ᵉ siècles* (Louvain-Paris, 1962), pp. 108-122.

9. As Bontinck points out, this observation was made chiefly for the benefit of the Portuguese Jesuits, most of whom were opposed to the use of the Chinese liturgy, in the hope that it might induce them to drop their insistence on Latin.

10. For similar care in expurgating even orthodox religious works in the earlier Japan mission, see Boxer, *Christian Century,* pp. 190-192.

11. For a balanced and judicious estimate of Navarrete, which takes adequate account of the views of his Jesuit opponents, see J. S. Cummins, *The Travels and Controversies of Fr. Domingo Navarrete, O.P., 1618-1686* (Cambridge, 1962).

12. Bontinck, *La Lutte,* pp. 130ff. Rouleau, in *"Emmanuel de Siqueira,"* p. 38, makes one of his rare errors when he states in his clear and concise account of Intorcetta's mission to Rome that the Sicilian advocated the ordination of "catechist-priests." On the contrary, Intorcetta stressed that none of the Jesuits in China favored ordaining their catechists: these were recruited from the lower classes, and if ordained would never receive the respect of the literati. Even individuals of their own social status would not want to receive the sacraments at their hands.

13. One of Daniel Papebroeck's arguments was that if the Protestant kings and princes of Northern Europe said they would return to the obedience of the Roman Catholic church, provided their respective national languages could be retained as the liturgical ones, the papacy would have no hesitation in agreeing to this request. For Buglio's Chinese missal and other liturgical works see Bontinck, *La Lutte,* p. 154.

14. Rouleau, *"Emmanuel de Siqueira,"* pp. 4 n, 38; Bontinck, *La Lutte,* pp. 246-252.

15. Bontinck, *La Lutte,* p. 252, points out that Pfister errs in calling him an Eurasian.

16. G. Mensaert, O.F.M. (ed.), *Sinica Franciscana,* vol. 5 (Florence, 1954), p. 180.

17. Bontinck, *La Lutte,* p. 264. L. Pfister, *Notices biographiques et bibliographiques sur les Jésuites de l'ancienne mission de Chine, 1552-*

1773 (Shanghai, 1932), has no record of Thomas à Cruce after 1735 but I have an autograph oath of his, swearing to observe the papal constitution *Ex quo singulari*, signed and dated "Xamhay" (Shanghai), 10 March 1744.

18. Bontinck, *La Lutte*, pp. 300–303.

19. Bontinck, *La Lutte*, p. 322.

20. Bontinck, *La Lutte*, p. 313.

21. Bontinck, *La Lutte*, p. 332.

22. Bontinck, *La Lutte*, pp. 322–344.

23. Bontinck, *La Lutte*, p. 348. See also Manuel Teixeira, *Macau e a sua diocese*, vol. 7, *Padres da diocese de Macau* (Macao, 1967), pp. 324 ff., for the names of the Chinese priests educated at Macao, whether at St. Joseph's or elsewhere. The Seminary of St. Joseph was reopened in 1780 under the Lazarists.

24. Bontinck, *La Lutte*, pp. 232–233, 347; Benno Biermann, O.P., "Briefe des ersten chinesischen Priesters und Bischofs Fray Gregório López O.P., 1683–84," in *Der einheimische Klerus in Geschichte und Gegenwart*, ed. D. J. Beckmann, S.M.B., suppl. vol. 2 (Schöneck-Beckenried, 1950), pp. 99–117; José Maria González, O.P., *Misiones Dominicanas en China, 1700–1750* (Madrid, 1952), pp. 23–24.

25. Bontinck, *La Lutte*, pp. 345–351, 356–358. In his *De Sacrosancte Missae sacrificio* (1740), Pope Benedict XIV, whose papal constitution *Ex quo singulari* of 1742 ostensibly put an end to the celebrated Chinese Rites Controversy, observed: "In the recent conversion of peoples, it is the responsibility of the Holy See to allow or to refuse the use of the vernacular in the divine offices, in accordance with the prevailing circumstances. But one can affirm that the Holy See inclines rather to the solution of teaching Latin to the most capable among these peoples than to concede the faculty of saying mass in the vernacular." (I have adapted Bontinck's French translation here.)

26. I have been unable to consult either A. Launay, *Journal d' André Ly, prêtre chinois, missionaire et notaire apostolique, texte latin* (Hong Kong, 1924), or J. M. Sédès, *Le Prêtre Chinois, André Ly* (Paris, 1943), which I presume to be the standard biography.

27. Joseph Krahl, S.J., *China Missions in Crisis: Bishop Laimbeckhoven and His Times, 1738–1787* (Rome, 1964), pp. 14–15.

28. Krahl, *China Missions in Crisis*, pp. 53–54, 109. The arrest of António José Henriques had a grave repercussion in Europe, since the Chinese magistrates accused the Padre of illicit relations with his female converts. The women denied this; but the allegation was believed by some Franciscan and other missionaries, obtained wide currency in Europe through Pombal's slanderous anti-Jesuit propaganda, and is

echoed in such contemporary works as *Authentic Memoirs Concerning the Portuguese Inquisition* (London, 1761), pp. 413–414.

29. Bernard H. Willeke, *Imperial Government and Catholic Missions in China During the Years 1784–1785* (New York, 1948).

30. "But we take into consideration the fact that they are ignorant people and were misled. They helped the Westerners and have been tempted by their financial assistance. We direct that after their case has been properly examined, they be banished to Ili and given as slaves to the Eleuths" (Willeke, *Imperial Government,* pp. 89–90). See also Georges Mensaert, O.F.M., "Le Père Pie Liu minor, Missionnaire au Shensi d'après sa correspondance, 1760–1785," in *Der einheimische Klerus,* vol. 2(1), pp. 143–161.

31. Georges Mensaert, O.F.M. (ed.), "Adrien Chu, prêtre chinois et confesseur de la Foi, 1717–1785," in *Nouvelle Revue de science missionaire,* 12(1956):19. For Paul Su and the vital work he performed in Fukien and elsewhere, see González, *Misiones Dominicanas,* index s.v.

32. Willeke, *Imperial Government,* pp. 161–167; J. Beckmann, B.S.B., "Beratungen der Propaganda-Kongregation über die Weihe Chinesischer Bischöfe," in *Missionswissenschaft und Religionswissenschaft* 3 (Münster, 1940), pp. 199–217.

33. Joseph Dehergne, S.J., "La Mission de Pékin vers 1700: Etude de Géographie Missionaire," in *Archivum Historicum Societatis Iesu,* vol. 22 (Rome, 1953), p. 315, n. 3.

34. A graphic account of these trials and tribulations will be found in Krahl's *China Missions in Crisis,* but the whole history of the Roman Catholic church in China is replete with them.

35. Typical example in González, *Misiones Dominicanas,* vol. 2, pp. 440–452, letter of Juan Alcober, O.P., dated 2 February 1730.

36. Rouleau, "Emmanuel de Siqueira," pp. 30–31, n. 73.

37. Krahl, *China Missions in Crisis,* p. 120; González, *Misiones Dominicanas,* vol. 2, pp. 455, 459, 506, et passim.

38. Henri Bernard-Maître, S.J., in *L'Histoire Universelle des Missions Catholiques,* vol. 2 (Paris, 1957), pp. 178–179; González, *Misiones Dominicanas,* vol. 2, pp. 112–113.

39. Willeke, *Imperial Government,* p. 25.

40. Krahl, *China Missions in Crisis,* pp. 5–8, for the experiences of Bishop Laimbeckhoven on his journey from Macao to the interior at a time when he knew no Chinese.

41. Renée Simon (ed.), *Le P. Antoine Gaubil, S.J., Correspondance de Pékin, 1722–1759* (Geneva, 1970), p. 639, Gaubil to Dom Vaissette, Peking, 22 November 1750.

Gujarati Merchants and the Red Sea Trade, 1700–1725

Ashin Das Gupta

The Red Sea at the turn of the eighteenth century provided the Gujarati merchants with their principal market, and, in addition to the annual fleet from the Mughal port of Surat, it attracted a large number of immigrants from Gujarat and Kathiawar. Hindu Bania settlers mainly from Kathiawar and Muslim shippers and merchants from Surat and Ahmedabad formed important elements in the urban population of Yemen and took some part in local political processes. The major attraction for the Gujaratis was the annual pilgrim market at Mecca where merchants from the far-flung cities of the Ottoman empire came to buy coffee and textiles, but the Gujaratis also helped clothe the inhabitants of the Red Sea area and Hadramaut with the products of the looms of western India. Europeans played only a small part in the trade to the Red Sea. In their main activities, the sale of spices and the purchase of coffee, they offered no competition to the Gujaratis. Insofar as they attempted to take part in the trade in textiles and to capture the carrying trade between Surat and Mocha they were, in the first quarter of the eighteenth century, held off by the Gujaratis. During this period, however, Gujarati trade was seriously undermined by forces within the Asian world, and the European merchants, particularly the English private traders, were left a relatively free field for their enterprise.

Figures for Indian trade are elusive and unreliable, but there is reason to believe that in a good year at the turn of the eighteenth century Surat's total turnover would have been over 16 million rupees. No more than 1.5 million of this would have been handled by European merchants: the rest would have been absorbed by the trade of the Indian Ocean, including trade with the cities of the Indian coasts, and handled by the Gujaratis themselves.[1] About twenty Gujarati ships sailed every year from Surat to Mocha and Jedda carrying pilgrims for the hajj as well as the annual trade of much of northern and western India. On average these ships were about 200 tons of deadweight carrying capacity, and it is possible they took with them 4 million rupees worth of textiles, which would yield a gross profit of around 50 percent if the hajj turned out a clement one.[2] The shipping was owned primarily by a small number of Muslim merchants of the city of Surat, but some Hindu merchants of Surat, Cambay, and Diu also owned ships and deployed them on the Red Sea run. Few European ships were seen on this route, and in size they were no different from the Gujarati vessels.

Because of attacks made by European pirates on the Red Sea fleet at the close of the seventeenth century, the Mughal government ordered the Dutch East India Company's lodge at Surat to provide escort vessels for the Gujarati ships on the Mocha run. Documents relating to the convoy, which lasted from 1696 to 1701, consisted of "instructions" issued by the lodge to the commanders of the Dutch vessels and "reports" turned in by commanders after the round trip. These documents provide us with interesting information about this fleet, known at Mocha as the "fleet of Hindustan,'' and about the trading season which in the Red Sea was marked by the appearance and departure of this fleet.

The Dutch never liked the Mocha convoy and gave it up as soon as they could. It is true that they took the opportunity to carry Gujarati freight to the Red Sea, turned the voyages into trading trips of their own, and even earned some money by providing this service to the Mughal government.[3] But the vexations of sailing with the Gujaratis were intolerable. The Gujaratis had little sense of sailing in formation. Each *nakhuda* (commander) was a little god on his own ship and displayed the waywardness of immortals. Every year before they set sail, the Dutch circulated copious instructions in good Persian relating to the convoy. It is questionable, however, whether many of the *nakhuda*s of Surat were fluent readers of Persian and, in any case, the numerous instructions about sailing procedures undoubtedly confused them. Some of the Gujarati ships were fast sailers and experienced in the Red Sea run while others were slow and had little familiarity with the route. Besides, each wanted to be first at the market and first to return, as the textiles sold better early in the season and the commercial intelligence which the ships brought back was vital for the market at Surat. There was also some virtue in being the last at both ends because, if the ship were a good one, it could pick up the late freight. Mulla Abdul Ghafur, the principal shipowner and merchant of Surat, knew these truths well, and the Dutch could do little about his ships, which were always the most numerous in their convoy.[4]

Under the circumstances the Dutch commanders did not feel they could provide protection for the entire convoy and fell back on the best alternative: they stuck as close as they could to the Mughal imperial ships under their charge. These Mughal ships, of which about two would usually make the voyage, were meant to be primarily pilgrim vessels but were much favored by the Surat merchants for carrying freight. Besides the fact that for some obscure reason they were regarded as "safer" than others, they enjoyed certain privileges at Mocha and Jedda which the freighter found attractive. All the Gujarati ships were overloaded with goods and passengers, but conditions on board the imperial vessels were probably even worse. Still they enjoyed great prestige, and the nucleus of the Hindustan fleet sailed with the Mughal ships.[5] The principal Mughal *nakhuda* was a person of great importance. He was an imperial official, a *mansabdar*, and he lived and behaved like a minor prince.[6] The world he carried with him on board ship would seem to have been the world of the Mughal court. Scattered data suggest that it was not marine expertise which conferred importance upon a person on an Indian ship but his social position. The *nakhuda* on any of the principal ships was seldom a maritime person. Sometimes a wealthy shipowner would himself come on board one of his vessels as its *nakhuda*. Occasionally he would place one of his sons, or another close relative, to act as his *nakhuda*. Eminent merchants of Surat often went as *nakhuda*s with the fleet of Hindustan. Amir Rezzak, a famous *nakhuda* of Mocha, was known in the Dutch documents as the *Arabishe landheer*, which may have meant an Arab landed magnate or simply an Arab aristocrat. The marine expert on board the Indian ships was the *sarang*, and whenever the Dutch commanders called a technical meeting to discuss the sailing of the convoy, it was the *sarang*s from the Gujarati vessels who would be in attendance. Most *nakhuda*s liked to ape the style of life set by the Mughal *mansabdar*s, and certainly the *nakhuda*s of Abdul Ghafur lived luxuriously, while their "superb conduct" often irritated the Dutch.[7]

A report written in 1701 on the voyage to Mocha and the season in the Red Sea by Dirck Clercq and Cornelis Snoeck for the edification of Hendrik Zwardekroon and the Dutch council at Surat is the best of its kind and gives a picture in the round of what the Red Sea run was like if one traveled with the fleet of Hindustan.[8] The fleet, such as it was, started very late. In fact several ships sailed away before the Dutch vessels, which waited obstinately for the Mughal ships to be ready. There were two imperial ships, the *Fateh Shahi* and the *Ganj-i-Sawai*, making the voyage this year. Hajji Muhammad Fazal was the principal Mughal *nakhuda* on board the *Fateh Shahi* while the *Ganj-i-Sawai* was under the command of Muhammad Mohsin. On 1 April 1701, when the Dutchmen were at the end of their patience and worried about missing the monsoon, the chief *sarang* of the *Fateh Shahi* presented himself on board the Dutch vessel *Nieuwburg* and conveyed the compliments of *nakhuda* Muhammad Fazal; he added that the imperial vessels were now ready to sail. The Dutchmen were happy to learn that both Mughal *nakhuda*s had written to the local governor praising them for waiting for the imperial ships, and the letter had been well received at the local *darbar*. It was agreed that they would sail the following day because the *sarang* said it was an auspicious time for Muslims. The Dutchmen were impatient, however, and tried to discover whether an earlier start was possible. Two hours after the *sarang* had departed, the *Nieuwburg* fired a gun as starting signal and lifted anchor along with her sister ship, the *Schellag;* but the Mughal ships did not move and the anchors had to come down again. A start was eventually made in the morning of 2 April 1701, but within a few hours of sailing the Dutch were alarmed to discover that the *Ganj-i-Sawai* of Muhammad Moshin was lagging about 4 miles behind the others. A meeting was called on board the *Nieuwburg* to which the chief *sarang* of the *Fateh Shahi* brought his *nakhuda*'s compliments and the information that the *Ganj-i-Sawai* was in no difficulty and was now catching up fast. "This is an accursed manner of sailing," the journal on board the *Nieuwburg* noted, "and each of the Moor ships contributes its best to our difficulty, one sailing ahead, another behind, so that in case of need, which the good God forbid, the Company's ships would be in no position to acquit themselves of their duty and protect the Moor vessels from the danger that may threaten."

In the night of 2/3 April 1701 the *Fateh Shahi* shot to the head of the convoy: "a very bad habit" said the *Nieuwburg*'s log, as it made holding the convoy together a matter of luck. There were other bad habits. On 7 April 1701 the *Nieuwburg* saw a ship approaching from behind. The *sarang* of the *Fateh Shahi* informed the flagship that it was one of Abdul Ghafur's which had started one day later from Surat. Indeed it was: the *Fateh Murad,* a fast sailer, which rapidly overhauled the fleet, saluted the imperial ships with its guns, did not recognize the Dutch, and went full sail ahead toward the Red Sea leaving the convoy in a tangle.

Except for the usual exasperations nothing interesting happened during the next two weeks. Once, in the night of 20/21 April, the *Ganj-i-Sawai* sailed ahead of the convoy while the *Fateh Shahi* lagged so much behind that the *Schellag,* in alarm, turned back to investigate. Nothing was wrong, however, and in the morning of 21 April Hajji Muhammad Fazal sent the *Nieuwburg* some fish caught by his boat and asked whether the Dutch officers would honor him with a visit. The invitation was, of course, accepted. On a fine morning, probably 22 April, the Dutchmen appeared on board the *Fateh Shahi* and were most hospitably received. Hajji Fazal took *opperhoofd* Dirck Clercg by the hand and led him into his own cabin where everybody was seated and served with coffee and numerous kinds of Persian fruits. As the company settled down to the repast, they were entertained by musicians playing Moorish instruments. The visitors formed a high opinion "of the civility of the *nakhuda,*" who was sorry when they rose to take their leave and offered them betel on parting. He walked with them "in great modesty and courtesy" to the deck and watched them get into their boat. As soon as the boat was well away, the guns of the *Fateh Shahi* fired a seven-gun salute while a salute of five guns came from the *Ganj-i-Sawai*. It had been hoped that the voyage would be finished in under a month, fast time for this route, but the fleet ran into calms for several days after sighting Socotra on 28 April 1701. It was not till 12 May that they anchored at Aden. The *Rampassa*, a Cambay ship which had joined the convoy in the last lap, did not wait at Aden, and probably many others went on to Mocha as well. The Dutch ships stopped because the imperial ships had decided to do so. Hajji Muhammad Fazal was interested in extending the concessions usually given to the Mughal ships by the Yemeni administration and exempting one of his ships from customs and to this end wrote off a letter to the imam's court. The Dutchmen did not know it at the time; they only felt depressed at the sight of the twelve or thirteen ships already at Aden and the knowledge that another fifteen or sixteen were at Mocha and a few at Jedda. "From this it can well be seen," said the *Nieuwburg*'s journal, "that this country is being traded to death by this enormous shipping and above everybody else by the merchant or to put it better that underminer of markets, Abdul Ghafur."

Hajji Muhammad Fazal did not obtain what he wanted from the imam's government and in pressing for it made rather a fool of himself. On arriving at Mocha on 16 May 1701 he decided not to land till the concession had been granted him in writing. He waited on board for two weeks, much to the delight of the town, which knew he was waiting in vain. Eventually he landed and, in the customary royal reception, was received outside the town walls by the brother of the town's governor with a retinue of a hundred soldiers or so. All the visiting *nakhuda*s were in the welcoming party, and all the ships in the road fired salutes as the Mughal *nakhuda* was carried in a palanquin to the blowing of trumpets and playing of many another musical instrument. "It seemed," wrote the Dutchmen at their lodge, "that the entire town had been brought to its feet."

The season turned out to be one of mixed fortunes. For

one thing, news came in from Jedda of a poor market, and there was much gloom among merchants selling textiles as their trade depended on Jedda. Information from Persia, however, was good. It seemed that the city of Basra after a temporary eclipse would revive under its Turkish administration. This news particularly cheered the merchants in the coffee trade as they expected larger sales. The Dutch sold their spices, sugar, and a few other imports like iron, lead, and alum well, and they bought 200,000 pounds of coffee at a substantial profit. One rather bizarre incident broke the monotony of an otherwise humdrum season. A fishing boat brought information to the port of a large, mysterious vessel anchored off the Bab el Mandeb. These were years of dreadful pirate attacks, and the town was at once in an uproar. "The principal *nakhuda* of the ships of Abdul Ghafur," noted the Dutch journal in discussing the panic, "ordered all his soldiers who were on land back on board their respective ships. He himself began to behave like a soldier and take all precautions in case his ships were attacked. This was not bad, but we believed firmly that in case of a real attack all these figures would vanish in the wind as soldierly qualities among people such as these comprised in nothing more than bravado when there is no danger." Fortunately for all concerned, the firm belief was never put to the test; no pirates appeared at the port.

By the middle of August, Gujarati vessels began to arrive from Jedda, their *nakhuda*s eager for the Dutch convoy on their homeward journey. On 19 August 1701 the journal noted the sailing of five ships for Kung in the Persian Gulf and the return of the only English ship of the season to Madras. "So the road begins to empty," it said, and noted the urgent requests of the Jedda *nakhuda*s to be away. But, of course, the decision had to be that of the imperial *nakhuda,* and, after a nerve-racking delay, the fleet of Hindustan, twenty-one vessels in all, set out for home on 30 August—only to run into all the problems of sailing in convoy. The *nakhuda*s of Ghafur in particular had no intention of remaining in convoy longer than they could help, and as soon as they were well clear of the Bab, and presumably the danger of piracy, several of them broke away and headed for home. This move was to have dreadful consequences for everybody concerned, but that story properly belongs to the history of Surat.

Here we may leave the account furnished us by Clercq and Snoeck of their voyage to the Red Sea from Surat in 1701. The importance of the Mughal *nakhuda* and the enigmatic presence of Abdul Ghafur emerge clearly from the narration. Ghafur owned eight of the nineteen vessels which sailed homeward with the Dutch ships that year. He had probably made his enormous fortune in the Red Sea trade and owned, besides warehouses, one of the largest mansions in the town of Mocha. His *nakhuda*s would stay in this house during the season and sometimes round the year to supervise the sale of his merchandise. Ghafur was a much honored man at Mocha and enjoyed special exemptions from customs at the port. Some of his principal *nakhuda*s were mentioned by name in the Dutch accounts and their doings were chronicled, although the Dutch did not have a favorable opinion of their master. There can be no doubt that the house of Ghafur at Mocha belonged to the high society of Yemen and was treated as such. It is more than likely that a few other wealthy merchants of Surat, like Muhammad Chellaby and Shaikh Hamid, received similar treatment at the Red Sea port.[9] There were other Muslim merchants from Gujarat who came and went every year, making their modest profit in the Red Sea trade. Such were the Bohras of Ahmedabad, none of whom were individually distinguished but who were of some importance as a community of merchants. In 1713, for instance, the merchants of Ahmedabad succeeded after long agitation in forcing the local administration to alter the price of gold in favor of silver. Ottoman merchants who brought gold had earlier persuaded the imam to favor them over the Indians, who dealt almost exclusively in silver.[10] This kind of triumph was interesting because the Gujaratis possessed only economic leverage against the local administration. Revenues from the ships of Surat were the mainstay of the imam's government at Mocha, and while Muslims from elsewhere, from Muscat for instance, were socially honored and financially favored, the Gujaratis won whatever concessions they could by their economic importance to Mocha.[11]

The curious paradox of economic importance and social inferiority was reflected in the manner of living of the Gujarati Banias. There were two kinds of Banias engaged in the Red Sea trade. There were those who came and went every year, doing their own trade and handling the business of others who remained at home in much the same manner as the Muslim merchants were wont to do. Banias from lower Gujarat, particularly from the cities of Surat and Cambay, were of this kind. Others had been long settled in Yemen and were found not only in every Yemeni city but in the port towns of Habash and the Hadramaut as well. Apparently Banias from Kathiawar, the Kapol Banias of the peninsula, were predominant among those who settled in Yemen, and immigrants from the ports of Gujarat and Kathiawar continued to come to Yemen throughout the first decades of the eighteenth century.[12] The Bania merchants of the Yemeni cities and the Habash ports controlled much of the commercial life of the area but, in Yemen at any rate, they lived like second-class citizens.

The importance of the Banias in the financial life of Mocha was evident in what was called the *nowroz:* the new-year system of payment. No one sold anything except coffee for cash at Mocha. For everything else, payment was deferred and was calculated according to the Bania calendar. The Banias closed their books as soon as the fleet of Hindustan sailed. Any sale after that date would automatically go on the next year's book and be paid on 100, 200, or 300 *nowroz:* that is, in January, April, and July. The Gujarati new year—Deevali, the festival of lights—followed closely on the departure of the Gujarati shipping. And at Mocha these were crucial dates of the trading season. Besides, everyone at Mocha kept book in an imaginary coin of account, usually called the Mocha dollar, occasionally the Bania dollar, which was fixed at 2½ percent below the Spanish dollar. The coin of account, the system of settling debts, and the calendar all demonstrated the ascendancy of the Bania merchants at the Yemeni port city.[13] In spite of their wealth and financial importance, these Hindu merchants were not welcome in the heartland of Islam. They were thought to be unclean infidels whose presence contaminated the spiritual atmosphere of Yemen. On this ground a "holy man" who emerged suddenly in 1700 arranged a massacre of three hundred Banias. Only resolute opposition from all Muslim merchants of Mocha prevented him from doing further good work.[14] Such passion for cleanliness was, however, not normal at Mocha; much more irksome were the restraints imposed upon the Banias by laws of the imam's government. They were not allowed any public performance of their religion. In the event that any of them died in Yemen, he was to be buried, not cremated. Banias were not allowed to bring their women into the country and were strictly forbidden relations with Arab women.[15] Officers of the administration fleeced them with impunity whenever the government was in need. Nevertheless Banias continued to come and make their little arrangements which would make life somewhat tolerable. They brought their Brahmans with them. On days which required public celebration of religious rituals they, with their priests, would go outside the town walls and hold their ceremonies under the sky.[16] Temples were not built, but several houses in town were used for worship, and officers of the administration were persuaded to wink at their presence.[17] The Banias married at home and would often return to India for prolonged periods. On these occasions they transferred whatever money they had accumulated in trade back to their ancestral city, which in most cases was Diu. The government knew this and made it difficult for rich Banias to leave Mocha. But it was natural that Banias who had grown old would wish to return home so that when they died they would have a proper Hindu funeral. No one was ever physically prevented from leaving.

In many ways, the Bania settlers of Yemen were admirable men. They knew they could expect no protection from the Mughal government,[18] and the government in Yemen barely tolerated their existence. They found themselves discriminated against at the customhouse and in business in general. But by their tenacious hard work, their thrift, and their expertise, they made whatever profit there was to be made in trade at Mocha. They were, of course, not ideal men. No one trusted them. They were quarrelsome, especially among themselves, and pursued their stupid vendettas with devotion. And occasionally their thrift outran their discretion, leaving them the laughingstock of the town. Thus it was said that on one occasion when the city was on fire, a number of Banias were seen arguing with the water carriers about how much should be paid for their services, unmindful of the conflagration in their homes.[19]

The family of Virachand, who had been born at Diu but made his fortune at Mocha, were among the leading Bania traders in Yemen at the close of the seventeenth century. Virachand was the broker for all European merchants at Mocha, for their East India companies as well as their private trade. Virachand was fluent in Arabic and spoke Portuguese, a qualification which not many Bania merchants apparently possessed. The first recourse of a European at Mocha was to the house of Virachand, where he would stay if necessary till proper accommodation was found in the town.[20] In 1711 Virachand, who was old and had been planning to return to Diu, died suddenly. He was survived by seven sons of whom the eldest, Mathura, inherited most of the property and took general charge of the family business. The brothers continued to live together, and for a long time to come the family was known at Mocha as "the sons of Virachand." Mathura did not know any European languages. Neither did the immediate younger brother Makhan who, till his death in 1719, managed the business of the family at the great coffee market at Beit al-Faqih. A third brother, Pitambar, much praised in the Dutch papers both for his linguistic abilities as well as his work, eventually took over the European brokerage.[21] But he did not stay at Mocha for long afterward, leaving for Diu in 1716 "to settle some family business." He never came back, and the European brokerage was taken over at his recommendation by his brother Trikam, who had for some time past been his deputy in that office.[22] The children of Virachand, in spite of their local eminence, suffered cruelly in the persecution of the merchants at Mocha in the 1720s. This persecution, directed especially against the Gujarati Banias, was the cause of the family's decline.[23]

The persecution of the merchants at Mocha caused not merely a decline in the fortunes of individual families but was at the root of the decline of Gujarati trade to the Red Sea. To understand the significance of this phenomenon, however, we must keep clearly in mind some of the features of trade and politics in the Red Sea during this period. For one thing the textiles which the Gujaratis brought to the Red Sea went in the main to the annual market at Mecca and were sold only partly to the inhabitants of Yemen, Habash, and Hadramaut.[24] It was stated repeatedly that trade at Mocha depended upon the market at Jedda—that is, the market of the hajj. The pilgrim caravans which came to Hejaz via Cairo brought money for those Yemeni merchants who sold coffee and for the Gujaratis who sold cloth. It was a complex and delicate network which reached Mecca through and from many another city of western Asia and northern Africa. Much could go wrong with this market, and once that happened, the Gujaratis were assured of "a poor season."

To some extent the Gujaratis were themselves to blame for a run of poor seasons at the turn of the eighteenth century. Whatever the reason, they had significantly expanded their shipping at the close of the seventeenth century and the large exports they sent annually to the Red Sea could not be absorbed in that market.[25] To this difficulty was added a somewhat mysterious falling away of the Ottoman demand in the second decade of the eighteenth century which hit the Gujaratis hard. The supply of money from Jedda to Mocha which the merchants of Mocha earned through the sale of textiles was disrupted in 1708. From this year complaints of "scarcity of cash" at Mocha because of the poor market for textiles at Jedda became common. The scarcity of money was so acute in 1714–1715 that half the main shops at Mocha remained closed after the season. The situation worsened for the Gujaratis because English private traders began large shipments of textile to the Red Sea at the close of the second decade of the eighteenth century. In the early 1720s there was panic in the town. Several merchants declared bankruptcy as they were unable to meet the demands for cash.[26] This acute depression affected only the market in Indian textiles and was caused by the failure of the hajj as far as the Gujaratis were concerned.

The market in Yemeni coffee on the other hand was doing well throughout the period and continued to prosper during the 1720s. Coffee was bought principally by "Turkish merchants" who came every year to Jedda with the hajj caravans. European purchase of coffee compared with the Turkish demand was small; the Indians bought very little.[27] Early in 1709, when the market in textiles was badly depressed, coffee rose sharply at Beit al-Faqil because of large purchases by Turkish merchants.[28] The price did not fall in 1710, although the Dutch East India Company bought nothing that year.²⁹ Similar information stressing the role of the Turkish merchants in keeping coffee prices high was recorded almost every year up to 1719. In the 1720s, with the European companies also buying largely, coffee prices became about double of what they were earlier.³⁰

The fact that textiles were depressed while coffee was doing well demonstrates that there was little connection between the two markets. Clearly some money earned by the merchants of Yemen, Arab, and Bania was used to buy Gujarati cloth. Much of it perhaps represented the local demand of Yemen and the immediately adjoining countries. What was declining in the early eighteenth century was the demand for Indian cotton cloth at the hajj, and the money which poured into Yemen every year for its coffee did little to rescue the merchant in the textile trade. To some extent the interests of the coffee merchant and those of the merchant in the Gujarati textile trade were conflicting, although the conflict was not a major one. The Dutch and the English financed their purchases of coffee to a large extent by borrowing money from merchants at Mocha and paying them at Surat. Gujarati merchants usually availed themselves of this method to remit their profits back to Gujarat, thus avoiding risks at sea and the customs at Mocha and Surat.³¹ But they and those who were associated with them in business were opposed to lending any money to the Europeans early in the season—it took money out of Mocha and into Beit al-Faqih at a time when they needed it at Mocha. At least once, in 1723, they made a determined attempt to stop this practice, but it appears that the coffee interest proved stronger and nothing eventually came of the move.³²

The trade in Gujarati textiles in the Red Sea was thus suffering from a glut at the turn of the eighteenth century, a glut created mainly by the Gujaratis themselves. By 1720 the position had worsened due to the falling demand for cottons at the hajj and the competition from English private traders. Yemen's bouyant trade in coffee, from which some Bania merchants doubtless derived considerable advantage, was no help to the main body of Gujarati merchants interested exclusively in textiles. The sustained civil war which erupted in Yemen in 1714 added a sanguinary element to the Gujarati tales of woe. The government at Sana, beset by rebellion, came to treat Mocha, its principal port, as a milch cow. The pressure from the central government for continuously increased contributions was naturally passed on by the administration at Mocha to the merchants of the city. The claim for much higher taxes at a time of declining trade eventually proved the undoing of Gujarati trade to the Red Sea.

It would, however, be quite wrong to suppose that high and arbitrary taxation was a new problem for the Gujaratis in the Red Sea. There had been complaints about rising taxes since at least the close of the seventeenth century.[33] Gujaratis trading at Mocha were accustomed to dealing with a complex structure of political power, elements within which kept shifting and adjusting continuously. The imam at Sana, head of the Zaidi Shia sect which ruled the country, was, in some sense, the man in control. But the *wazir*, the imam's chief minister at Sana, was often the ruler's eyes and ears. The *wazir* kept the imam informed, but the minister in his turn had arrangements with the governors of the various towns so that part of their extralegal takings went to him. A governor at Mocha operated with the *wazir* and the imam at one end and "the notables of the city" at the other. Principal merchants from Surat as well as the visiting Mughal *nakhuda* would usually be included among the local notables, but none of the Banias in the city. The Gujaratis keenly watched the continuous shifts within the structure of power which stretched from the quays at Mocha to the palace at Sana. They had but one intention: to pay as little as possible for permission to carry on their commerce. They did not, however, act as one common body to protect their interests. Whatever may have been said about Gujarati mercantile organizations, the evidence indicates that the Gujaratis had not evolved institutions to take care of their common interests. They saw one another as competitors rather than fellow merchants. And the administration at Mocha treated the Gujaratis with varying degrees of severity. Those who were better treated saw no point in combining with the others who had the worst of everything.

In Yemen in the early eighteenth century trade and politics were closely intertwined. The imams of the period took a close and personal interest in the India trade. Two ships of the Zaidi imam were annually deployed on the Gujarat run, and it was said that the imam established a personal monopoly in certain Indian textiles at Sana.[34] The involvement of the governors of Mocha in the trade of the port probably began no earlier than 1704, but once begun by Governor Saleh Horebi it was continued and soon became a considerable nuisance at least for some merchants.[35] In the 1720s, local Arab merchants who were close to the government operated a monopoly in certain commodities. High officials of the imam's government, besides the governor of Mocha and his favorites, also took part in the Indian Ocean trade throughout the period. In the town of Mocha factions were formed around the intertwining networks of trade and politics, and official "oppression" could be understood in terms of the prevailing realities of the situation.

The European documentation never comes to grips with the formation and dissolution of factions at Mocha. But there are stray bits of evidence which indicate even if they do not illuminate a fluid situation. The bizarre story of the murder of the *qanungo* of Mocha by the visiting Mughal *nakhuda* in 1698 was an illustration of this instability. Saleh Bhai was the *qanungo*—the official who represented the interests of the foreign merchants at the port. He and his brother Kasim Bhai,[36] a high official at the court of Sana, were deadly enemies *(dood uijand)* of the Mughal *nakhuda* who visited Mocha in supreme command of the two imperial ships, the *Fateh Shahi* and the *Ganj-i-Sawai,* in 1698.[37] The *nakhuda,* oblivious of the fact that the monsoon was ending, made a journey to Sana and, it was said, paid 26,000 dollars to the imam, who "made over" Kasim Bhai and the Mocha *qanungo* to him. The *nakhuda,* before he left for Surat, had the *qanungo* murdered but took Kasim Bhai away to India with him. A senior official of the Sana court, Ali Wazir, was sent to the Mughal court as ambassador of the imam, and he appears to have acted with the *nakhuda* in the matter and left Mocha on board one of the Mughal ships. The imam changed his mind about the matter and ordered the governor of Mocha to leave the two brothers alone, but his orders arrived too late. When the imam learned of it, he punished not only the governor but several leading Arab merchants of the city who were thought to have ganged up against the late *qanungo.*[38] The ambassador to India, Ali Wazir, on his return to Yemen settled down at Mocha as a private merchant and "tried to provide for his very large family from the profits of trade." The decision not to return to the political life of Sana presumably was connected with the unpleasant aftermath of the murder of Saleh Bhai. Unfortunately for Ali Wazir, Shaikh Saleh Horebi, who had by 1709 established some sort of a monopoly at Mocha, forbade him all trade at the port.[39] Governor Horebi at the time was working closely with Amir Rezzak, the imam's *nakhuda,* and Qasim Turbati, the leading merchant of Mocha.[40] His interests at Sana were protected by the *wazir,* Faqih Musa. This combination was indeed very strong; nevertheless, as Ali Wazir found himself without any means of subsistence, he complained to the imam. His letter fell into the hands of Faqih Musa, who suppressed it and warned Horebi. Horebi promptly banished Ali Wazir from Mocha. The aggrieved man went off to Jedda, where he began to agitate among the merchants of that port against the governor of Mocha. The agitation was eminently successful. Soon a large delegation from Jedda waited on Imam Al Mahdi to explain to him the pernicious practices of Saleh Horebi and Faqih Musa. The imam confessed himself totally surprised that such monopolies had been established by his officials. He then arrested Musa and recalled Horebi from Mocha.[41] Both Rezzak and Turbati were arrested and heavily fined as "bosom friends" of Horebi.[42]

Saleh Horebi was out of power at Mocha for about a year when a Turkish aristocrat who had fled to Mocha from Mecca and was living as a merchant was appointed governor. Horebi maneuvered him out of the office partly by stratagem and partly by luck. The new governor was discredited because of a fluke attack of the Muscat men-of-war upon the fleet of Hindustan which he was unable to deal with.[43] At the same time, Horebi cornered the grain market at Mocha and neighboring cities. Prices rose so much at Mocha that his successor was unable to remit the usual tribute to Sana. In 1710 Horebi was reinstated as governor of Mocha, although he continued to live at the imam's court while his deputy, Abdur Rahman, ruled the port. It is possible that the understanding he reached with the imam was that henceforth he would share his monopoly profits with the ruler.[44]

The Imam Al Mahdi was at the time a feeble old man in his eighties, and a struggle for succession had already begun at Sana. Sidi Ibrahim, the eldest son of Al Mahdi, was faced with a strong bid for power by Sidi Qasim, a nephew of the imam's and the most successful general of the Sana government. Saleh Horebi, Amir Rezzak, and Qasim Turbati were supporting the faction of Sidi Qasim. The Mughal *nakhuda* who arrived at Mocha in 1712 knew nothing of these complexities and was not interested in them. He was an exalted nobleman of the Indian empire, a commander of five thousand horse, and, it was said, a former governor of Gujarat. His rank, in fact, was so high that it was considered inappropriate to call him a *nakhuda*—by tacit agreement everyone called him Mirza Saheb. Now such a grandee from the Mughal court had seldom come to Mocha, and Bania merchants with their many complaints of ill treatment at the port flocked to him. Mirza Saheb was patently unhappy with the deputy governor of Mocha, Abdur Rahman, and the Mughals at least on one occasion came to blows with the local soldiery. Some of the complaints which Mirza Saheb heard at Mocha made him particularly furious.[45] As there was no redress at Mocha, the high Mughal *mansabdar* made the journey to the imam's court with considerable difficulty. The results were all that could be desired. Sidi Ibrahim appears to have jumped at the chance of wiping out the Horebi faction at Mocha which this unexpected embassy provided. Two of his slaves quickly appeared at Mocha with the imam's orders to bring up Abdur Rahman and his Bania counselor Manji to the court. Both had to pay a fine before they set out. A second order imposed heavy fines on Turbati and several other merchants, presumably of his faction, and all of them were banished from Mocha. Rezzak, however, was untouched and Horebi himself retained his position at Sana.

Eminent Muslim merchants from Surat appear to have supported the Horebi faction at Mocha throughout these years and were allowed to continue their business unmolested, whatever may have happened to the smaller fry from Gujarat. Amir Rezzak, who went every year to Surat, was closely connected with the shipowners of that city.[46] Qasim Turbati, when exiled from Mocha, went and lived at Surat with his entire family. He was, in fact, so close to the Gujaratis that there was speculation at Mocha that he was partly responsible for the journey of Mirza Saheb to Sana for redressing the complaints of the visiting merchants from India's west coast.[47] Turbati and his family maintained this close rapport at least till the 1720s, as was evidenced in the important meeting in 1723 at the house of Abdul Ghafur which was attended by a son of Turbati's.[48]

The political revolution in Yemen between 1714 and 1716 placed power in the hands of Sidi Qasim, who became Imam Qasim Mutwakil Bilah. At once Amir Rezzak was raised to even greater consequence at Mocha. Turbati appears to have fallen out with Rezzak for a time and faced bankruptcy as a result of official exactions. But he came through and dominated Mocha for several more years. Conditions created by the upheaval were, however, such that merchants of Mocha in general came under heavy financial pressure and the Gujaratis, residents of Mocha as well as visitors, fell victim to the change. The new imam engaged in sustained armed conflict with his relations and was forced to spend ever more on retaining the loyalty of his armed forces. Customs at the seaports and all other sources of public revenue were farmed out to officials. The port of Mocha, richest source of revenue for the imam's government, faced continuous demands for extraordinary contributions. Matters went very badly with the hapless Banias from Kathiawar, but no merchant was now spared.[49]

Documents written at Mocha—letters, diaries, memoirs— from around 1716 make dismal, occasionally harrowing, reading. As repeated demands for money reached the town from Sana, local merchants were called upon to provide the cash. Banias from Diu and Porbandar were usually overassessed at customs by 100 percent, and Muslim merchants from Gujarat and elsewhere were treated little better. Soldiers would sometimes be billeted on the homes of the Gujarati Hindus, which for them meant disaster. There was at least one occasion when even distinguished Hindu merchants were mercilessly beaten till they paid what was asked. There are repeated references to merchants leaving Mocha and occasionally fleeing to a mosque outside the town walls for sanctuary. The intensity of the persecution varied. Those who could protect themselves least suffered the most. But evidence in the 1720s indicates that even the house of Ghafur was not exempt from the extortions of the government. Individual misfortunes were nothing new at

Mocha; sporadic official tyranny was known. But the sustained attack on mercantile property was a fatal innovation. The tragedy for the Gujarati merchants lay in the fact that they were at the same time exposed to similar persecution at Surat and other Gujarati cities. It was this simultaneous breakdown of administration in Mughal Gujarat and Zaidi Yemen which more than anything else destroyed the Gujarati trade to the Red Sea.[50]

Competition or collaboration with European merchants had little role in the mainstream of Gujarati commerce with the Red Sea. Of the Europeans the Dutch East India Company at the turn of the eighteenth century sold some spices at Mocha and bought coffee, neither of which interested the Gujaratis. The English company, which began significant operations in the Red Sea during this period only in 1716, was exclusively interested in coffee. It is true that without the assistance of the family of Virachand no European could hope to succeed at Mocha, but compared to the operations of great Gujarati families like that of Mulla Abdul Ghafur, the Virachands were not of much consequence. Again, it is true that the two European companies derived some advantage from the use of Gujarati money at Mocha to buy their coffee while the Gujaratis used this method of transfer to Surat, but the amounts involved, compared to what must have been the total Gujarati trade, were small.[51]

In two minor areas of trade there were, however, minor confrontations between the Gujarati and the European merchants. The Dutch company traded in a small way in textiles to the Red Sea, and textile imports by English private traders became heavy toward the very end of the second decade of the eighteenth century. Besides, there was, throughout, the question of the carrying trade which both the European and the Indian shipowners wished to capture, although at the time the competition was not keen from the European side. The Gujaratis held their own in both branches of trade. The Europeans had to be content with little profit in textiles and what little freight they could obtain on the Red Sea run. As long as the structure of trade was not undermined by political pressure, there was no question of anybody driving the Gujaratis out of the Red Sea market.

In European circles reflections on the textile trade were uniformly gloomy. Besides the fact that throughout the period only gluts and low prices characterized the Red Sea market, the seeming ability of the Gujarati merchant to carry on, regardless, was offensive. "It is impossible for us," a despondent Pieter Ketting informed Batavia in 1698, "to make out the accounts of the Muslim and the Bania merchants in their trade to Mocha as we do not know whether they buy cheaper than us or sell dearer." He did think the former was more likely. Besides—they were more expert at smuggling, they spent less on equipping their vessels, they bought little ammunition, and their employees, who were given no diet money, earned less than their counterparts in the Dutch service.[52] Whenever the Dutch factors at Mocha tried to sell the costly Madura textile their company sent them, they found the Gujaratis with their cheaper cloth and their immense imports, a well-nigh insuperable barrier. "It is almost unbelievable," wrote a much chagrined Ketelaar from Mocha in 1709, "how badly the textile prices slumped this year." He was mortified because he had been warned to sell his imports before the Gujaratis arrived and had not done so. Once the first ships of Abdul Ghafur hove to at Mocha, textile prices tumbled between 20 and 30 percent. "Each one of the merchants from Surat present here," added Ketelaar, "will have it that the *nakhuda*s of Ghafur sold far below their cost price. It is thus unintelligible how these gentlemen would account for their conduct to their master, unless we are to accept what diverse merchants from Surat report that Mulla Abdul Ghafur seeks only to establish a monopoly in the trade to Mocha and Jedda for himself and his people."[53] In 1720 factors of the English company, whose large imports of textiles were making the prevailing glut much worse, were equally discouraged by the strength of the Gujarati position in the market. Even though the Gujaratis paid 9 percent customs, which was 6 percent higher than the rate allowed the English, they bought their goods 15 percent cheaper.[54]

The Europeans fared no better in the struggle for the carrying trade. While it was true that European ships were more secure and better handled than Indian vessels, they charged higher freight, a difficulty made worse by the additional taxation of 2 percent called *verar*. The *verar* probably originated as an additional tax on freight goods as distinct from goods shipped by the owner of a vessel. Some distinguished owners, like the Mughal emperor or the two North European companies, were allowed by the administration at Mocha to have for themselves the *verar* on the freight their vessels brought. During the early years of the eighteenth century, however, the Mocha governor began to claim at least half the *verar* on the European ships for the government, while the Europeans were unwilling to relinquish their privilege. The upshot was that Indian freighters on European bottoms often paid at least 1 percent more on their goods.[55] A further deterrence was the prevalence of private arrangements made between European skippers and other officers and the Indian freighter. Whereas these arrangements for private freight appear to have been widely made, the Indians had no redress in case they had complaints: the European companies officially knew nothing of them.[56] The Dutch convoy ships to the Red Sea at the turn of the eighteenth century therefore carried no impressive amount in Gujarati freight. When the Dutch factors made it a special point to obtain Gujarati freight, they had to invent pirates prowling off the Bab el Mandeb.[57] In 1720, when the English factors at Mocha discovered that, contrary to their expectations, the English company's vessel the *London* had obtained little freight on the Surat-Mocha run, the only explanation they could offer was that it was the *verar* on board an English ship which still kept the Gujarati freighter away.[58] The struggle in the textile market and the competition for the carrying trade were to be intensified in the 1720s, but by then the Gujarati merchants had already been eroded.[59]

NOTES

1. For a discussion of the figure for the total turnover in 1698–1699 see my article "Trade and Politics in 18th Century India" in *Islam and the Trade of Asia,* ed. D. S. Richards (Oxford, 1970). As to European trade at the time, according to the figures given by Jan Schreuder, Dutch *directeur* at Surat during the 1740s, the total trade of the Dutch company, by far the largest European concern at the close of the seventeenth century at Surat, was 1.2 million rupees during that season. The English company exported 39,737 pieces of cloth from Surat in 1699 and 34,144 pieces in 1700. The figures for 1698–1699 are not known; neither is the value of the export for which the quantity is known. But the value of annual English exports cannot have much exceeded the figure of a lakh of rupees. Other European trade, official and private, virtually did not exist at Surat at the time. For the quantities of English exports, I am indebted to Dr. K. N. Chaundhuri; the figures given by Schreuder are in his "Memoir of Free Trade," H[ooghe] R[egeering] 837, para. 263 at the Algemeen Rijksarchief at The Hague.

2. The figures for shipping between Surat and Mocha are available in the Dutch documentation. The fleet which the Dutch cruisers escorted every year from Surat to Mocha and back would be swelled by a few vessels from Gujarati ports other than Surat; on the return journey they would include one or two non-Gujarati vessels. Writing his official memoir at Surat in 1710, J. Grootenhuijs, retiring Dutch *directeur,* said that the annual import of treasure by the Gujarati vessels, which had been 6 million rupees, had recently fallen to half that figure. See H.R. 834, p. 188. As to profits in the Red Sea trade, 60 percent gross was regarded by the Gujaratis as satisfactory. See the report of the Mocha factors in 1699, K[oloniaal] A[rchief], The Hague, 1517, p. 131.

3. A "capital ship" detached for escort duty would, according to instructions from the Mughal court, obtain 20,000 rupees for the Dutch company. These charges were paid in the first two years but were later stopped. For this and other details about the profits the Dutch sought to earn from the task forced upon them, see the "instructions" of 1700 in K.A. 1527, pp. 177a–178.

4. A typical instance of the regulations about sailing in convoy would be the *seing brief* issued to the Gujarati *nakhuda*s by the Dutch commanders in 1699. It contained twenty-four different points which, among other things, dealt with procedures for setting sail, changing direction, anchoring by night, and keeping clear of one another. In case a stray vessel wished to rejoin the convoy, it would be hailed by the word "Orange," to which it was to answer "Nassau." See K.A. 1517, pp. 143–147.

5. Jan Jillisz, a navigator who was lent to the Mughal government for service on board the *Ganj-i-Sawai* in 1694, wrote several letters while on this duty to his superiors at the Dutch lodge at Surat. Jillisz found the ship so abominably overcrowded that he was certain none of its guns could be brought into action in an emergency. In spite of large expenditures officially sanctioned for its maintenance, the imperial vessel was in fact badly neglected. In the season 1694–1695 the *Ganj-i-Sawai* returned to Surat, leaking badly, shortly after it had set out for Mocha. For the letters written by Jan Jillisz and the abortive voyage of the *Ganj-i-Sawai*, see the Surat *Dagh-Register* for the year 1694 in K.A. 1493, pp. 415a–416, 480a–486a.

6. While it is true that all Mughal *nakhuda*s were distinguished men, some were more illustrious than others. Later in this essay I present details about an eminent person who came out to the Red Sea as a Mughal *nakhuda* but was reverently called Mirza Saheb.

7. A distinguished family of Turkish merchants, the Chellabies of Surat, usually placed members of their own clan as *nakhuda*s on their ships. This name therefore often appeared in the shipping lists. Jillisz was disgusted to notice that while the *Ganj-i-Sawai* was limping back to Surat, partially submerged, there were some who absolutely exhausted themselves pumping while others stood about. Dutch chronicles of the Mocha voyage mentioned the *nakhuda*s of Ghafur almost every year with considerable irritation.

8. The "Mocha Report," dated 22 September 1701, is in K.A. 1552, pp. 772–808a. Minutes of technical meetings held on board the *Nieuwburg* are in the same document, pp. 811–812.

9. Some details about the privileges which Abdul Ghafur had at Mocha are given in Ketelaar's memoir written at that town in 1709. See K.A. 1689, p. 65.

10. For the Ahmedabad Bohras at Mocha and their agitation to alter the gold-silver exchange in favor of silver, see the memoir of Christiaan van Vrijbergen, 1713, K.A. 1735, pp. 47–48.

11. The privileges of the Muslims from Muscat were mentioned by Ketelaar in his memoir, K.A. 1689, p. 64. The exemption which Muscat-

men enjoyed from local taxation was mentioned in the English factory's letter to London, 5 August 1725, Factory Records, Egypt and the Red Sea, G/17/1, at India Office, London, no pagination. The fact that the local government was heavily dependent upon the customs from Gujarati ships was stated often in the documentation.

12. The fact that Banias from Kathiawar had settled in all Yemeni towns was mentioned occasionally in connection with other business. Thus in 1721, while attempting to obtain a pair of desert mules for the governor of Ceylon, the Dutch factors at Mocha asked their broker, a Bania from Diu, to get into touch with "his caste which had settled as far as the territories of the Imam extended." The broker was asked particularly to sound the Banias of Sana, Taiz, and Beit al-Faqih. See minutes of the council, 1 July 1721, K.A. 1875, p. 77. Theodor Zas in his report on Abyssinian trade in 1699 referred to thirty or forty Banias who lived at Massowa and dominated trade at that port. He also wrote of the more numerous Banias of northern Yemen who controlled the trade at Suakin. See K.A. 1517, p. 158. Evidence about Gujarati Banias migrating to Yemen is occasionally encountered in the documentation, especially in the later years. In 1723 a ship "sardine-packed" with Banias was reported from Somnath Patan. See K.A. 1881, p. 111a. In 1724 a Portuguese ship from Diu arrived at Mocha "with a large number of Banias": K.A. 1898, p. 2830a.

13. There are references almost every year to the importance of the Banias in the commercial life at Mocha. Ketelaar in his memoir referred in particular to the coin of account they had devised around 1693–1694. See K.A. 1689, pp. 59–60. The best discussion of the *nowroz* system of payment and the Bania custom of closing their books with the sailing of the fleet from Hindustan is in the writings of Vrijbergen. See especially his letter from Mocha, 30 August 1713, K.A. 1735, p. 4, and his memoir in the same document, p. 46.

14. See K.A. 1527, pp. 909–909a. The holy man was also unhappy about the permission given to Jews to settle in Yemen. The small Jewish colony at Mocha faced occasional persecution. Though not of any economic importance at Mocha, Jewish merchants controlled the mint at Sana.

15. See Ketelaar's memoir, K.A. 1689, p. 65. The Banias also paid the *jizya* (poll tax levied on non-Muslims) in Yemen. For a false but dangerous accusation against a Bania that he was having relations with an Arab woman, see *Dagh-Register*, 19 October 1724, K.A. 1914, p. 2480.

16. Festivities of the Gujarati Banias were noted each year by the Dutch diarist. For instance, it was said on 9 October 1723: "Today is the Bania feast for the new year and so one can scarcely find a Bania in the

town. But outside [the town] one can see them making merry in the fields and under the hillocks." See K.A. 1898, p. 2806. Twenty days later the Gujaratis were still celebrating their new year by a display of fireworks: ibid., p. 2808a. The celebration of *holi* was noticed on 7 March 1724: ibid., p. 2827. On 26 September 1724 the diary recorded that Banias with their Brahmans went out of the town for the day to perform their religious rituals, the occasion being their new year. See K.A. 1914, p. 2460.

17. Late in the 1720s this toleration appears to have broken down, doubtless because the Banias could no longer afford to buy it. On 4 March 1728 the *Dagh-Register* noted that the governor had demanded 20,000 dollars from the Banias for the use of their temples comprising four houses in the town. The Banias told him he could take over the houses if he wished, but they had no money to give. See K.A. 2041, p. 6183.

18. For the only instance of what may be called "Mughal protection" in these years, see the episode of Mirza Saheb.

19. See *Dagh-Register,* 30 October 1708, K.A. 1676, p. 1881a.

20. In 1705, when J. J. Ketelaar, chief of the Dutch trading venture for the year, landed at Mocha on 13 November, he and his council lived with Virachand till 24 December following; they then moved out to a rented house. Three years later Virachand bought the house which was rented for Ketelaar and it became the Dutch company's lodge at Mocha. The Bania broker was thus the landlord of the Dutch company at Mocha. See *Dagh-Register* for 1705–1706 in K.A. 1610, pp. 1208a, and *Dagh-Register* 1708–1709 in K.A. 1676, p. 1836a. For similar hospitality given by Virachand to an English private trader see *Dagh-Register,* 20 April 1706, K.A. 1610, p. 1243a. The Dutch company could never persuade Virachand or his successors to forsake the other Europeans. The Banias always pointed out they had no guarantee that Dutch trade to Mocha would not be suspended, and in case it was, they would find it difficult to win back the brokerage of the other European concerns. For the views on this point of Ramji Nakra, Virachand's successor, see C. Vrijbergen's letter from Mocha to Batavia, 19 August 1711, K.A. 1704, pp. 118–119.

21. Actually it was Ram Nakra, a deputy of Virachand's for the previous fifteen years, who took over the brokerage in 1711. At a ceremony at the governor's palace on this occasion Ramji, Mathura (head of the Virachand house), and Pitambar (deputy to Ramji) were presented with shawls. See Vrijbergen's letter cited above. Ramji, who knew Portuguese and Arabic and was much praised for his civility, returned to Diu with a considerable amount of money in 1714. He had some difficulty in leaving Mocha, as the governor was opposed to his departure. Before he

left, he said that he would return in a year or two but never did. He remained active in the Red Sea trade, however, and occasionally his ships from Diu were reported at Mocha. For details about Ramji see the memoir of Christiaan van Vrijbergen, written at Mocha, 20 August 1713, K.A. 1713, K.A. 1735, p. 40, and Mocha to Batavia, 22 August 1715, K.A. 1777, pp. 7, 13a; for a later report of a ship of Ramji's at Mocha see *Dagh-Register,* 7 April 1720, K.A. 1827, pp. 2260–2260a. Details about Pitambar are also given in these letters and papers.

22. Pitambar when he left for Diu was planning to return "early next season." For Pitambar's departure and the assumption of the brokerage by Trikam, see Abraham Pantzer's letter from Mocha to Batavia, 22 August 1716, K.A. 1768, pp. 2352a–2353.

23. The persecution of the merchants at Mocha began around the time Pitambar left for India and was at its height in the 1720s. Writing his memoir in 1719 at the Yemeni port, Pantzer regretted that no one as able as Pitambar was available any longer to take over the brokerage. Even more regrettable was the fact that Bania merchants in general and the Virachand family in particular no longer had any money which they could lend the Dutch company for the purchase of coffee. They all concealed their wealth for fear of being fleeced by the administration and sent what money they could away to Diu. Whenever the Bania merchants of Mocha were forced to pay the government, the Virachands paid more than others. Pantzer warned his successor, for whom the official memoir was written, not to be surprised if occasionally soldiers came to drag the company's broker, or his relations, away to jail for refusing to pay a forced contribution. It happened to all of them at one time or another. See K.A. 1856, pp. 104–105. In the 1720s the family lost the English brokerage because the English felt that under the circumstances no Bania merchant could suitably represent their interest. See Robert Cowan's letter from Mocha to William Phipps at Bombay, 10 February 1724, R[obert] C[owan] P[apers], India Office, London, microfilm reel 2013, no pagination.

24. It is possible that as much as two-thirds of the Gujarati exports to the Red Sea were sold at Mecca. Estimates made at Surat in 1710 suggested that two consecutive failures of the hajj market had reduced the import of bullion from the Red Sea into that port from 60 lakhs of rupees to between 30 and 20 lakhs. Jano Grootenhuijs in his memoir written at Surat in March 1710 thought the import of bullion had fallen to about 30 lakhs. See H.R. 834, p. 188. C. Besiun, writing from Surat shortly after, said that bullion import from the Red Sea had fallen to a third of what it had been. Both agreed about "previous imports" having been of the order of 60 lakhs of rupees. For Besuin's letter to Batavia, 27

April 1710, see K.A. 1689, p. 207. A small amount of coarse cloth was sold at the Habash ports like Suakin, Massowa, and Zeila. For a good account of this trade written by Theodor Zas at Mocha in 1698, see K.A. 1517, pp. 133–134, 158–159. Sana was an important element in what can be called the local demand for Gujarati textiles. But other Yemeni cities like Beit al-Faqih, Taiz, and Zelba also required the imported cloth. For an interesting discussion see Vrijbergen's memoir in K.A. 1735, p. 48, Mocha to Batavia, 21 August 1714, in K.A. 1748, p. 22, and Mocha to Batavia, 22 August 1715, in K.A. 1777, p. 55.

25. Complaints about overtrading by the Gujaratis in the Red Sea area were common at the close of the seventeenth century. Typical of these years was the gloom expressed by Hendrik Zwardekroon in his "instructions to the Mocha convoy" in 1700: K.A. 1527, p. 780.

26. For the failure of the hajj in 1708 see Ketelaar's letter from Mocha to Batavia, 24 August 1708, K.A. 1644, pp. 1831–1832. Complaints about scarcity of money at Mocha because of a failure of supplies from Jedda were repeated in 1709, 1710, 1713, and 1714. These complaints all related to the market in textiles. For the closure of the Mocha bazaar see K.A. 1777, p. 21a.

27. Both Ketelaar (1709) and Pantzer (1719) emphasized the overwhelming importance of "the Turkish merchants" in the coffee market. Later English and Dutch estimates agreed that even in the 1720s, when European demand for coffee was high, European purchases amounted to a small fraction of what was bought by "the Turks."

28. On 22 January 1709 information reached Mocha via Beit al-Faqih of the arrival of a large number of vessels at Hodeida, the roadstead the Ottoman merchants used for their coffee exports. It was said that numerous merchants had arrived on these vessels to buy coffee and as a result the price had risen sharply. On 8 February 1709 Qasim Turbati told the Dutch at Mocha that the civil war within the sharifian clan which had dislocated trade at Jedda was now terminated and coffee could be exported freely to Grand Cairo. In that city, the trade of the Christian merchants dealing in coffee had been under an embargo for some time past. But now the Turkish governor of Cairo had lifted the prohibition and the coffee market was expected to rise further. The next day Turbati heard from Hodeida that 300,000 Spanish dollars had been sent there from Jedda for the purchase of coffee. See *Dagh-Register* in K.A. 1678, pp. 1920–1920a, 1941–1941a. On 5 May 1709 it was noted that Turkish merchants had brought 600,000 Spanish dollars to Beit al-Faqih for buying coffee: ibid., p. 2102a.

29. Daniel Haagdoorn at Mocha mentioned the fact in his annual letter to Batavia and said that the English bought coffee at 118 or 119 Spanish dollars per *bahar* at Beit al-Faqih. See K.A. 1704, p. 70.

30. For comments on the topic see Mocha to Batavia, 30 August 1713, K.A. 1735, pp. 14–15; Mocha to Batavia, 21 August 1714, K.A. 1748, pp. 28–29; and the memoir of Pantzer, 1719, K.A. 1856, p. 112. In 1721 Dutch council minutes noted that coffee at Beit al-Faqih had risen to between 133 and 136 dollars per *bahar:* K.A. 1875, p. 36. English documents of the middle 1720s give prices as well over 200 dollars.

31. They had, of course, to pay a price for it. Spanish dollars at Surat by their intrinsic worth fetched usually about 217 Surat rupees for 100 dollars. In July at Mocha, when the Gujaratis usually were eager to buy European bills of exchange, they would not obtain anything more than about 205 rupees for 100 dollars.

32. The *Dagh-Register* of 1723–1724 recorded several "unheard of cases" of bankruptcy among merchants of Mocha and the general fear of failure. A meeting was held "at the house of Abdul Ghafur" between the leading Muslim merchants of Mocha and the visiting Gujaratis. At the end of this meeting the governor of the town was unanimously urged by the participants to take steps which included a rescheduling of all debt payments and a prohibition against the lending of money early in the season, which was in the interest of the trade in coffee. See K.A. 1881, pp. 57a–61a.

33. Discussing increasing taxation in 1700, the visiting Dutch factors noted that this kind of oppression began twelve years earlier when the Imam Al Mahdi came to power by force. See K.A. 1527, p. 908a.

34. For references to the imam's monopoly in some varieties of Gujarati cloths which were widely used for making sleeping bags at Sana, see *Dagh-Register,* 6–7 January 1725, K.A. 1914, p. 2481.

35. The beginning of Horebi's trade was noticed by Ketelaar when he visited Mocha in 1704. He wrote that Mocha that year was facing famine and many merchants had left town. It was this desertion which prompted Saleh Horebi to try his luck in trade. See "Mocha Report," 1704, K.A. 1606, pp. 141–142.

36. The names 'Sallawij and Cossombij, if indeed I have reconstructed them rightly from their Dutch incarnations, seem to indicate that they were Bohra Muslims from Gujarat.

37. The name of this *nakhuda* is now given in the documents. Pieter Ketting, *directeur* of the Dutch lodge at Surat, in a letter to Batavia dated 22 November 1698, said that the *nakhuda,* "a drunken rascal," wasted so much time in pursuing his vendetta in Yemen that he delayed the Red Sea fleet and many of the ships missed the monsoon. As a result Amanat Khan, governor of Surat, was very angry with the *nakhuda:* see K.A. 1517, pp. 23, 44. Doubtless it was as a consequence of this misadventure that this unnamed *nakhuda* was replaced by the courtly if somewhat obtuse Hajji Muhammad Fazal.

38. Besides Ketting's letter to Batavia cited in note 37, the details of this incident were given by Nicholas Welter and Adrian van den Heuvel at Mocha in their letter to Surat, 12 December 1698, K.A. 1517, pp. 126–128.

39. Horebi's trade, which began in 1704, was not generally objectionable in the earlier years. The Dutch company, for instance, was quite content to sell him their imports, for which he paid cash, which was unusual at Mocha. By 1709–1710, however, he was being denounced as a "monopolist" who forced importers to sell to him and then, in turn, sold again to the Bania merchants of Mocha at 25 percent profit. Horebi appears to have been far more interested in the imports made by the Europeans than those of the Indians. Eminent Gujarati merchants almost certainly supported the Horebi faction at the time. For relevant details see Ketelaar's reports from Mocha and the *Dagh-Registers* of 1704 to 1709 in K.A. 1606, pp. 141–142, K.A. 1610, pp. 1217–1219, K.A. 1644, pp. 1831–1832, and K.A. 1676, pp. 2190–2193. Writing to Batavia, 19 August 1711, Vrijbergen denounced "the shameful monopoly" of Horebi. See K.A. 1704, pp. 128–129.

40. Amir Rezzak, "the Arab landed magnate," went every year to Surat in supreme command of the two ships of the imam. On his return to Mocha, he would pay a courtesy call at the Dutch lodge. J. J. Ketelaar, who received Rezzak at the lodge in 1709, was most favorably impressed with the latter's cosmopolitan outlook, which contrasted sharply with that of the other Arabs who never went abroad. See *Dagh-Register*, 27 April 1709, K.A. 1676, pp. 2079a–2080. Amir Rezzak became the governor of Mocha in 1718. His son, Sidi Ali Rezzak, who married a daughter of Qasim Turbati, was governor of Mocha for a period in the 1720s. For details about these developments see K.A. 1796, p. 241, K.A. 1898, p. 2824, and K.A. 1925, pp. 3608–3608a. Qasim Turbati was one of the leading merchants of Mocha as early as 1699. For a reference to his position in that year see K.A. 1517, p. 115. With some misfortune, as occasionally his faction lost power at Mocha and Sana, Turbati maintained his eminence for about thirty years. He was said to be an austere man, and although he maintained "a large nousehold of many wives and slaves," public opinion at Mocha compared the simplicity of his personal life favorably with the riotous living in the Rezzak household. Turbati consented to the marriage of his daughter with Sidi Ali Rezzak only on condition that Rezzak would get rid of his slave girls beforehand. For comments on Turbati and his household, see Abraham Pantzer's memoir in K.A. 1856, pp. 95–96. On 15 January 1719 the *Dagh-Register* noted that governor Amir Rezzak in a drunken orgy had fallen down and hurt his back and this had scandalized Mocha town. The diary added that

Qasim Turbati, "whose manner of living is of an entirely different kind," had remonstrated gently with Rezzak about his conduct. See K.A. 1810, p. 2005. The details of the Turbati-Rezzak marriage arrangements are given in K.A. 1925, pp. 3608f.

41. The account of Horebi's struggle against Ali Wazir is in the *Dagh-Register* for 1709, K.A. 1676, pp. 2189a–2193.

42. See Mocha to Batavia, 22 August 1710, K.A. 1704, p. 21.

43. The attack on the fleet which resulted in the loss of two ships within gunshot range of the Mocha forts was described by Daniel Haagdoorn in his letter to Batavia, 22 August 1710, K.A. 1704, pp. 56–61.

44. Ibid. And for complaints in 1711–1712 that the imam had sanctioned Horebi's monopoly and was sharing its profits, see K.A. 1704, p. 129, and K.A. 1735, p. 4.

45. The details of one such complaint are worth recording. A Bania of Cambay had sent an agent to Mocha in 1711 with goods worth 15,000 dollars. The ship on which the agent was traveling lost the monsoon and put in at Socotra. The agent died while on the island and his principal, the Bania of Cambay, also died at about the same time. Before his death at Socotra, however, the agent had handed over the Cambay Bania's business to another compatriot. This new agent appeared at Mocha and sold the goods which were the property of the late Bania of Cambay. Of these goods 3,000 dollars worth were sold to the deputy governor, Abdur Rahman. Now the evil genius who guided Abdur Rahman's actions was himself a Bania by the name of Manji. Manji came to discover the complexities of this affair and informed Rahman. When, therefore, the new agent asked the deputy governor for payment he was told not only would he receive nothing of the 3,000 dollars but he must give an account of what he had done with the rest of the money, which belonged to the government as it was masterless. For this complaint and other facts relating to the sojourn of Mirza Saheb in Yemen, see K.A. 1735, pp. 23f.

46. In 1706, for instance, Rezzak informed the Dutch at Mocha that he would be bringing back four ships instead of his usual two from Surat that year. Surat at the time was blockaded by the Dutch, who would not allow any vessel of a subject of the Mughal to pass. Under such circumstances a favorite dodge of the Gujaratis was to transfer their vessels temporarily and fraudulently to non-Mughals from Arabia and Persia. It is almost certain that Rezzak was performing this service for his Gujarati friends. See K.A. 1610, p. 1270a. In 1704, while Rezzak commanded the imam's ships, a *ghurab* of Saleh Horebi's joined Rezzak's vessels on their voyage to Surat. The *ghurab* on this occasion was under the com-

mand of Muhammad Aref, who was described at the time as a *stuurman* or *sarang* of Abdul Ghafur's. Aref was later to rise to prominence and become a principal figure in the Bohra faction at Surat. See K.A. 1606, p. 182.

47. For Turbati's banishment to Surat and his return from there in 1714, see K.A. 1748, pp. 43–44. He employed his vessels regularly on the Gujarat run. In 1716 Turbati sent a ship to Surat with one of his sons as *nakhuda*. On the return voyage the young man managed to blow up the vessel and kill himself: K.A. 1768, pp. 2343a–2344. The role of Turbati in the Mirza Saheb affair was common gossip at Mocha at the time. Probably there was nothing more behind it than the prevalent knowledge of Turbati's close involvement with the Gujarati merchants. Some tension within the Horebi–Rezzak–Turbati alliance cannot, however, be ruled out.

48. For this meeting see note 32.

49. Apart from the detailed notes preserved in the *Dagh-Register* there are two good accounts of the assumption of power in Yemen by Qasim Mutwakil Bilah written by Abraham Pantzer, who was at Mocha from 1714 to 1719. See Pantzer's letter to Surat, 20 August 1717, K.A. 1796, pp. 24–33, and Pantzer's memoir in K.A. 1856, pp. 76–96. It was Amir Rezzak who brought the garrison of Mocha over to the new imam in 1716 and was eventually rewarded with governship of the town in 1718. Saleh Horebi became *wazir* at Sana but was not altogether happy at the changes which now occurred. He certainly lost his monopoly trade to Rezzak. Turbati was alienated from Rezzak for similar reasons, but by the time Pantzer came to write his memoir he had patched matters over and proceeded to establish an ascendancy over the Rezzak family.

50. The persecution of the merchants, particularly severe for the businessmen from Kathiawar, was graphically described by the *Dagh-Register*. On 7 August 1717, for instance, the diary recorded that at the customhouse merchants from Diu and Porbandar were being assessed 50 dollars for goods they had sold at half that price. Merchants from Ahmedabad and Turkish merchants paid customs on 30 dollars for goods they had sold at 20 dollars. The flight of the two Bania *nakhuda*s to the mosque outside Mocha was recorded on 19 July 1717. On 9 February 1718 it was noted that, as fresh demands had come from Sana for 6,000 dollars, Moor (i.e., Gujarati Muslim), Bania, and Turkish merchants were called up by the deputy governor. The Banias, "who were the most fearful of imprisonment and violence," offered the keys to their houses to the official. They said he was free to take away what money there was, if only he would leave them at liberty and do them no violence. On 10 February 1718, the merchants paid 2,500 of the 6,000 dollars being

demanded. Three days later soldiers were sent to the houses of the Banias and the rest of the sum was hastily made up. See *Dagh-Register* in K.A. 1796 under relevant dates.

51. The practice of buying and selling bills at Mocha on Surat was really a characteristic of the 1720s. Earlier there is little evidence of it. Thus the Dutch factors sold no bills in 1698 and in 1699 they had one Bania merchant buy 2,332 dollars worth in Surat bills from them. There is nothing on this topic till 1713, by which time the Dutch purchase of coffee had gone up from about 200,000 pounds to over the million mark. In 1713, however, the Gujaratis, who had had a very poor market, could afford to buy only 18,000 dollars worth in Dutch bills. See K.A. 1735, pp. 19, 24. This pattern remained typical for the following few years.

52. See Surat to Batavia, 22 November 1698, K.A. 1517, p. 6.

53. Ketelaar's comments are in K.A. 1689, pp. 16–17. For repeated comments on the vast import of textiles from Gujarat and the absolute domination of the Gujarati merchant in this market, see K.A. 1610, pp.1235–1236, K.A. 1676, pp. 2012a–2013, and the general assessment in the memoir of Christiaan van Vrijbergen in K.A. 1735, p. 50.

54. See Mocha to London, 25 July 1720, in Factory Records, Egypt and the Red Sea, G/17/1, no pagination.

55. The origin of the *verar* as a special tax upon the freighters was mentioned by Ketelaar in his memoir written at Mocha in 1709. He said that *verar* for all freighters was 2½ percent. See K.A. 1689, p. 64. In 1701 the Dutch *directeur* of Surat, Hendrik Zwardekroon, gave special instructions to the convoy ships about treating the Gujarati merchants well so that they were induced to freight on Dutch bottoms. He added a word of caution about the unique privilege of *verar*, which, he said, was enjoyed at Mocha only by the vessels of the Dutch company besides the ships of the Mughal. See K.A. 1552, pp. 762a–764. Difficulties about the *verar* and the claim of the Mocha officials for at least half of it began as early as 1699. For details see K.A. 1517, pp. 111–113.

56. Instances of such "private freight" cropped up occasionally in the official papers. In his instructions to the convoy in 1699, for instance, Pieter Ketting asked the Mocha factors to watch whether the Dutch commanders arranged for unofficial freight "as indeed has happened before." See K.A. 1517, p. 121. In 1701 three Bohra merchants of Ahmedabad complained to the Dutch lodge at Mocha that by the miscarriage of private arrangements, which they had made the previous season for freighting bullion to Surat, they had been forced to pay 25 percent. See K.A. 1552, pp. 677–678.

57. Pirates off the Bab were first invented in 1699. Further and more

legitimate efforts were also made to obtain the bullion freight of the Gujaratis. At a meeting with the Gujarati *nakhudas* and merchants that year at the lodge at Mocha, the Dutch factors told the Gujaratis they were aware of the reluctance to freight on Dutch vessels because of higher charges. But the Gujaratis were free to offer whatever seemed ''reasonable.'' The Gujaratis pointed out that they were under instructions from their principals to distribute their bullion freight among the various ships and thus reduce risks. See K.A. 1517, pp. 106–107. For a similar situation in 1704 see K.A. 1606, pp. 162–164.

58. See Mocha to London, 21 July 1721, in G/17/1.

59. The reader will have noticed that this study is based almost exclusively on the unpublished documentation of the Dutch East India Company, and in particular I have relied often on the Mocha *Dagh-Register*. In this connection I wish to thank Dr. Elizabeth Munro of St. Antony's College, Oxford, who by a most kind and impressive sleight of hand produced a grant from the ''Private Papers Fund'' of the college so that I could obtain a set of the *Dagh-Registers* in microfilm.

Dutch Commercial Policy and Interests in the Malay Peninsula, 1750–1795

Sinnappah Arasaratnam

The general declining state of the Dutch East India Company (VOC), the futility of much of its commercial and political policies, and the unprofitability of some of its trade had been noted since the beginning of the eighteenth century by many of its officials in the east. A detailed and precise statement of this continuing decline was made in 1741 by Baron van Imhoff, the designated governor-general, before his departure to Batavia to assume that office.[1] Imhoff noted three general causes for the unsatisfactory position of the company. Firstly it had grown too large for its good health both in territory and in its commercial enterprises and was not in a position to manage these enterprises exclusively. Secondly there had been a general worsening of terms and conditions of eastern trade. This situation was caused both by the confusion of the company's extended trading network as well as by the entry of more and more competitors in the field, especially from the early years of the eighteenth century. Prices had risen and Asian traders and producers supplying the Europe/Asia trade were in a more advantageous position. In the context of rising prices and lessening profits, large organizations such as the VOC, with vast capital outlay and fixed capital costs were the worst affected. Thirdly the company was not as well served as before by officers who could attack these evils and bring about necessary remedies. Imhoff went on to suggest a number of radical measures to rehabilitate and revitalize the company.

One region of long-standing Dutch commercial interests where these factors operated with great intensity was Malacca and the Malay peninsula. Dutch conquest of Malacca in 1641 and subsequent Dutch commercial policy had turned this entrepôt into a place of relative insignificance and had led to the rise of rival centers of trade in the Malacca Straits. While the Dutch wanted naturally to retain the entrepôt character of the trade of Malacca, this aim could not be reconciled with the company's policies in eastern trade which sought control over the supply of commodities and their prices through monopoly. Nowhere is this situation more clearly demonstrated than in that important commodity of the trade of the Malacca Straits, tin. The bulk of the tin supply came from the lands adjoining the western and eastern shores of the Malacca Straits, on the island of Sumatra and the Malay peninsula. A great deal of energy was expended in the second half of the seventeenth century in entering into trading contracts with rulers of various tin-producing states of the region requiring the sale, at fixed prices, of all, or a stipulated share of, the produce of tin in each state. But it has been clearly established by recent studies that these treaties produced little results and were often breached soon after they were signed.[2]

Yet the Dutch persisted with these regulations. By the end of the seventeenth century, Malacca had been hedged in by a long list of price and quantity controls, exclusive monopolies, and shipping restrictions. The purpose of these regulations was twofold. In the first place they were intended to engross as much as possible of the trade of the straits and peninsula. The traditional right of Malacca, enjoyed under the sultanate, to channel through this port all the export and import of the area was to be asserted and maintained. The second aim was to make Malacca fit into the Dutch trading system of Southeast Asia, centered at Batavia (Jakarta). Nothing was to be done in Malacca that would endanger the dominant position of Batavia in Southeast Asian trade. In this way Malacca was stifled by the restrictive policies of the Dutch and by the hostility of the Dutch Supreme Government at Batavia toward a rival trading entrepôt. Malacca thus lived in the shadow of Batavia, and it was possible for the governor-general and council to write to Amsterdam in 1698: "It has been known for a long time that Malacca has been more a place of necessary residence and garrison than of trade."[3] Imhoff, in his report of 1741, compared Malacca with Malabar as a deficit post of the company: it produced little trade and was of no importance in relations with indigenous states. It could be reduced in size but not completely abandoned because of its strategic position.[4]

Thus through the seventeenth century Malacca stagnated because of faulty commercial policies. In the eighteenth century, however, new developments in the trade and politics of the area produced a new activity and necessitated new policies. One of these new developments was the change in eastern trade from the 1720s with the discovery of the possibilities of importing Chinese tea into Europe. The English were the first to realize its importance but were soon followed by the Dutch and the Danes. In the course of a decade the quantities imported into Europe had increased by geometric proportions.[5] But the increase in imports from China intensified the problem of remittances for the China trade. At all times the variety of goods demanded by the Chinese was small, and this sudden enlargement of Chinese imports had to be financed by the export of bullion, a commodity all traders were short of and wished to save. At first the English and the Dutch sought to increase the sale of pepper in China, but there was a limit. Another possibility was tin, for which there was always a demand in China. In this context the tin-producing areas of the Malay peninsula and Sumatra assumed importance, and thus Malacca itself became the seat of Dutch power there.

The increased need of the Dutch, together with their competitors the English and the Danes, to procure tin and pepper in Southeast Asia to finance the China trade caused a stir in the region. The English increased their penetration into Southeast Asian trade in those areas the Dutch had not expropriated to themselves and later even challenged the Dutch monopoly. A major aspect of this English challenge was the growth of the "country" trader, a phenomenon perceptively analyzed by Holden Furber.[6] He characterizes the changes that resulted from the expansion of Asian trade in the course of the mid-eighteenth century as a commercial revolution. An element of this revolution, becoming more pronounced after the 1770s, was the English dominance of the country trade between Coromandel and Malaya. Much of this traditionally important trade had been diverted to Madras, and the English conquest of Nagapatnam in 1780 during the fourth Anglo-Dutch war (1780–1784) facilitated this dominance.[7] Nagapatnam had been an important port for the trade between India and Malaya—in fact, the Dutch had been able to secure their share of that trade by their sovereignty over this port. The voyages of the English country vessels from Calcutta and Madras to Malayan ports outside Dutch control record a drastic increase from this period, a factor noted with much regret by the Dutch in Malacca. The Danes and Portuguese too were taking advantage of these new opportunities and using Malayan markets to feed their China trade both in partnership with the English and separately. The Danes, in particular, for want of other commodities of import to exchange for pepper and tin, were engaging in a lucrative armaments trade.[8] Malay and Bugis rulers were hankering for arms at this time, and the English and Danes took full advantage of this opportunity. Opium also became a savior of the import trade to Southeast Asia at the same time, just as decades later it was to solve all remittance problems as far as the China exports were concerned. This evolving pattern of east Asian trade and the Southeast Asian role in it caused considerable movement in the area and set in train a chain of events which engulfed the Dutch, the Malays, and other power groups in the area.

The second major factor that changed the commercial and political situation of the Malay peninsula and Malacca Straits was the rise of Bugis power in the area. The Bugis were a well-knit group of people organized into a number of small states in the southwestern part of the Celebes islands. They were excellent traders and courageous fighters who roamed the seas of the archipelago carrying on trade and offering their services as mercenaries to anyone who made payment. When the Dutch conquest of Macassar (1667) and their nearly complete domination of the spice trade of the Moluccas disrupted the Bugis trading pattern, they began their migratory movement. In time, some of them came and settled in the Malay peninsula. They founded their first settlements in the sparsely populated districts of Klang and Selangor, and toward the end of the seventeenth century their services were being sought by Malay rulers in their dynastic disputes. It was these factors that helped them finally to establish themselves in Johore, the most powerful kingdom in the area and putative successor to the Malacca sultanate. A Bugis confederation of five brothers succeeded in securing the sultan of Johore under their control in 1722 and began an era of Bugis dominance in the affairs of Johore. One of the brothers, Daing Merewah, was made *Yam-tuan Muda* or underking of Johore. The other brothers established themselves as lords over various strategic districts along the coast. One of their descendants elevated himself as sultan of Selangor, a dependency of Johore.[9]

This political penetration of the Bugis in Johore and Selangor was followed by an intensive participation in the trade of these places. In particular, the Bugis had their eye on the tin of Johore and its dependencies in the hinterland of Malacca, a commodity that was rising in demand from Dutch and other European traders as well as from Chinese merchants who came to these ports. At first the Bugis were trading with the Dutch and wished to cultivate good commercial relations with them as the long-established traders of the region. Consequently in the early decades of the eighteenth century they helped to augment the delivery of tin at Malacca. But it was not long before the incompatibility of the interests of the two parties revealed itself. With their successful political penetration in the area Bugis ambition broadened to a monopoly of the trade of these states, an aim similar to that of the Dutch as contained in their many monopoly contracts with these states. The Dutch found the Bugis the main instruments for the violation of these trading contracts and a widening hostility developed between them.[10] This feature provides another backdrop to the commercial relations of the Malay peninsula in the second half of the eighteenth century.

The emergence of these factors influenced the Dutch to make a renewed and vigorous attempt at expanding their naval and military presence and, through this, their trade in the area. Writing in 1750, the outgoing Dutch governor of Malacca, W. B. Albinus, reviewed the trade of Malacca and the Malay states and the politics of the area in relation to Dutch interests.[11] The Bugis controlled all the tin of Johore and had the young sultan in their power. Most of the tin from the hinterland districts of Malacca—Sungei Ujong, Sri Menanti, Muar, and Linggi—was marketed in Riau or Selangor or taken by land to Trengganu and Pahang on the east coast of the peninsula. The Dutch could not secure enough tin to meet the European demand. Though the Dutch had an exclusive contract with Perak, some nobles there were encouraging the transport of tin to Kedah with Buginese help along the rivers and overland. In Kedah there was a free market for tin and for import commodities such as textiles and opium, whereas in Malacca all these goods were subject to Dutch monopoly. Albinus recommended constant patrolling of the seas before Larut by a sloop to stop smuggling and force all vessels from Siam, Cambodia, and China which had bought tin at Kedah, to call at Malacca and surrender all the tin.

To strengthen Dutch rights in Perak, Johore, and a number of subordinate states, a diplomatic offensive was launched. Old treaties were reconfirmed and the punitive provisions strengthened. The political situation was rather favorable to the Dutch as the Bugis had overplayed their hand. Their dominance of trade and politics was threatening the Malays, who showed some disposition to seek a Dutch alliance against the Bugis. The first success of this offensive was in Perak, a state which was in many ways crucial to the Dutch purchase of tin. In 1745, the Supreme Government at Batavia had ordered the reoccupation of the fort at Pulau Dinding, off the mouth of the Perak River, which had been sacked a few times by the Malays and successively abandoned and reoccupied. Backed by a strengthened Dutch naval presence in these waters, the sultan of Perak, Muzaffar Shah III, was persuaded to come to a new contract with the Dutch signed on 25 July 1746.[12] By this treaty the sultan agreed to sell all the tin found in his kingdom to the Dutch at 26 new ducatrons (32 Spanish dollars) a *bahar* and a duty of 2 Spanish dollars a *bahar* to the sultan.[13] Permission was obtained from the sultan to erect a fort at a suitable point on the Perak River. In 1748 a fortified factory was erected up the river on Tanjong Putus from where the Dutch could enforce the sale of tin from all boats passing downriver. All vessels of Perak and those that came from outside were to call at the Dutch fort to be inspected; all the tin on board was to be sold to the Dutch at the fixed price. Vessels caught smuggling were to be confiscated together with the cargo and shared equally by the sultan and the Dutch. This treaty was reconfirmed in March 1753 on the accession of a new sultan.[14] The provisions were similar to those of the earlier treaty, the price of tin being fixed at 32 Spanish dollars a *bahar* and 2 Spanish dollars duty. The sultans of Perak were persuaded to enter into such agreements by the hope of Dutch assistance and protection against the Bugis. It does appear that some nobles thought the sultan had gone too far in his commitment to the Dutch. Two well-known leaders of the anti-Dutch faction, Raja Alim and Orang Kaya Muda, were brought to Malacca and put under guard there.[15] The benefits from these treaties were immediately visible. In 1749 the Malacca officials were able to fulfill the total demand in tin of 200,250 Dutch pounds for Europe, 200,000 Dutch pounds for the China trade, 200,000 Dutch pounds for Surat, and 100,125 Dutch pounds for Batavia.[16]

At the same time, opportunities arose for renewing the contracts with Johore and reestablishing Dutch influence there. Sultan Suleiman and the Malay party in Johore led by the sultan of Trengganu were getting tired of Bugis dominance and showed signs of looking to the Dutch for assistance. A Dutch officer at Malacca, Undermerchant Claes de Wind, was sent on an embassy to Johore. De Wind was instructed to impress strongly on the sultan the fact that there was extensive violation of treaty obligations in the admission of Chinese to trade in Riau and in the smuggling of tin. Complaint over these violations was made in letters from the governor and council of Malacca to the sultan and to the Bugis underking dated 16 November 1745. In the negotiations, the sultan agreed to cede the trade of Siak to the Dutch in return for their support against his rival Raja Alam, the ruler of Siak. Siak was a dependency of Johore on the island of Sumatra across the Malacca Straits. It was important to the Dutch for the tin it could supply and the gold trade for which it was famous. It was to be subordinated to Johore and a ruler favorable to the Dutch set on the throne.[17] The agreement was incorporated into a treaty signed on 3 November 1754. This pact gave the Dutch permission to erect a fort on Pulau Gontong, an island at the entrance to the Siak River. No cloth was to be imported except from Malacca and no vessels were to sail upriver except with a pass from Malacca.[18]

A Dutch expedition set out from Malacca in December 1754 to the Siak River to attack Raja Alam and install Raja Muhamad as ruler under the overlordship of Johore. This task was accomplished by August 1755, and the Dutch had seized and fortified the island of Pulau Gontong at a strategic point on the entrance to the Siak River. With this demonstration of Dutch naval power, the sultan, who had dragged his feet while the attack on Siak was going on, proceeded hastily to Malacca to conclude a new treaty with the Dutch.[19]

The sultan of Johore saw signs of the revival of Dutch power and interest in the area and wanted to take advantage of this opportunity to reestablish his authority in Johore and Johore's authority over its far-flung dependencies. The Dutch saw here a means to divide the Malays from the Bugis, expel Bugis power from the Johore kingdom, and thus reestablish their control over the tin trade. These motives alone explain contravention of their traditional reluctance to be embroiled in the internal disputes of native powers of the peninsula. By article 1 of the treaty of 1756 with Johore, the Dutch promised to help their "old friend" the sultan of Johore to bring all his lost lands back under his authority. Dutch influence in Siak was strengthened by the commitment that the sultan's nominee there must meet with Dutch approval. The provisions of the earlier treaty (of November 1754) giving the Dutch dominance over the

trade of Siak were strengthened. The Dutch took this opportunity to reaffirm, by article 9, that the tin at Selangor,
Klang, and Linggi was to be sold only to the Dutch at 32
Spanish dollars a *bahar* and 2 Spanish dollars per *bahar* as a
gift to the local ruler. If the tin were brought to Malacca it
would be paid at 45 rix dollars a *bahar* (36 Spanish dollars)
and 3 rix dollars for the ruler. No foreign European nations
were to be admitted in any part of the entire Johore kingdom except with Dutch passes.

This new Dutch offensive was not to go unchallenged by
the Bugis. All those forces affected by a revival of Dutch
monopoly naturally came together. Raja Alam, the defeated
claimant to Siak, joined forces with Daing Kemboja, the
Bugis underking of Johore, and the Bugis sultan of Selangor, who were all disadvantaged by Dutch claims on the tin
trade and their cruising of the traditional Bugis exit points
of the tin trade at Linggi and Selangor. In April 1756 they
assembled a combined naval might and attacked Dutch
shipping in the straits. They closed in on Malacca, laid
waste its hinterland, and launched a daring attack into the
heart of the city, burning down houses and plundering settlements. The Dutch hastily put together a naval force
under Captain Cornelis Eijke and took the offensive against
the Bugis in the end of July 1756. This force was insufficient. The Bugis, joined by the Menangkabau from Rembau and the hinterland of Malacca, pressed on Malacca,
again causing much damage and laying siege to the city. At
the same time Raja Alam threatened the new Dutch fort at
Gontong, which had to be relieved from Malacca.[20]

It was the arrival of naval reinforcements from Batavia in
July 1757 that saved the situation. Now the Dutch felt
strong enough to attack Daing Kemboja's stronghold in
Linggi, and an expedition set out on 19 November 1757
under Major Faber. At the same time, Sultan Suleiman arrived with his son-in-law the ruler of Trengganu to support
the Dutch. The combined force attacked Linggi and sacked

it. In December 1757, the ruler of Trengganu, on behalf of his overlord the sultan of Johore, ceded to the Dutch the territory of Rembau, with its nine districts and dependencies, and the territory of Linggi up to the Klang River, which now became the boundary between the Dutch and the kingdom of Johore. The only condition was that the Dutch should not effect any changes in the practice of the Islamic faith in these lands.[21]

A few days later Daing Kemboja also came to terms with the Dutch and the treaty of 1 January 1758 was signed.[22] Daing Kemboja and the other ruling chiefs of Linggi submitted to the Dutch and were allowed to retain their positions. All trade with foreign European nations was to cease. All the tin of Linggi, Rembau, and Klang was to be sold to the Dutch at the price already agreed upon in the treaty with Johore—32 Spanish dollars per *bahar* and 2 Spanish dollars for the ruler. In addition the rulers of Rembau were to give the Dutch the traditional tribute to the overlord of 500 Spanish dollars worth of tin. No vessels were to pass along the coast from south to north and vice versa without touching at Malacca to get passes.

At the same time the sultan of Selangor and his chiefs were brought into a contract with the sultan of Johore which was also countersigned by the Dutch in January 1758.[23] By this treaty the rulers and people of Selangor promised to obey the sultan of Johore as their lawful sovereign and to consider the Dutch as their faithful ally. Only those vessels which had Dutch or Johorese passes were to be allowed to trade in Selangor. All the tin of Selangor was to be sold to the Dutch at 32 Spanish dollars a *bahar* and 2 Spanish dollars for the rulers. If the tin was brought to Malacca by the Selangor suppliers, it would be paid at 45 rix dollars (36 Spanish dollars) a *bahar*. No Selangor vessel was to be allowed to sail down the coast without touching at Malacca and getting a pass. As part of this diplomatic offensive, a treaty was entered into with the ruler of Indragiri, the pepper state in east Sumatra.[24] The treaty mainly repeated the provisions of the previous agreement of 1664 and made two significant additions. The ruler promised not to let any opium into the land other than that of the Dutch Opium Society of Batavia. Vessels were to be inspected to see whether the opium chests bore the chop of the Dutch society. All traffic out of the kingdom was to be to Malacca or eastward to Patani, Siam, Cambodia, and Batavia and was to be provided with passes from Batavia or Malacca.

Armed with these renewed contracts and buttressed by the temporary presence of a sizable naval force, the Dutch set about to reinforce the restrictive trading regulations of the seventeenth century and introduce some new ones. The Dutch stronghold at Pulau Gontong was in a favorable situation to control the trade of the straits and regulate east-west passage. Vessels coming from the west, particularly from Bengal, were prohibited from going to Siak to trade in tin, pepper, and opium. The traffic from Palembang and Bangka to the straits was also forbidden in order to prevent the smuggling of tin. Vessels coming from Batavia and Macassar to Malacca were not to call at any other place and were specially forbidden from proceeding to any place northwest of Malacca. Traffic to the Siak River was forbidden to all these vessels, and traffic east of Malacca was forbidden to traders from Johore and Riau. The trade to Siak and Indragiri was permitted to subjects of Malacca with passes—provided they sold all the gold bought there to the Dutch at fixed prices.[25]

The struggle between the Bugis and the Malays was by no means concluded. The Bugis were merely biding time. They desired above all to get back the influence they had enjoyed in the Johore court at Riau. From there they could more effectively carry on their trade against the Dutch blockade. The Dutch found that their control of the trade at Siak was by no means secure. Raja Muhammad, whom they had helped to set on the throne, had ceased to be a protégé and refused to be confined by the restrictions on his trade imposed by the Dutch. He encouraged smuggling and piracy in the straits. The Dutch trade at Siak was worth a trifle—totally insufficient to support the expense of a fortified establishment at Pulau Gontong. Just as they were considering withdrawing this post, Raja Muhamad fell on the Dutch garrison there and massacred it in November 1759.[26] This was a grave blow to the Dutch. It showed them that in the shifting politics of the region one did not know one's enemies from one's friends. The Batavian government felt they had gone too far in siding with the Malays and instructed Malacca to move toward a neutral line in the dispute between Malays and Bugis. They accepted Daing Kemboja's overtures for friendship and signed a treaty with him on 11 November 1759.[27] By the treaty, the Dutch offered to increase the fixed price of tin to 38 Spanish dollars a *bahar*, inclusive of ruler's tax, in the hope that this would serve as an incentive to the exclusive delivery to the Dutch of the tin of Linggi, Rembau, and Klang. The death of Sultan Suleiman and the minority of his successor enabled Daing Kemboja and the Bugis to return to Riau, where they reestablished their power. It was largely with the aim of avenging the rout at Pulau Gontong of November 1759 and rehabilitating Dutch prestige in the straits that it was decided to support Raja Alam against the earlier ally Raja Muhamad and help him recapture Siak. This he accomplished after a costly and prolonged expedition in June 1761.[28] An agreement was entered into with Raja Alam ensuring Dutch control over the import trade of Siak.[29]

That this was a prestige-building operation was clear from the progress of trade in Siak. The Dutch reconstructed the fort at Pulau Gontong. The new ruler Raja Alam was no more faithful to the terms of the contract than was Raja Muhamad. The trade of Siak showed no increase. The followers of the previous sultan roamed the area, plundering and obstructing trade. Those whose subsistence by legitimate trading had been denied by the monopoly regulations became pirates. The post at Pulau Gontong was proving to be expensive and futile, and so the Dutch withdrew it in October 1765.[30] The costly war had brought nothing, proving again the hopelessness of relying on contracts and pretended allies.

The effects of the militant policy lasted longer at least as far as Perak was concerned. Treaties were negotiated with every new sultan as he ascended the throne. In September 1765, Everhard Cramer was sent from Malacca to Perak to negotiate a treaty with Sultan Muhamad Shah. A treaty was signed in the following month with the standard provisions for tin monopoly.[31] The price was fixed at the previous level of 34 Spanish dollars a *bahar*. All vessels, including those of the king and the chiefs, were to touch at the Dutch fort to be inspected. When a new sultan, Mansur Iskander, ascended the throne, a fresh treaty was negotiated with him in December 1773 by Abraham Werndly.[32] The provisions were repeated, but the price was reduced to 32 Spanish dollars to reflect a fall in the market price. By and large, the sultans of Perak in the 1750s and 1760s seem to have been faithful to the treaties: the supply of tin at Malacca in these years was steady. In 1763 a record amount of 1,138,134½ Dutch pounds was exported from Malacca.[33]

The return of Daing Kemboja and the Bugis to Riau in 1761 began a series of new developments which complicated the commercial and political relations of the straits lands. Until his death in 1777, Daing Kemboja was able to wield a dominance over Johore, and particularly over Riau, much greater than that exercised by his predecessors. After his death, his son Raja Ali succeeded as underking and overlord of Riau. This period coincides with the commercial revolution, outlined above, which brought the English company and country traders in increasing numbers to Malayan waters. The Bugis began to take full advantage of their presence to develop Riau into a major entrepôt. Riau itself produced nothing of commercial value. It was an archipelago of sheltered islands, swampy in many parts, but providing safe anchorage to large vessels as well as creeks into which small native *prahu* could sail. Under the Bugis it developed in the 1760s and 1770s into a place where the produce of neighboring states of the peninsula and Sumatra could be assembled and transshipped by the oceanic traders who came with the monsoons.

The Dutch records have left us a vivid picture of the trade of Riau. The major commodities were opium, tin, pepper, piece goods, and China goods. The English and Portuguese brought opium from Bengal. The Bugis bought it from them at 280 to 300 Spanish dollars per chest and sold it to the Chinese for 300 to 350 Spanish dollars. Tin was brought overland from the Johore dependencies and by sea from Palembang and Bangka. It was bought by the Bugis for 13 to 14 Spanish dollars a *picul* (39 to 42 Spanish dollars a *bahar*) and sold to the English, Portuguese, and Chinese at 15 to 16 Spanish dollars a *picul* (45 to 48 Spanish dollars a *bahar*). Pepper was brought both from Johore and by sea from Palembang, Jambi, Indragiri, and other places in Sumatra as well as from Borneo. The buying price was 9 or 10 Spanish dollars a *picul;* the selling price was 12 to 13 Spanish dollars. Textiles of various varieties were brought from Coromandel, Bengal, and Surat by the English and Portuguese. These goods were then bought by the Bugis and sold to the indigenous traders of the region who brought tin and pepper. The Chinese junks that now began to come in large numbers brought the China goods and took back tin, pepper, and opium. The Chinese established good relations with the Bugis rulers of Riau. There was a headman among them, or Capitan China, who managed the affairs of the numerous Chinese traders. An assortment of Siamese, Cambodian, Malay, and Achinese vessels came to buy opium, piece goods, and China goods. The European vessels took in the tin and pepper on their way to China and on their return loaded the remaining tin for the India trade or Europe.[34] All this was going on in direct contravention of the provisions of the treaties and in defiance of the Dutch. Thus in 1777 the Dutch estimated that the English took over 500,000 pounds of tin from the Malacca Straits—which was about 78,000 pounds more than the Dutch bought in that year. Of this amount about 440,000 pounds were said to have been taken from Riau alone.[35]

The reasons for this rise of Riau are not far to seek. The revival of Dutch naval power and commercial monopoly had created new problems for the indigenous traders and suppliers. In the seventeenth century and the first half of the eighteenth, they had got by largely on account of the inefficiency of the monopoly system. Now in the 1750s and 1760s the Dutch had tightened their hold on the two major producer states of the area, Johore and Perak. They had, for the time being, by their revived naval presence in these waters, succeeded in driving away the vessels from the traditional outlets near the centers of production. In the search for replacement centers, the ports of Kedah, outside the reach of the Dutch, and Riau became important. In Riau the freedom of navigation and trade was preserved by the exertions of the Bugis. A glance at the prevailing prices of commodities in this port, as compared with the fixed prices of the Dutch, explains its popularity. The selling price of tin was 45 to 50 Spanish dollars a *bahar* while the Dutch fixed price was 34 to 36 Spanish dollars. Pepper was generally bought by the Dutch through their contracts at 9 Spanish dollars a *bahar* while the selling price in Riau to Europeans was 12 to 13 Spanish reals. Further, there was the advantage of a free market in textiles, which in Malacca was largely a company monopoly. Opium in Riau was subject to competitive bidding while Dutch opium was a monopoly of the Opium Society of Batavia. By the arrival of the Chinese junks, the traders of the region had a wide assortment of China goods to purchase on their return. The Dutch decision in 1758 to prohibit Chinese junks from calling at Malacca in order to centralize all the Chinese trade at Batavia further helped the rise of Riau. There was thus every reason for the growing prominence of Riau in Southeast Asian trade in these years.

The real beneficiaries of all this activity, and in a sense its agents, were the English. They now posed a serious challenge to Dutch influence and commerce in the area. The English search for an entrepôt and staging post on the route to China, somewhere in Southeast Asia, was dictated both by strategy and by commerce. English interest in the trade of the area had become so great that it would have been greatly convenient to have a permanent port of their own in these waters. The English country traders were pushing hard from the 1770s for such a settlement. Edward Monckton had attempted to conclude a defensive alliance with the Bugis and obtain permission for an English military post at Riau in 1772. Some years later, Thomas Forrest had worked hard on a project to open a small trading post at Riau. Captain Glass, another country trader of the area, was a great friend of the Bugis and was apparently working toward the same end and functioning as liaison between the English company and rulers of the area. These were parts of a common search which embraced Acheh, Kedah, Ujang Selang, and Trengganu, among other places, and culminated in the lease of Pulau Penang in 1786 by Captain Francis Light from the sultan of Kedah.[36] During the fourth Anglo-Dutch war (1780–1784), the British attacked the Dutch fort in Perak and expelled the garrison.

In the face of this erosion of their share of commerce and the gathering threat of an English challenge to their influence, the Dutch decided on another phase of militancy to reestablish both. In Riau, Raja Haji succeeded to the dominant role held by Daing Kemboja. He was a romantic figure in Malay annals, fearless warrior and monopolist, who continued the policy of developing Riau as a great trading entrepôt. He did everything possible to undermine Dutch monopoly and flout the regulations. An occasion arose for a dispute between them when a ship belonging to the English company, *Betsy*, anchored on the roads of Riau with a valuable cargo, was seized by the French privateer Captain Barbaron with Dutch connivance in March 1782. Raja Haji demanded half the prize and when rebuffed started hostilities against the Dutch. He was joined by the sultan of Selangor and the rulers of Linggi and Rembau, and soon an anti-Dutch alliance was forged among neighboring rulers. This combination attacked the Malacca seas, plundered vessels in sight of that port, and brought trade to a standstill. The Dutch counterattacked by laying siege to Riau but were unsuccessful in breaking the power of the Bugis. Raja Haji returned to the siege of Malacca, closing to the east while the sultan of Selangor pressed to the west, putting the place in dire distress.[37]

The Malacca government requested urgent help from Batavia. Fortunately for Malacca, a Dutch squadron had arrived in March 1784 from Europe under Commander van Braam with the general purpose of restoring Dutch naval power in the east. Van Braam was sent to Malacca in April 1784 to attack Raja Haji, expel him and the Bugis from Riau, and reestablish the authority of the Malay sultan of Johore. In June the squadron attacked Raja Haji's positions 5 miles east of Malacca and chased the Bugis out. Raja Haji was killed in battle. The Bugis retreated to Riau and prepared their defenses under Raja Haji's nephew, Raja Ali. The Dutch then proceeded to Selangor, where they drove away Sultan Ibrahim, who had been an ally of Raja Haji, and installed a protégé on the throne. A treaty was entered into with the new sultan, Muhamad Ali, in August 1784.[38] By this treaty Selangor was declared as having been won by the Dutch by right of conquest and the sultan was recognized as having received the kingdom as a fief from the

Dutch for himself and his successor. There were the customary provisions for the tin monopoly and the fixing of prices. Article 10 further stipulated: "The Malay rulers having discovered the evil consequences of admitting Buginese into their kingdoms, it is in the interest of the king of Selangor to admit them as little as possible and so the king binds himself to drive them away and not to entrust any ports of importance to these people." Other articles empowered the Dutch to station a garrison in the kingdom for the security of the ruler as well as to reoccupy the fort in Kuala Selangor which had been abandoned. Every succession had to be regulated by the governor of Malacca and confirmed by the Supreme Government at Batavia.

Having settled the affairs of Selangor, Van Braam proceeded to Riau to deal with the Bugis. His strong fleet blockaded Riau and called upon the sultan of Johore to expel the Bugis. Faced with this naval might, the Bugis fled from Riau with all their belongings under cover of darkness on the night of 31 October 1784. Now the sultan accepted all the conditions set by the Dutch and a peace treaty was concluded. Provisions of this treaty were similar to those of the treaty with Selangor.[39] A right of conquest was declared over the territories of Johore, and Sultan Mahmud and his successors recognized this right and received the kingdom as a lawful gift from the Dutch under the conditions stipulated. Every succession had to be confirmed by the Dutch. A Dutch garrison was to be stationed at Riau, and the sultan undertook to assist in its maintenance as well as in the maintenance of any fortifications the Dutch might put up. By article 9, the sultan agreed not to allow any Bugis to settle in Riau, to expel all their families and descendants, and never to appoint them as underkings or put them in any government post. Other provisions gave the Dutch freedom of trade in the ports of Johore and the exclusion of all other Europeans from these ports. Restrictive regulations providing for the Dutch tin monopoly were laid down. Every vessel sailing in and out of Riau had to call at the Dutch fort for inspection.

The Dutch protégé at Selangor could not keep his throne against his Bugis predecessor, Ibrahim. After the withdrawal of the Dutch squadron, Ibrahim attacked Selangor, drove out the incumbent Sultan Muhamad Ali, and regained his throne. Hastily the Dutch withdrew their garrison from the fort. Ibrahim now urgently sought English assistance to back him up against the Dutch. He wrote to the English governor-general in Calcutta in August 1784 asking for an emissary to be sent to him ("Light or Scot or any other Captain") to enter into an alliance with the English.[40] He welcomed the English to Selangor to trade with the Bugis. At the same time, the expelled Bugis ruler of Riau appealed to the English for help in reestablishing Bugis trade. He asked to be taken under English protection and to be able to live and trade under their flag.[41] Shortly after the conquest of Riau by the Dutch, the sultan of Johore also appears to have had more than a taste of Dutch commercial dominance in Riau. He too made overtures to the English. He wrote Captain Light, informing him of the Dutch conquest of Riau, complaining of their policies, and asking for English help from Bengal as the English had "the power of relieving the oppressed."[42]

Thus the resurgence of Dutch power in the Malacca Straits and the west coast of the Malay peninsula, with the conquest of Riau and Selangor, was most disturbing to the indigenous powers and traders. They were looking around for allies to counterbalance Dutch power and, with the establishment of the English at Penang, they pinned their hopes on the English. However, the English were not disposed to come to a confrontation with the Dutch. They were at peace with the Netherlands at that time, and with the acquisition of Pulau Penang they had secured their aim of a staging post and entrepôt in Southeast Asia. In the course of acquiring it, they had had a full taste of involvement with native states in the region and their relations with Kedah were still not ironed out. Moreover, Pitt's India Act (1784) had made it more difficult for the company's government in India to engage in wars and make treaties at will. The mood in England was to discourage territorial involvement in Asia. So these urgent requests for assistance went unanswered and the rulers were forced to make their accommodation with the Dutch as best they could. The sultan of Selangor, after waiting a year in vain for English help, came to terms with the Dutch in July 1786.[43] He accepted vassal status to the Dutch: he received his kingdom as a fiefdom from them and they had the right to regulate succession. All provisions ensuring Dutch monopoly of trade were confirmed. Sultan Mahmud of Johore too thought it wiser to strengthen his bonds with the Dutch than to look for uncertain friends elsewhere. By the treaty of 7 February 1787, the Dutch hold on Riau was tightened. They now controlled customs, the administration of the port, the affairs of all foreign merchants, and justice.[44]

The increased Dutch naval and commercial dominance was by no means as overpowering as the treaties make it appear, however. No doubt Dutch physical presence had extended into Selangor and Riau, which now recognized Dutch overlordship. But it was soon withdrawn from Selangor, and their weakness in Riau was revealed after the departure of Van Braam's squadron. In May 1787 a strong fleet of Lanun pirates of Sulu, probably under the instigation of the Bugis, attacked the Dutch fort at Riau and the Dutch had to abandon the fort and retreat to Malacca.[45] The Dutch suspected that the sultan of Johore was an accomplice to this attack, for he did nothing to help them. Under the leadership of the sultan of Johore and the ruler of Trengganu, there was an attempt at a Malay coalition against all Europeans in the peninsula. A Malay fleet was assembled which first attacked the Dutch fort at Perak and then besieged Malacca. It attacked European vessels in the straits and captured many private as well as company vessels. But it was successful against neither the Dutch nor the English.[46] The Dutch reoccupied Riau in May 1787 and strengthened its defenses.

The reoccupation of Riau was the occasion for a review of policy in relation to the tin trade of the straits and the development of an entrepôt in the area. Opinion in Batavia was not in favor of the reoccupation of Riau but for its abandonment after being rendered commercially unusable. The officials of Malacca, however, had different ideas, which they recommended for the consideration of the Supreme Government. They were still reeling under the impact of the establishment of an English station at Fort Cornwallis in Pulau Penang, about 250 miles north of Malacca, in 1786. They were following the progress of this settlement closely and, despite the obvious bias, Dutch records of this period are among the best sources for the early history of Penang. They were impressed by the measures taken by the English officials there to attract trade to Penang and develop it as an entrepôt of Southeast Asian trade. The prices that could be got there for pepper were high. The tin price of 50 Spanish dollars a *bahar* was the highest in the region. As the sultan of Selangor wrote to the Dutch, the English were keeping the prices at Penang a good 20 percent higher than the Dutch prices.[47]

The policy was beginning to bear fruit. The Achinese had begun to sail to Penang with their pepper, bypassing Malacca. The vessels from Rangoon, Mergui, and other ports of the kingdom of Ava, which used to come to Malacca to fetch archipelago produce in exchange for the produce of their lands, now went instead to Penang. Then there was the now increased smuggling of tin and pepper from the contracted states of Perak, Selangor, and Palembang overland and by sea to Kedah and Penang. Furthermore, the English had forbidden ships of their flag from calling at Malacca, further reducing the revenues of this port in harbor dues and services to the large number of English vessels that used to call there.[48] A breakdown of the revenues of Malacca shows that these dues made up a great proportion of the total income.[49] The Dutch officials were thus aware that a great threat had been posed to their Malacca and straits trade. The conquest of Riau was not going to make any difference. The English were adding to this alarm by a propaganda war. Their country captains went around the area singing the praise of Penang and predicting the ruin of Malacca. What is more, after the establishment of Penang there appeared a statement in the Calcutta newspapers that by this establishment the English sought to avenge the Amboyna "massacre."[50]

On the other hand, the Dutch officials were convinced of the future of Dutch trade in the area—especially now that the major indigenous rival entrepôt at Riau had been neutralized—if only wise commercial policies were followed. They were not very impressed with the suitability of the place the English chose for their settlement. It was too much to the north, as far as the direct route to China was concerned, and even as far as the archipelago was concerned. It had physical disadvantages in that the passage between the island and the mainland had submerged cliffs and rocks and was dangerous for large vessels. All sailing had to be done round the island, on the ocean side, thus adding to the distance. Further, they were following, with evident enthusiasm, the political difficulties of the English with the sultan of Kedah and the possible impact on tolls and tariffs and increased cost of provisions and supplies. They were aware of the obvious advantages that Malacca offered, as contrasted with the drawbacks of Penang, and they had confidence that, given a free hand, they could bring about the liquidation of the Penang settlement.[51]

The measures now proposed by Dutch officials were so radical that they represented a major reorientation in thinking and a repudiation of the fundamental VOC monopoly system. They in fact amounted to a free trade movement among these officials, reflecting the movement toward the abolition of monopolies and the freeing of economic forces in the Netherlands and western Europe. The Malacca officials appear to have been influenced by the success of English policies and methods of trade. Now they were trying to adapt these methods to the Malacca situation. Among the most forceful statements of this policy was the memoir of De Bruijn, governor of Malacca from 1776 to 1785. His successor Abraham Couperus (1787–1795) took up the crusade for Malacca and was largely instrumental in persuading the Batavian government to retake Riau in 1787. Their views were reinforced by Van Braam Houckgeest, the VOC supercargo at Canton with some fifteen years' experience in the China trade. During a stay in Malacca in 1790 on his way to China to assume duty as officer in charge of the Canton factory, he studied the situation and compiled a report on the tin trade of Malacca for the attention of his superiors. His interest was roused by the importance of tin for the import trade to China, and he was concerned that the Dutch should procure as large a share of this tin as possible.

These officials were all disillusioned with the monopoly contract method of trading and questioned these contracts both from an economic and from a moral standpoint. Couperus asked: "What is the best means for the Company to remain master of this trade? Must one enforce the rights of the Company and the promises made by sworn treaties through armed force or must one take resort in an indulgent alteration of the contract in the present time?"[52] Van Braam argued that a plausible contract is one which must contain advantages to both sides. And he went on to ask: "But how are the contracts between the rulers of Palembang, Perak and Selangor and our Company in respect of the delivery of tin? Can one with any appearance of justice pretend or even expect that these kings would keep to their word, while the English are around everywhere and will take away the tin for a much higher price than we will pay?''[53] Although the governing price for tin in the area had gone up to 50 Spanish dollars a *bahar*, the Dutch were still fixing their price at an upper limit of 38 Spanish dollars. The rulers of Perak and Selangor were pressing for an increase in the fixed price and declaring their helplessness at forcing producers and local traders to part with tin at that price. The officials showed an appreciation of the difficulties. Cruising the waters, a time-honored Dutch method of enforcing contracts, would achieve nothing. They had now become aware of the migrant nature of the mine workers and knew that force in one place would only encourage them to pack up and leave for another place away from the reach of the armed forces. Even the sultan could not prevent this migration: mining land was in abundance and miners were in great demand. Van Braam showed his concern with the moral aspect of the problem as well. He recalled that when it suited them the Dutch requested a reduction of the fixed price—the market price of tin was lowered in 1774, for example. The sultan of Perak was gracious enough to agree to a lowering of the price fixed by contract. In Palembang, despite the exclusive tin monopoly, sometimes the Dutch accepted only certain quantities and refused to buy up the whole product. He went on to ask: ''Is it because we as Christians claim to possess more exalted principles than these heathens that we dare to carry on such shameful injustice?'' He concluded that the request for a higher price of about 44 Spanish dollars a *bahar* of tin made by the sultan of Perak was, apart from its basic economic justification, a righteous request.[54]

This widespread disillusion with the contract system was combined with an attack on the restrictive trading regulations in Malacca and those ports where Dutch had authority. Van Braam went furthest in this respect when he asserted that, though Malacca was a possession of the VOC, the Malacca Straits were a free waterway and the Dutch had no right to regulate its traffic: "The course of commerce brooks no force, it is like a river whose flow permits no opposition but takes its own free course."[55] There was unanimous condemnation of the policy of trying to regulate the commerce of the peninsula and the archipelago with the aim of centering it on Batavia to develop that port into the dominant entrepôt of Southeast Asia. This policy had led to the decline of Malacca without contributing to the increased growth of Batavia and had resulted in a decreasing Dutch share of the total volume of trade in the region. It was now helping the growth of Penang, which was benefiting from the trade restrictions of Malacca.[56]

So the officials recommended greater freedom of trade at Malacca—that is, greater scope for the company's commercial personnel there to buy and sell in the open market. They ought to be given the freedom to cut and raise prices, following the latest trends in the area and especially following the governing prices at Penang. Besides increasing the price of tin, they suggested an increase in the purchase price of pepper so that Achinese and those of Rembau and Johore could be persuaded to come to Malacca with their pepper instead of going to Penang. Opium should be freely sold at Malacca, without upsetting the monopoly of the Opium Society, through the society's agents. The textile trade should be thrown open to all and the company's monopoly abolished. That step would attract indigenous traders there to secure their supplies of piece goods. Chinese junks should be permitted an unrestricted sailing to Malacca. In this way, while the share of the trade directly engaged in by the company in Malacca might decrease, the incomes of that port would increase measurably through tariffs and port dues and through the prosperity of its citizens.[57] Van Braam also used the argument that it is restrictive regulations which lead to underhand dealings by officials. If trade is free and prices follow the market, officials have less scope to look for private gain.[58] When Malacca resumed its traditional significance as a center of peninsular and Sumatran trade, through the new policies that were proposed, it could sustain itself and dispense with the necessity to import specie from Batavia or Europe. It could thus pay for its purchase of tin from the profits of the trade and revenues and might even be able to send surplus cash to Batavia. De Bruijn estimated the potential profits and showed that a total of 300,000 rix dollars (750,000 guilders) would accrue to the company—more than enough to pay for the tin.[59] Van Braam suggested a direct sailing from Malacca to China, without touching at Batavia, with tin, rattan (Malacca cane), and other local goods and returning with Chinese goods for sale in Malacca. Likewise he proposed a direct sailing from Malacca to the Netherlands so the government could be provided with its necessities for consumption and trade from Europe. This measure would bring about a direct relationship between Malacca and Europe. Directors could then keep a direct eye on a place too important to be left under the sole control of the Supreme Government at Batavia.[60]

These recommendations struck at the fundamentals of the VOC's trade and policy in the east. They would have revised very radically the relationship between Batavia and Malacca and would have devalued Batavia in importance as the center of Dutch trade. The free sale of monopoly commodities such as opium and textiles would have affected the market for these goods in Java and the eastern islands. The opening of a free market in Malacca would have influenced traders of that area to sail there for their supplies. The markets that the Dutch had gained at much expense in Java and the eastern islands would have slipped from their control. The increase in price of pepper and tin would have attracted merchants of east Sumatra to Malacca and thus reduced the supply in Batavia. Free sale of tin and pepper in Malacca would have harmed the sale of these goods shipped by the Dutch from Batavia to China. The unrestricted admission of Chinese junks to Malacca might have slackened their traffic to Batavia. These fears were uppermost in any consideration of these proposed changes.[61]

At about the same time, the Nederburgh Committee had been appointed in Holland to effect a complete reorganization of the VOC's system of trade and government. These papers were forwarded to the committee for consideration as part of its overall review of policy. The committee arrived in Batavia in November 1793. It soon got tied up with the establishment deeply entrenched in Batavia and was not the body from which such radical reforms could be expected.[62] By 1794, the revolutionary wars of Europe had extended to the Netherlands. The Dutch stadhouder, William V, took refuge in England, and, armed with a letter from him, the famous Kew letter, the British took possession of Malacca in August 1795. Thus ended the Dutch proposals to effect a rehabilitation of Malacca. And thus, for the duration of the Napoleonic wars, ended all Dutch trade in the Straits of Malacca.

NOTES

1. "Consideratiën over den tegenwoordigen staat van de Nederland-sche Oost-Indische Maatschappij met relatie voornamentlijk tot haar Bestier, Handel, Scheepvaart en Huijschoudinge in Indien, vervat in eenige Poincten, meer dan andere van opmerkinge ter aantoninge van het algemene verval harer zaken, en op wat wijse men deselve veel ligt soude kunnen redresseeren" [Considerations on the present state of the Dutch East India Company with particular relation to its administration, trade, shipping, and management in the Indies, including some points in demonstration of the general decline of its affairs and in what manner this could be very easily redressed], G. W. van Imhoff, 24 November 1741. *Bijdragen tot de Taal-, Lande-, en Volkenkunde,* Deel 66, pp. 445–555.

2. G. W. Irwin, "The Dutch and the Tin Trade in Malaya," in *Essays*

on the *Social and Economic History of China and Southeast Asia,* ed. J. Chen and N. Tarling (Cambridge, 1970), pp. 267–287; S. Arasaratnam, "Some Notes on the Dutch in Malacca and the Indo-Malayan Trade 1641–1670," *Journal of Southeast Asian History* 10(3)(1969):480–490.

3. Cited in Irwin, "Dutch and the Tin Trade," p. 287.

4. "Consideratiën," Deel 66, p. 521.

5. K. Glamann, *Dutch-Asiatic Trade 1620–1740* (Copenhagen, 1958), pp. 213–243; E. Pritchard, *Anglo-Chinese Relations during the Seventeenth and Eighteenth Centuries* (Urbana, 1930), pp. 121–126.

6. H. Furber, *John Company at Work* (Cambridge, Mass., 1951), pp. 160–190.

7. Furber, *John Company at Work,* pp. 171–173.

8. Ole Feldbaek, *India Trade under the Danish Flag 1772–1808* (Odense, 1969), pp. 14–20.

9. Some facts of their political expansion in Malaya are to be found in E. Netscher, *De Nederlanders in Djohor en Siak 1602 tot 1865* (Batavia, 1870); R. Winstedt, "A History of Johore 1365–1895," *Journal of the Malayan Branch, Royal Asiatic Society (JMBRAS)* 10(3)(1932):51–66; and R. Winstedt, "A History of Selangor," *JMBRAS* 12(3)(1934):3–10. See also Leonard Y. Andaya, *The Kingdom of Johor 1641–1728: Economic and Political Developments* (Kuala Lumpur, 1975).

10. Dianne Lewis, "The Tin Trade in the Malay Peninsula during the Eighteenth Century," *New Zealand Journal of History* 3(1)(1969):59–62.

11. Memoir of W. B. Albinus, governor of Malacca, 15 February 1750, in *JMBRAS* 27(1954):24–31.

12. F. W. Stapel, *Corpus Diplomaticum Neerlando-Indicum,* Vijfde Deel (1726–1752), *Bijdragen,* Deel 96, pp. 430–432.

13. A new ducatoon was worth slightly less than 1¼ Spanish dollars or reals—the common currency of payment and accounting for trade in the region. A Spanish dollar was fixed in this period at a value of 3 Dutch guilders or 5 English shillings. A rix dollar was worth 2½ Dutch guilders or 3s. 8d. One Dutch guilder =1s. 10d. The *bahar* was a standard of weight varying according to region and commodity weighed. In respect of Malayan tin it was equal to 375 Dutch pounds. Three *picols* made one *bahar.* One Dutch pound = 1.09 English pounds.

14. Stapel, *Corpus Diplomaticum,* Zesde Deel (1753–1799), pp. 1–2.

15. Memoir of Albinus, *JMBRAS* 27(1954):27.

16. Memoir of Albinus, *JMBRAS* 27(1954):26.

17. Governor and council of Malacca to sultan of Johore and Pahang; governor and council of Malacca to *Rijksbestierder* of Johore and Pahang: Netscher, *De Nederlanders in Djohor,* apps. 10, 11, pp. xxvi–xxix.

18. *Corpus Diplomaticum,* Zesde Deel, pp. 22–23.

19. *Corpus Diplomaticum,* Zesde Deel, pp. 77–80.
20. Netscher, *De Nederlanders in Djohor,* pp. 87–92.
21. *Corpus Diplomaticum,* Zesde Deel, pp. 148–149.
22. *Corpus Diplomaticum,* Zesde Deel, pp. 149–151.
23. *Corpus Diplomaticum,* Zesde Deel, pp. 152–155.
24. *Corpus Diplomaticum,* Zesde Deel, pp. 159–161.
25. Points of consideration, necessary for a good administration of Malacca . . . by governor-general and council, 8 March 1758, cited in Netscher, *De Nederlanders in Djohor,* pp. 96–98.
26. Netscher, *De Nederlanders in Djohor,* p. 105.
27. *Corpus Diplomaticum,* Zesde Deel, pp. 185–188.
28. Netscher, *De Nederlanders in Djohor,* pp. 115–126.
29. *Corpus Diplomaticum,* Zesde Deel, pp. 215–218.
30. Netscher, *De Nederlanders in Djohor,* p. 133.
31. *Corpus Diplomaticum,* Zesde Deel, pp. 255–258.
32. *Corpus Diplomaticum,* Zesde Deel, pp. 377–379.
33. Dianne Lewis, "The Dutch East India Company and the Straits of Malacca 1700–1784," Ph.D. dissertation, Australian National University, Canberra, 1970, p. 98.
34. Memoir of P. G. de Bruijn, governor of Malacca, 15 June 1785, *JMBRAS* 26(1953):56–62.
35. Governor and council of Malacca to governor-general and council, 11 June 1778, cited in Netscher, *De Nederlanders in Djohor,* p. 167.
36. R. Bonney, *Kedah 1771–1821* (Oxford, 1971), pp. 27–52; D. K. Bassett, *British Trade and Policy in Indonesia and Malaysia in the Late Eighteenth Century* (New York, 1971), pp. 50–71.
37. Netscher, *De Nederlanders in Djohor,* pp. 170–185.
38. *Corpus Diplomaticum,* Zesde Deel, pp. 534–540.
39. *Corpus Diplomaticum,* Zesde Deel, pp. 551–559.
40. King of Selangor to governor-general and council, 22 Shaban 1199 (A.H.), *Journal of the Indian Archipelago,* New Series, 2(1857):187–188.
41. King of Riau, Raja Ali, to governor-general, 16 Ruthee Assanie 1199 (A.H.), *Journal of the Indian Archipelago,* New Series, 2(1857):187–188.
42. Sultan Mahmud of Johore to Captain Light, 29 Muharran 1202 (A.H.), *Journal of the Indian Archipelago,* New Series, 2(1857):152–153.
43. *Corpus Diplomaticum,* Zesde Deel, pp. 573–578.
44. *Corpus Diplomaticum,* Zesde Deel, pp. 579–584.
45. Netscher, *De Nederlanders in Djohor,* pp. 212–216.
46. Netscher, *De Nederlanders in Djohor,* pp. 226–227.

47. Sultan Ibrahim to governor of Malacca, 5 March 1789: Netscher, *De Nederlanders in Djohor,* p. 235.

48. Abrahim Couperus, governor of Malacca to Johannes Siberg, councillor of Indies, 13 September 1788, *Bijdragen,* Deel 77, pp. 607–614.

49. "Memorie over Malacca en den thinhandel aldaar, ter speculatie van de WelEdele Achtbare Heeren Bewindhebberen der Nederlandse Oost-Indische Compagnie" [Memoir on Malacca and the trade there, for the consideration of the Honourable Directors of the Dutch East India Company], A. E. Van Braam Houckgeest, 1790, *Bijdragen,* Deel 76, p. 293.

50. Governor-general and council of Indies to directors, 29 December 1787, cited in *Bijdragen,* Deel 76, p. 295. The incident of 1623 in which all the occupants of the English factory at Amboina were put to death by the Dutch after a hurried trial became a sore point in Anglo-Dutch relations in the seventeenth century and in subsequent centuries an issue in Anglo-Dutch historiography. The English always describe it as a "murder" and a "massacre," and any reference to it in the company era would provoke English emotions against the Dutch.

51. Couperus to Siberg, 13 September 1788, *Bijdragen,* Deel 77, pp. 607–610; "Memorie over Malacca," Van Braam Houckgeest, 1790, *Bijdragen,* Deel 76, pp. 295–297.

52. Couperus to Siberg, 13 September 1788, *Bijdragen,* Deel 77, p. 608.

53. "Memorie over Malacca," Van Braam Houckgeest, 1790, *Bijdragen,* Deel 76, p. 297.

54. "Memorie over Malacca," Van Braam Houckgeest, 1790, *Bijdragen,* Deel 76, pp. 297–298.

55. "Memorie over Malacca," Van Braam Houckgeest, 1790, *Bijdragen,* Deel 76, pp. 302–303.

56. Couperus to Siberg, 13 September 1788, *Bijdragen,* Deel 77, pp. 612; Memoir of P. G. de Bruijn, governor of Malacca, 15 June 1785, *JMBRAS* 26(1953):60–62.

57. Memoir of P. G. de Bruijn, *JMBRAS* 26(1953):56–60.

58. "Memorie over Malacca," Van Braam Houckgeest, 1790, *Bijdragen,* Deel 76, p. 303.

59. Memoir of P. G. de Bruijn, *JMBRAS* 26(1953):60–61.

60. "Memorie over Malacca," Van Braam Houckgeest, 1790, *Bijdragen,* Deel 76, p. 307.

61. Memoir of P. G. de Bruijn, *JMBRAS* 26(1953):61.

62. H. H. M. Vlekke, *Nusantara, A History of Indonesia* (The Hague, 1959), pp. 235–236.

Masters and Banians in Eighteenth-Century Calcutta

Peter Marshall

It is an obvious truism that the European empires in Asia depended both for their establishment and for their continued existence on consent as well as force. They required not merely the passive acquiescence of the great mass of the population but also the active cooperation of important groups within Asian society. British dominion in India was no exception. It could not have come into being unless certain Indians had been prepared to give their services to the British. Yet crucial as the role of the collaborators was, who they were, how they gave their help, and what they got in return are questions which remain largely unexplored, although a recent study has made interesting suggestions as to how the Muslim grandees in the last days of the independent nawabs of Bengal sought to come to terms with the British.[1] This essay examines the role of another group of collaborators—those whom the British called their "banians," men who cooperated with them in many different functions from the beginnings of English trade with Bengal in the seventeenth century until well into the nineteenth century.

The term "banian" was used loosely by contemporaries. Europeans were in the habit of referring to almost any Indian who had dealings with them in Bengal as a banian, and historians have tended to use the word equally widely. But nearly all contemporary Englishmen seem to have recognized that the term also had a more precise meaning. A European of any consequence in Bengal was expected to have his personal banian, an Indian agent who managed his private affairs for him. In his *Considerations on India Affairs*, published in 1772, William Bolts wrote of banians employed by "the English gentlemen in general . . . to transact all their business."[2] Two years later Warren Hastings told a newcomer to Bengal that he would have to appoint a banian "to be your *minister*." "These are the people through whom every concern of whatever nature passes to their masters," he explained.[3] It is in this special sense of personal service to an individual European that the term "banian" will be used in this essay. Indian merchants trading on their own account or Indian officials holding office under the company are, for instance, excluded. Personal service to a European was the criterion of a banian in the specialized definition of the term understood by eighteenth-century Englishmen.

For most banians personal service was primarily financial and commercial. "Our buying and selling," a company servant wrote in 1770, "is carried on by the means of a Banian i.e. a Bengal man who has acquired some knowledge of our language and accompts. He mentions the price offered or demanded for any articles and when approved closes the sale with the black merchants. He is also cash keeper . . . so that you trade sometimes without either seeing the cash or the goods you purchase. Your business is only to keep the accompts in which you must be very exact or fall a sacrifice to the Banian who misses no opportunity of benefitting by your folly or neglect."[4] But a banian's duties could be much more wide ranging. Bolts described a banian as "interpreter, head book-keeper, head secretary, head broker, the supplier of cash and cash keeper and in general also secret keeper."⁵ In brief, the banian was his master's contact with the Indian world, a world with which most Englishmen, lacking the linguistic skill and other expertise required, felt themselves unable to deal at first hand. The banian managed his master's household, engaged and dismissed his servants, paid his bills, even lent him money for his commercial concerns. Moreover, the banian bought and sold on the Englishman's behalf, acted as his intermediary when his official duties required transactions with Indians, and for some employers at least acted as undercover agent in dealings from which Europeans were formally excluded.

If a good banian was indispensable for a substantial European fortune, service with a good employer was highly profitable for a banian. Most banians appear to have been paid wages. Hastings' banian, the famous Cantoo Babu (Krishna Kanta Nandi), is said to have been paid 15 or 20 rupees a month in his early service.⁶ But giving evidence in 1751, a banian said that instead of wages he received a commission of 1 anna 3 pice in the rupee (about 10 percent) on "what business he transacts for his master," and a European added that "there are a hundred banians in this place who receive no wages."⁷ The main lure of service for a banian was not, however, the wages or the officially permitted commission but a whole range of profits of which his employer might have only the haziest knowledge, if he was aware of them at all: the merging of the banian's commercial activities with his master's, deductions from his master's profits, commissions on supplies for his house, douceurs from those desiring access to him or employment under him. The banian of a powerful European was extremely well placed to acquire land, revenue, farms, or contracts with the company, sometimes with his master's collusion, sometimes without.

Mughal aristocrats seem to have employed servants whose functions were very similar to those of the English banians,⁸ as no doubt did the Portuguese. The derivation of the term remains, however, obscure, even puzzling the redoubtable authors of *Hobson-Jobson*. The English presumably adopted the Portuguese corruption of *vaniya* and, as they had done, applied the title "bania" to Hindu and Jain merchants in western India. But it is not clear why a more specialized meaning should have come to be attached to the term, apparently only in Bengal; in Madras the equivalent of the Bengal banian was known as a *dubash*. Banians in Bengal were certainly not drawn exclusively from the Hindu trading castes, who could be described as "banias"; Brahmans, Kayasthas, and even Muslims[9] were all serving as banians in the later eighteenth century. Whatever its origins, the Bengal usage was an old one. Company servants were talking about their "house banian" in 1676.[10] Ten years earlier, the French traveler Thevénot had written: "Aussi chacun a son banian dans les Indes et il y a des personnes de qualité qui leur confient tout ce qu'ils ont."[11]

Historians who have written about banians have chiefly been concerned with them as an example of the social upheavals caused by British conquest. Banians have been portrayed as "men of humble origin" who made spectacular fortunes by cooperating with the British and founded families which were able to attain "high social status in one or two generations" and dominate Calcutta society for much of the nineteenth century.[12] There certainly were conspicuous success stories of this kind. But any attempt to apply such a stereotype to banians as a whole encounters certain difficulties. In the first place, the years in which immense fortunes could be made overnight by banians were only an episode in the long history of banian-European connections in Bengal. In the thirty years or so after Plassey the nawabs' administration was overthrown, but no closely regulated British regime took its place. Opportunities for taking bribes, misappropriating revenue, and speculating in salt greatly enriched a number of Englishmen and, inevitably, their banians as well. Easy profits from access to political power had not, however, been available to banians before Plassey and were not generally to be open to them again after the 1780s. For most of the two hundred years or so in which Englishmen and banians were linked in Bengal, banians made their living by means which were both slower and more prosaic. Generalization is hazardous, but it also seems to be the case that most banians whose origins can be traced were already men of some substance when they entered the service of Englishmen. It is of course possible that the families of prominent banians had gradually worked their way up through dealings with European traders going back perhaps to the seventeenth century, but rags to riches sagas in a single life span seem to be rare. Indeed, Bolts was writing by the 1770s of "many persons of the best Gentoo families" who "take upon them this trust or servitude."[13] As for the classic question regarding the effects of foreign conquest on indigenous societies, in the case of the Bengal banians conquest seems to have confirmed the position of men already dominant who were able to adapt themselves to new opportunities, rather than enabling new groups to rise to the top.

If quick fortunes made out of politics were not the normal lot of most banians, huge gains were nevertheless made by some in the post-Plassey years. The man who seems to have been the pioneer for the later fortune makers was called Ruttoo Sircar by the English. He was clearly an important banian by 1751, when he gave evidence about his work,[14] and already a rich man before Plassey: he put forward claims for compensation for losses in the sack of Calcutta in 1756 which amounted to 180,000 rupees.[15] The inventory of his estate, proved in 1764, showed that he had invested very largely in property in Calcutta, which was valued at 71,318 rupees—eight of his nineteen houses or gardens were rented to Europeans. He also had some 70,000 rupees owed to him on bond by eleven Europeans, not counting considerable bad debts in European names.[16]

An even more spectacular fortune was acquired by Na-

bakrishna, or Nobkissen as he was usually called by the
English. The younger son of a revenue official, he took his
chance in the crisis year of 1756. He became a Persian
secretary to the company and accompanied Clive on the expedition which overthrew Siraj-ud-daula, according to leg-
end helping himself liberally to the ex-nawab's treasury in
the process.[17] He appears to have remained in Clive's service
until the Englishman left India in 1759. He then became
banian to Major Adams, who commanded the company's
troops at the beginning of the war with Mir Qasim. On
Clive's return to Bengal in 1765, Nobkissen was appointed
banian to the new Select Committee, also managing Clive's
household. Titles were gathered for him by Clive from the
Mughal emperor. Under Clive's successor, Verelst, Nobkissen remained in office as what was called the company's
"political banyan," but finding that he did not enjoy the
governor's confidence, he withdrew from business.[18] Although never formally employed by a European again, he
was still a figure of great influence in Calcutta politics,
much courted by Europeans and Indians alike, until his
death in 1797. His fortune was huge. Apart from any coup
that he may have been able to bring off at Murshidabad in
1757, he was involved in some very profitable revenue
speculations, such as that which put the huge *zamindari* of
Burdwan under his control in 1780.[19] He lent large sums of
money to many Europeans from the governor to the most
junior newcomer, apparently telling one such that he could
make him "a great man, as he said he had made others."[20]
In Calcutta he obtained possession of Sutanuti and Bagh-
bazar, "the most valuable part of this town, being inhab-
ited by all the principal merchants," while he built up a
landed estate in scattered properties paying revenue of over
a lakh of rupees a year.[21] He was reputed to have spent half
a million rupees on the *shradh* of his mother[22] and to have
died worth a crore or 10 million rupees.[23]

Although his family background was one of service to the

nawabs, Nobkissen's career is perhaps an example of one that depended solely on skill and luck in a situation of violent change.[24] Other meteoric fortunes acquired after Plassey had more solid beginnings. Gokul Ghosal, a kulin Brahman, went to Chittagong in 1760 as banian to Harry Verelst, who was establishing the company's rule in the province which had just been ceded by Mir Qasim. In 1779 he died an immensely wealthy man, leaving thirteen separate *zamindari* properties, the largest being in Chittagong and Dacca, the salt farm of the island of Sandvip off the coast of East Bengal and large claims on salt produced west of the Hughli in the late 1760s, claims for uncollected revenue on other lands which he had farmed, and twenty-four houses in Calcutta. The assets still to be collected on behalf of the estate four years after his death amounted to over 5 million rupees.[25] Service with Verelst had obviously been of enormous value to Gokul Ghosal, but, according to his nephew, himself banian to a European at Dacca, he had inherited a large fortune from his father Kandip Ghosal, one of the company's early revenue farmers.[26]

The story of Cantoo Babu is in some ways a similar one. A most illuminating study of him being prepared by his descendant, Maharajkumar S. C. Nandy of Kasimbazar, shows that in the period in which he was banian to Warren Hastings and Francis Sykes, he purchased a substantial landed estate, undertook large farms for the company, was deeply involved in the salt trade, carried on a silk business, and transacted a great deal of miscellaneous trade as well. But his descendant's researches also show that if service as a banian helped make a princely fortune for Cantoo, his father had been an important silk merchant at Kasimbazar and he himself had been actively engaged in trade on his own account before he entered European service. Hazari Mal, a Punjabi who had financial connections with most of the prominent Europeans of Calcutta in the 1760s and was claimed as banian by one of them in 1759,[27] was a man of

great wealth long before he began to use his influence with
the company's servants to gain revenue farms or set up a
short-lived bank under Hastings' patronage. Hazari Mal was
in fact the brother-in-law of the famous Omichand, almost
certainly the richest single merchant of any nationality in
early eighteenth-century Bengal, and was the administrator
of his estate, said to be over 4 million rupees.[28] Another
man of substantial means who entered European service is
Nimaicharan Malik. He is said to have inherited 4 million
rupees.[29] He became banian to James Ellis and Nicholas
Grueber in the salt business in the late 1760s[30] and died in
1808 worth 8 million rupees.[31]

These careers suggest a roughly similar pattern. All were
greatly enriched by service as banians, but all were men of
some substance already. Less is known about the origins of
other notable banians of the post-Plassey period. Santiram
Sinha, a Kayastha who had served Samuel Middleton, resident at the nawab's durbar, left a fortune of over 2 million
rupees, even though his employer died insolvent owing him
275,000 rupees.[32] Kashinath (usually rendered as Cossinaut
Baboo) is a name that constantly appears in the company's
salt and revenue records. Details of his personal connections
with Europeans are, however, obscure. He was described before Plassey as "one of the Company's banyans,"[33] is said
to have served Clive,[34] and appears as the security for the
banian of a free merchant called Edward Hardwicke in
1762.[35] Ramlochan, founder of another famous Calcutta
family, was the banian of John Holme[36] and yet another
dealer in salt and farmer of revenue. Another who had
abundant opportunities for enriching himself, although the
degree of his success is uncertain, was Ramcharan Ray, who
was employed by Clive in his first governorship, became
Henry Vansittart's banian from 1760 to 1764, and later "attracted the attention" of General Richard Smith.[37] Ramratan Tagore, another banian, served James Alexander and
then attached himself to the opulent Richard Barwell.[38]

Profits from territorial revenue collecting or salt farming appear to have contributed the major part of these great post-Plassey fortunes as well as of numerous smaller ones whose details cannot now be traced. As more and more of Bengal came under direct British control, banians were able to establish themselves as farmers, or temporary collectors of revenue, over large areas and in some cases to carve out for themselves sizable *zamindari* estates. Opportunities for monied men to buy land or invest in revenue farming had existed under the nawabs, but there was much more scope for them under the British—especially after 1772, when the company systematically let out land to the highest bidder. It was rumored that after 1772 a third of Bengal's revenue was being collected by Calcutta banians. Hastings thought this figure grossly exaggerated but was prepared to concede that a tenth might be in their hands.[39] Their stake in the manufacture and sale of salt was also considerable. Under the nawabs the salt trade had been let out to merchants who purchased a monopoly. Under the British the monopoly at first passed to private Europeans until 1768 when their participation was forbidden; in 1772 it became an official company monopoly. The formal exclusion of the Europeans was the banians' opportunity. Men like Gokul Ghosal, Cossinaut, and Cantu made huge purchases in the late 1760s.

Some of the banian involvement in territorial revenue and salt trading after Plassey was simply European involvement in disguise: Europeans could counter official prohibitions by acting under cover of their banians. But many banians were also acting for themselves. If the company offered tempting revenue farms or salt contracts, banians, because of their wealth and their contacts with Europeans, were the obvious people to take them up, whether their masters were concerned or not. Cantoo Babu farmed lands for over half a million rupees after 1772,[40] "taken and held," according to Hastings, "without my advice and almost all without my knowledge."[41] The banians of lesser men had lesser stakes in the revenue. As Hastings put it, "young and inexperienced men, . . . some totally ignorant of the language of the country" would inevitably "give their authority and influence to the people who had either acquired their confidence by long personal service or the right of creditors to exact it."[42] Apart from the profits of their own revenue farms, banians could also do well out of douceurs from *zamindars* or other farmers who hoped for their masters' favor. The list of banians accused of taking money from the Burdwan *zamindari* between 1768 and 1773 is a roll call of most of the eminent banians of Calcutta: Nobkissen, Cossinaut, Cantoo, Krishna Chatterjee (another employee of Hastings), Ramcharan Ray, Kaliprasad Bose (banian of Charles Stuart), Ramballabh and Ramratan Tagore (banians to James Alexander), Harikrishna Tagore (banian to Richard Becher), as well as the cashiers of John Graham and George Vansittart.[43]

The great banian fortunes as well as some sizable ones made by men much more difficult to trace may have come from being associated with Europeans exercising newly won political power, but this point should not be allowed to obscure the fact that, except in the immediate post-Plassey period, the banian-master relationship was essentially a commercial one. For historians of the British in India banians are perhaps chiefly important as the agents who enabled British business activity to develop in Bengal to the point where by the mid-nineteenth century houses of agency and other private British concerns were beginning to stand on their own without Indian support. By comparison with their long commercial connection, the banians' role as the intermediaries for the new administrators was short-lived. It began after Plassey and was virtually brought to an end in the 1780s and 1790s. By then the reforms of Lord Cornwallis were cutting down the private profits of officials on which banians could batten. Significantly, Cornwallis was the first governor who did not himself employ a banian or take a "native of any distinction" into his service as "moonshee or dewan."[44] At the same time, new revenue policies were eliminating opportunities for banians to acquire large farms. Purchase of *zamindari* lands outright was still possible under the Permanent Settlement's provisions for defaulters' lands to be sold, but recent studies suggest that Calcutta banians were not heavily involved in such purchases.[45] Finally, a strictly enforced company salt monopoly after 1781 was reducing the high profits made from dealing in salt in the past.

Banians continued, however, to play an important role in European trade in Bengal until well into the nineteenth century. In commercial matters the relationship between the banian and his master was a partnership in which both sides had clearly defined parts to play. The banian was expected to provide linguistic skill and a knowledge of markets, local conditions, and creditworthiness of Indian merchants which the European could not hope to have on his own. But above all he was expected to provide his master with capital. It was not until the late eighteenth century that European trade came to be financed to any large extent from European funds. Men in India able to offer bills of exchange on their relatives in London could usually obtain money from another European who wanted to remit his fortune home, while some men who had gone home were prepared to let part of their wealth stay behind in India in order to earn Indian interest; but most Europeans had to borrow extensively from Indians in order to carry on their trade. It was generally recognized to be the banian's duty to find the money himself or arrange loans from others. In 1774 a senior company servant replied to a request for a loan from another European by asking "Does not the man who serves you as banian furnish you with money? It is customary that this should be done."[46]

Young men newly arrived in India tended to run up debts with their banians even for setting up house, especially if they were in the company's service and thought it incumbent on them to cut a figure in the world. The words of an affidavit presented to the Supreme Court in a vain attempt to recover something from the exiguous estate of a company servant long dead echo what must have been the lamentations of generations of banians: "Yet he was very extravagant and by borrowing money from several gentlemen and natives in Calcutta and getting considerably in debt to this deponent, contrived to keep a number of horses, dogs, carriages and other things and to spend from three to five thousand rupees a month."[47] More prudent young men who turned their minds to thoughts of trade naturally looked to an experienced banian, "a man of property," to finance their first ventures.[48] Well-established European merchants were able to attract loans from a wide circle of investors, but their banians still seem to have contributed on a sizable scale. For instance, Santiram Sinha was owed 275,000 rupees out of immense bonded debts of 1,500,000 rupees or so left by his master Samuel Middleton.[49] George Vansittart owed 65,000 rupees to his banian, Jagat Ram, out of his total borrowing of about 150,000 rupees in 1772.[50]

Loans to Englishmen were obviously an attractive form of investment for banians, although those whose resources enabled them to do so seem to have chosen to spread their risk widely. Judging by the number of times his bonds are mentioned in litigation, the inventories of estates, or private correspondence, Hazari Mal must have made up to twenty loans at a time to various Europeans in the 1760s or early 1770s; Nobkissen and Cantoo appear to have distributed their favors almost as widely. Four years after his death, the estate of Gokul Ghosal still had claims on no less than forty-eight Europeans.[51] The interest paid on such loans was much lower than that available on loans to *zamindars* and seems generally to have been less than Indian merchants were obliged to pay. From the Europeans' point of view, however, the rates were disagreeably high, rarely falling below 9 percent and often reaching 12 percent, the maximum enforced by the British courts. For the banian any loss of interest seems to have been outweighed by the relative security of loans to Europeans. They could be brought to book in the British courts in India, and persistent banians resorted to employing European attorneys to pursue their quarry to England and even to bring them before the courts in London. Young men likely to die before they had become acclimatized, leaving a few bottles of wine and a pile of IOUs as their only assets, were, of course, a less secure proposition. The willingness of banians to lend even to them suggests that a tolerably secure investment yielding a reasonable return was not their only inducement. In the partnership between master and banian the Englishmen had real services to offer. In return for his banian's expertise and capital, the master was expected to contribute the privileges and authority attached to his position as a European.

These privileges became much more valuable after Plassey, but even in the early eighteenth century they were substantial, especially for the company's servants. In the first place, it was they who distributed the contracts to Indian merchants for providing the piece goods and raw silk needed for the London market. It was often alleged that a servant's banian stood a particularly good chance of being chosen. In 1732, for instance, specific charges were made that certain senior servants were guilty of "introducing their own banyans" as the company's merchants.[52] An even more important privilege which banians hoped to gain as a result of their service was the right to move goods throughout Bengal without paying the nawabs' customs or even submitting to inspections, which involved delay, harassment, and exactions by their officials. This privilege had been claimed by the English company and its servants in the seventeenth century, but it was given a much more effective basis by the famous grant of customs exemption in the farman issued by the Emperor Faruksiyar in 1717. Thereafter the private goods of company servants as well as the official trade of the company traveled under a *dastak* or seal, which was subject to some limitation on the goods it could be used to cover but otherwise gave virtually complete immunity. Indian merchants naturally coveted the *dastak* too. Goods which they supplied to the company or European imports which they bought from it were always regarded as being entitled to *dastak*s, but beyond that they could only be obtained through the favor of individual Europeans. One of the strongest incentives for an Indian merchant to become banian to a European was to get *dastak*s and thus to "borrow a name for his trade and cheat the government of their dutys."[53] When confronted with allegations that company servants antagonized the nawabs by issuing *dastak*s to many who had no right to them, a governor of Bengal replied: "Persons for the sake of commission on the goods belonging to the natives will apply for dusticks . . . and it's probable they do it frequently to oblige their banians."[54] The number of would-be banians was thought to have increased in the years after 1753 when the company began a new policy of obtaining goods directly through its own agents rather than buying them from Indian merchants. So-called *dadni* merchants, such as the Sett families,[55] who had in the past obtained *dastak*s for supplying the company and therefore "rarely before that period stooped to be banians to the gentlemen," now "condescended to serve" and obtained "the Company's dusticks . . . chiefly from your junior servants."[56]

Service as a banian became increasingly attractive after 1757. The prospect of sharing in his master's spoils from his office in the new administration was now dangled before the banian's eyes, but there were obvious advantages too for those who wished to prosper as merchants. Limitations on the goods covered by the *dastak* were quickly broken down, thus greatly enhancing its value as salt and other "inland" commodities began to move custom-free. With Europeans beginning to assert their authority over more and more of Bengal, an apparent connection with one of the new rulers must have seemed increasingly desirable insurance for an Indian merchant to take out to protect his trade. There are conspicuous examples of notable families seeking banian status after Plassey. Omichand, who on his own account had provided a third of the company's investment in a single year,[57] seems never to have linked himself with a European; Hazari Mal, the administrator of his fortune, did so immediately after Plassey. The Basaks, who had been prominent *dadni* merchants closely associated with the Setts, like them seem to have entered European service round about the time of Plassey.[58] By 1780, a witness told a House of Commons committee, most of the "considerable native merchants" in Bengal preferred to trade "with the assistance and countenance of some English gentleman."[59]

If Indian merchants found it convenient to become banians, it should not be assumed that they necessarily compromised their independence to any significant extent. In commercial matters the banian was his master's partner rather than his servant and there can be no doubt that in many partnerships it was the banian who was the senior partner, making the decisions and merely paying a commission for the use of his master's name and his *dastak*. A company servant was said to be able to get "20 or 25 per cent by a trade in which he runs no risque and has no trouble, merely for procuring to his banyan permits or dustucks."[60] In one case of trading ventures in Oudh the banian provided the stock and managed the concern; "in consideration of the advantages to be derived from the use of the name and influence and interest" of his master, he agreed to make over half the profits to him after deducting 12 percent interest.[61] In another case, a banian called Ramdulal Mishra told a young company servant that "very great advantages were to be made by trade in purchasing various sorts of goods, wares and merchandize in Calcutta . . . and sending such up the country to various marketts and aurungs." When the young man pointed out that "he had not a capital of his own for such a business," he was told that "it was not material"—he had "only to execute and deliver his interest bond or bonds to him from time to time." Periodic reports (which ultimately proved to be fictitious) came from Ramdulal Mishra about the dealings of a partnership to which the master had contributed nothing beyond putting his signature to various pieces of paper.[62]

If these stories are typical, a great deal of what passed as European trade can only have been European in the most nominal sense. Statements about Indian merchants being driven out of business by European competition after Plassey may also need to be treated with skepticism. It is in fact extremely difficult to determine degrees of ownership in many transactions where banians and Europeans are involved. There is a wide spectrum between salt contracts where the banian's name provided cover for his European master, on the one hand, and cases where a European merely allowed a banian to "use his name in making contracts for buying and selling goods and merchandize and borrowing money" on the other.[63]

The formal language used between banian and European may have been the language of master and servant, but for many Europeans the reality was very different. As the collector of a district frankly admitted when he asked a correspondent who hoped he would bring pressure on Nursingh, Cantoo's brother: "What can I do with him; he is a much greater man than I am."[64] Hastings at least believed that banians must be treated with proper consideration, reproving a young company servant who borrowed money from Nobkissen's nephew and then turned him out of his service and "left him to shift for himself."[65] In bad trading conditions in 1770 it was said that "the banyans take advantage of the English laws, and throw their masters into court; so that many are obliged to fly the country, or keep themselves concealed.''[66]

Rather than driving Indian merchants out of business altogether, the British conquest of Bengal seems to have forced them to come to terms with the conquerors and either enter into genuine partnerships with them or become their nominal clients, buying their protection for a share of the profits. For their part, Europeans continued to need their banians as partners in trade for many years to come, above all as a source of capital. In time, however, European funds became much more plentiful. From the 1780s most officials were forbidden to use their money directly in trade and thus tended to invest it with those outside the service who were permitted to trade. The characteristic unit of European trade was also beginning to change from the individual and his banian to the much larger and longer-lasting partnerships which came to be known as houses of agency. Houses of agency raised their capital increasingly from "the savings of the civil and military servants" and used it in a wide range of activities: shipowning, developing indigo plantations and sugar factories, banking, insurance.[67] Most houses of agency employed banians who still had important functions, such as raising short-term funds. But the success of the nineteenth-century European business enterprises no longer depended on the services of their banians as the eighteenth-century private traders had done. For the banians themselves the outlook was changing. Some individuals, such as the immensely wealthy Ramdulal De, who died in 1825,[68] continued to operate successfully on their own. But the future for most ambitious Indian businessmen in Calcutta ultimately lay in becoming partners in existing houses of agency or in founding their own companies on European lines, such as Rustomjee Turner and Company of 1827 or Carr Tagore and Company of 1834.[69]

Banians may have outlived some of their usefulness by

the 1850s, but their services to the British had been of great value for more than two hundred years. Like other Europeans in other parts of Asia, Englishmen in Bengal in the seventeenth and for much of the eighteenth century were seeking to establish themselves in a commercial world of great complexity which they lacked the power to shape to their own purposes. They were forced to trade on Asian terms, not on their own. It was not until the early nineteenth century that the military power and accumulated wealth of the British were such that they could begin to dictate the terms of trade. In the long period in which the English were just another of the many groups of Asian and foreign traders operating round the Indian Ocean, their banians were the essential intermediaries who enabled them to compete in alien conditions. Much as most Englishmen might abuse their banians, using epithets like "a race of vermin" or "the dregs of the people," they could hardly have done without them.

The impact of the banians on their own society is less easy to determine. They have been seen both as the filter through which western knowledge was to reach the Bengali intelligentsia of the nineteenth century and as the creators of the wealth which enabled an elite to cultivate such knowledge. Most banians must certainly have been shrewd and careful observers of Europeans and their ways. Some learned to speak English with a fair degree of facility. Nobkissen, for instance, was described as "well acquainted with and understanding the English language."[70] All must have understood European methods of keeping accounts and mercantile procedures, and many resorted to the English courts. As stewards of households, there is little they cannot have known about English domestic tastes. The way of life of a man like Nobkissen might show some of these influences at a superficial level in such matters as the building of his great Calcutta house. But in essentials banians appear to have remained totally committed to the Hindu system of values. Their ambitions were of the most traditional kind. They sought improved caste status and used their wealth in temple building, charitable distributions, and colossally lavish celebrations of *shradhs*.[71] In the eighteenth century successful banians were able to challenge the cultural leadership previously exercised by prominent *zamindari* families and turn Calcutta into a center of Bengali Hindu culture in a way the old Mughal capital of Murshidabad had never been.[72]

There is, however, little evidence, at least for the eighteenth century, that banians had been westernized to any real degree by close contact with Englishmen. The official and commercial communities of Bengal had been dealing with foreigners for generations—with Mughal noblemen, Arab, Armenian, Portuguese, Dutch, and French traders, as well as with Englishmen—while English law courts and municipal administration had been established in Calcutta since early in the century. Consequently it seems probable that the British conquest of Bengal did not present any strikingly new cultural or intellectual challenges to the inhabitants of Calcutta, at least until the arrival of the missionaries and their schools[73] or the setting up of Fort William College.[74]

In cultural as in other matters the impression of continuity between the first fifty years after Plassey and the preceding period is a strong one. In the early eighteenth century Bengal was already a commercially sophisticated society with a large volume of internal and foreign trade. There was no shortage of rich men willing to seek additional profit by easing the entry of Englishmen into Bengal's commercial system and later to share the spoils of conquest with them. So important were the services of such men to the English that they could not be dispensed with until well into the nineteenth century. The master-banian relationship was in many respects a partnership of equals offering substantial benefits to both sides.[75]

210 • *Masters and Banians in Calcutta*

NOTES

1. A. M. Khan, *The Transition in Bengal 1756-1775* (Cambridge, 1969), pp. 3–16.
2. W. Bolts, *Considerations on India Affairs* (London, 1772–1775), vol. 1, p. 84.
3. Letter to E. Impey, 12 October 1774, B[ritish] M[useum] Add. MS 29125, ff. 365–366.
4. E. Law to J. Law, 15 January 1770, Public Record Office, PRO 30/12/17/2, pp. 39–40.
5. Bolts, *Considerations,* vol. 1, p. 84.
6. I[ndia] O[ffice] R[ecords], B[engal] S[ecret] C[onsultations], 8 May 1775, Range A, vol. 28, p. 2143.
7. IOR, Mayor's Court Proceedings, 16, 17 December 1751, Range 155, vol. 24, evidence of Ruttoo Sircar and H. Cole.
8. M. Athar Ali, *The Mughal Nobility under Aurangzeb* (Bombay, 1968), p. 161.
9. See, for example, Sadr-ud-din's account of his services with John Graham and Richard Barwell: *A Complete Collection of State Trials,* compiled by T. B. Howell and T. J. Howell (London, 1816–1826), vol. 20, p. 1200.
10. *Diaries of Streynsham Master,* ed. R. C. Temple (London, 1911), vol. 1, p. 353.
11. H. Yule and A. C. Burnell, *Hobson-Jobson* (London, 1886), p. 64.
12. S. N. Mukherjee, "Class, Caste and Politics in Calcutta 1815-38" *Elites in South Asia,* ed. E. R. Leach and S. N. Mukherjee (Cambridge, 1970), pp. 46–48.
13. Bolts, *Considerations,* vol. 1, p. 84.
14. IOR, Mayor's Court Proceedings, 16 December 1751, Range 155, vol. 24.
15. IOR, B[engal] P[ublic] C[onsultations], 18 September 1758, Range 1, vol. 30, f. 319.
16. IOR, Mayor's Court Inventories, Range 154, vol. 63, ff. 66–67.
17. *A Translation of the Seir Mutagherin* (Calcutta, 1901–1903), vol. 2, pp. 287–288.
18. Nobkissen to Clive, 26 March 1772, I[ndia] O[ffice] L[ibrary], MS Eur. G. 37, box 63, ff. 136–137.
19. P. J. Marshall, "Nobkissen v. Hastings," *Bulletin of the School of Oriental and African Studies* 27(1964):390–391.
20. Calcutta High Court Records, Mayor's Court, Nobkissen v. Goold.
21. Sunker Dutt to C. Manningham and others, 5 April 1778, North-

amptonshire Record Office, A xxxiii, 10. Nobkissen's *taluks* are listed in IOR, Bengal Board of Revenue Proceedings, 2 February 1798, Range 73, vol. 29 (I owe this reference to Dr. R. Ray).

22. P. Sinha, "Approaches to Urban History: Calcutta (1750–1850)," *Bengal Past and Present* 87(1968):114.

23. A. Stirling, "Account of the Late . . . Nubkissen," IOR, Home Miscellaneous, vol. 773, p. 887.

24. Sinha, "Approaches," p. 113. For further details of Nobkissen's career, see N. N. Ghose, *Memoirs of Maharaja Nubkissen Bahadur* (Calcutta, 1901).

25. See the papers on his estate in IOR, B[engal] R[evenue] C[onsultations], 26 November 1784, Range 50, vol. 55, pp. 222–223, 241ff., 294–295. For the subsequent history of the *zamindari* properties, see IOR, Bengal Board of Revenue Proceedings, 20 April 1798, Range 73, vol. 31.

26. IOR, BRC, 26 November 1784, Range 50, vol. 55, pp. 158–159.

27. By G. Williamson, Calcutta High Court Records, Supreme Court, Plea Side, J. Doe *v.* Bolakee Sing.

28. N. K. Sinha, *Economic History of Bengal* (Calcutta, 1956–1970), vol. 1, p. 245.

29. L. N. Ghose, *The Modern History of the Indian Chiefs* (Calcutta, 1881), vol. 2, p. 67.

30. Calcutta Bar Library Club MS, Supreme Court Notes, vol. 2, p. 424.

31. Sinha, *Economic History,* vol. 3, p. 90.

32. Calcutta Bar Library Club MS, Supreme Court Notes, vol. 16, pp. 26, 270–271.

33. S. C. Hill (ed.), *Bengal in 1756-7* (London, 1905), vol. 1, p. 58.

34. Ghose, *Indian Chiefs,* vol. 2, p. 39.

35. Calcutta High Court Records, Mayor's Court, Hardwicke *v.* Cossinaut.

36. IOR, Calcutta Committee Proceedings, 8 December 1777, Range 67, vol. 68. Ghose, *Indian Chiefs,* vol. 2, pp. 81–82.

37. IOR, BRC, 12 January 1773, Range 49, vol. 38, pp. 562–568.

38. He was still alive in 1802 (W. Jackson to R. Shawe, 16 February 1802, British Museum Add. MS 29178, f. 250).

39. IOR, BSC, 7 December 1775, Range A, vol. 32, p. 143.

40. Listed in *9th Report of the Select Committee,* 1783, app. 35B, *Reports from Committees of the House of Commons* (London, 1803– 1806), vol. 6, pp. 195–199.

41. IOR, BRC, 28 June 1775, Range 49, vol. 54, p. 896.

42. Letter to G. Vansittart, 3 March 1777, British Museum Add. MS 29128, f. 34.

43. IOR, BRC, 31 October 1775, Range 49, vol. 56, pp. 532-584.

44. S. Turner to W. Hastings, 19 September 1786, British Museum Add. MS 29170, ff. 210-211.

45. R. Ray, "Changes in Bengal Agrarian Society," Ph.D. dissertation, Cambridge, 1973, pp. 279-282; M. S. Islam, "The Permanent Settlement and the Landed Interest in Bengal from 1793 to 1819," Ph.D. dissertation, London, 1972.

46. G. Vansittart to Capt. Roberts, 5 May 1774, Bodleian MS dep. b. 94, p. 108.

47. Calcutta High Court Records, Supreme Court, Equity, Ramdullol Missere *v.* Miller.

48. G. Bogle to R. Bogle, 11 April 1771, Mitchell Library, Glasgow, Bogle MSS.

49. IOR, Mayor's Court Inventories, Range 155, vol. 6, no. 64; Calcutta Bar Library Club MS, Supreme Court Notes, vol. 16, pp. 270-271.

50. Bodleian MS dep. b. 99, pp. 1-2.

51. IOR, BRC, 26 November 1784, Range 50, vol. 55, pp. 241-245.

52. S. Greenhill to directors, 9 February 1732, IOR, Home Miscellaneous, vol. 74, p. 162.

53. J. Holwell's "Hints on Bengal Affairs," 1757-1758, IOR, Correspondence Memoranda, D/106.

54. IOR, Correspondence Reports, 23 November 1732, D/19.

55. On them see B. Ghosh, "Some Old Family-Founders in Eighteenth-Century Calcutta," *Bengal Past and Present* 79(1960):42-55.

56. J. Z. Holwell, *India Tracts*, 3rd ed. (London, 1774), p. 427.

57. IOR, BPC, 8, 10, 25 June 1747, Range 1, vol. 19, ff. 276, 277-278, 297.

58. D. Basu, "The Early Banians of Calcutta," *Bengal Past and Present* 90(1971):38-40.

59. Evidence of W. Harwood, *9th Report of the Select Committee*, 1783, *Commons Reports*, vol. 6, p. 267.

60. G. Bogle to R. Bogle, 5 September 1770, Mitchell Library, Glasgow, Bogle MSS.

61. Calcutta High Court Records, Supreme Court, Equity, Hyde *v.* Ojagur Mull.

62. Calcutta High Court Records, Mayor's Court, Bateman *v.* Ramdullol Missere.

63. Calcutta High Court Records, Supreme Court, Equity, Ramdullol Missere *v.* Miller.

64. Richard Barwell to Roger Barwell, 25 January 1773, IOL, MS Eur. D. 535, pt. ii, f. 128.

65. Letter to W. Pye, 28 June 1774, British Museum Add. MS 29125, f. 325.

66. G. Bogle to R. Bogle, 5 September 1770, Mitchell Library, Glasgow, Bogle MSS.

67. J. Crawfurd, "A Sketch of the Commercial Resources and Monetary and Mercantile System of British India," *The Economic Development of India under the East India Company*, ed. K. N. Chaudhuri (Cambridge, 1971), pp. 276–277.

68. A. Tripathi, *Trade and Finance in the Bengal Presidency 1793-1833* (Calcutta, 1956), p. 139.

69. For the role of banians in the nineteenth century, see B. B. Kling, *Partner in Empire: Dwarkanath Tagore and the Age of Enterprise in Eastern India* (Berkeley, 1976), pp. 56–58; D. Basu, "The Banian and the British in Calcutta, 1800-1850," *Bengal Past and Present* 92(1973):157–170.

70. Marshall, "Nobkissen *v.* Hastings," *Bulletin of the School of Oriental and African Studies*, 27(1964):383.

71. N. K. Sinha, *Economic History*, vol. 3, pp. 96–101; P. Sinha, "Approaches to Urban History," *Bengal Past and Present* 87(1968): 113–114; "The Territorial Aristocracy of Bengal: no. 5, the Kasimbazar Raj," *Calcutta Review* 57(1873):94–95.

72. P. Calkins, "The Role of Murshidabad as a Regional and Subregional Centre in Bengal," in *Urban Bengal*, ed. R. L. Park (East Lansing, 1969), p. 26.

73. M. A. Laird, *Missionaries and Education in Bengal 1793-1837* (Oxford, 1972).

74. D. Kopf, *British Orientalism and the Bengal Renaissance* (Berkeley, 1969).

75. I am indebted to Professor B. B. Kling, Dr. John McGuire, and Maharajkumar S. C. Nandy of Cossimbazar for valuable information and helpful criticism.

Alien and Empathic: The Indian Poems of N. B. Halhed

Rosane Rocher

The attitudes of the British in India have been the subject of a vast literature. Most often, the people whose reactions are analyzed were administrators, diplomats, soldiers, missionaries, and their wives—persons whose avocations and bent of mind did not predispose them to accept their Indian surroundings. Whether in their professional capacity or in fiction,[1] they revealed themselves as foreigners on an Indian scene. Orientalists were different: although most of them had come to India in some other capacity, and with no more preparation than their fellow British citizens, they often underwent a process of—partial—conversion to things Indian. Their attitudes have been studied at the hand of their scholarly disquisitions.[2] The present study follows a different line of approach; it examines productions of an orientalist which are not of a scholarly nature. A picture will emerge of a man who was genuinely fascinated by India, through a medium that does not require the self-conscious drive for objectivity which is the hallmark of scientific activity. The picture may not look as sharp as others; it may appear as a blurred superposition of partial images with different foci. It will

reveal the complexity of a man at once attracted and re-
pelled, loving and lordly, and forever at odds with Britain
as well as India.

Nathaniel Brassey Halhed (1751–1830) went to India in
1772 for the same reasons others did: to make himself a fortune. He was, however, better educated than most of the
young writers in the service of the East India Company. He
had studied at Harrow and Oxford. He knew Persian.[3] As a
poet, he had published jointly—and anonymously—with his
friend Richard Brinsley Sheridan, a versified English version
of Greek erotic prose.[4] His first year in Bengal was a miserable experience, as he indicated in the clearest terms in a
letter to his friend Samuel Parr on 5 November 1773:

> Give me then leave to inform you that India (the wealthy, the
> luxurious, and the lucrative) is so exceedingly ruined and ex-
> hausted, that I am not able by any means, not with the assis-
> tance of my education in England, and the exertion of all my
> abilities here, to procure even a decent subsistence. I have
> studied the Persian language with the utmost application in
> vain; I have courted employment without effect; and after hav-
> ing suffered much from the heat of the climate, spent whatever
> money I brought into the country, and seen the impossibility of
> providing for myself for some years to come, I have taken the
> resolution of quitting so disagreeable a spot, before the necessity
> of running deeply into debt confines me here for years (perhaps
> for life). . . . You must grant, as my postulate, that Bengal is
> beyond conception exhausted. . . . I say, therefore, that as
> Bengal is so much altered for the worse that I find it impossible
> to get my bread, I have formed the plan of leaving it before my
> health and constitution be totally debilitated.[5]

Halhed's fate changed dramatically in early 1774. His
knowledge of Persian finally paid off when Warren Hastings
chose him to translate into English the compendium of
Hindu laws which he had commissioned and which had
been translated into Persian.[6] By the time Halhed had composed a long preface,[7] he was a genuine orientalist, curious

about Sanskrit language and literature and Hindu antiquities. He was to pursue this interest with a grammar of Bengali[8] and several works he did not care to publish.[9] Thanks to Hastings' patronage and continuing interest,[10] the young man who in November 1773 had been concerned only with making a quick fortune and returning to England as soon as possible became a scholar of considerable merit. Through the vicissitudes of a checkered career, two constants remained unchallenged: his interest in Hinduism and his devotion to Hastings.

The first of Halhed's Indian poems which have been preserved—most of them are unpublished—was addressed to Hastings on 22 May 1774 while Halhed was engaged in translation of the *Code*. It is a panegyric. Hastings is heralded as protector of science, patron of Sanskrit learning, and restorer of the ancient laws—the sphere of activity in which Halhed had been set to work. He is presented as deeply concerned with the welfare of the people, a "guardian," "the parent, not the ruler of the state." Through Hastings, the role of the British in India is profiled as benevolent paternalism. In the triangle British–Hindu–Muslim, the mission of the British—and Reason—is to free Hindus and protect them from the despotic power and bigotry of the Muslims. Under British tutelage agriculture, the rule of law, arts—and trade!—will bloom. Even though they may not appreciate it now, the people will one day be duly thankful. Is is characteristic—though surprising, considering that Halhed read Persian fluently and had but a smattering of Sanskrit—that the authentic representative of India is the Hindu *par excellence,* a Brahman. The poem, entitled "The Bramin and the River Ganges," is introduced with a quotation from Virgil: *si Pergama dextra/defendi possent, etiam hac defensa fuissent.*[11]

Silent and sad (where Ganges' waters roll)
A care-worn Bramin took his pensive way,

Proscient of ill, in agony of soul
    Tracing his country's progress to decay.
Age on his brow her furrow stamp had wrought,
    While sorrow added to th' impression deep:
And melting Nature at each pause of thought
    Snatch'd the indulgent interval to weep,
Thus straying, as he wearied out with pray'r
    Each fabled guardian of that hallow'd wave;
To soothe the misery of vain despair
    The river's goddess left her oozy cave.
"O lost to thought and obstinately blind!
    Weak man!" she cried, "thy baseless passion cease:
Rouse from this torpid lethargy of mind,
    And wake at last to comfort and to peace.
Smile, that no more ambitious spoilers range
    Thy labour's fruits relentless to devour:
Smile to obey (and hail th' happy change)
    The rule of reason for the rod of pow'r.
Hast thou forgot how Tartar fury spurn'd
    The suppliant meekness of the patient sage;
How bigot zeal the groves of science burn'd,
    While superstition sanctified the rage?
Hast thou forgot each prostitute decree,
    Each venal law the plaint Coran sold:
While the fleec'd suitor famish'd on his plea,
    And judges wallow'd in extorted gold?
What could Mahommed's race degen'rate teach,
    Themselves to spoil alone and ruin taught?
Neglected commerce wept her silent beach,
    And arts affrighted distant dwellings sought.
Think then on what ye were—destruction's prey—
    How low, how worthless in the scale of things!
While havock stain'd with Indian gore her way,
    And deserts whiten'd with the bones of kings.
Ingrateful Hindûs! when a tender hand
    Pours balm into your wounds; is't right to weep?
Your guardian's anxious efforts to withstand,
    Who wakes to labour but that you may sleep!
Are murmurs, then, and tears the tribute just,

Are plaints, to wisdom and to mercy due,
   That rais'd your groveling functions from the dust,
And open'd life and freedom to your view?
   The frail exotic might as well accuse
   Th' officious kindness of the planter's care,
That shelters it from autumn's sickly dews,
   And blunts the keenness of December's air.
Say, is it nought, that no insulting lord
   With riotous arms the lab'ring plough impedes?
Nought, to behold your country's laws restor'd,
   The moral system of the slighted Vedes?[12]
Nought, that deliver'd from a tyrant's chain
   Diffusive trade re-m——s[13] the busy strand?
That arts invigorated bloom again,
   And favour prospers each inventive hand?
Go, go, vain mourner! thy glad homage show
   To *Him* who broke despotic slav'ry's tie:
Who gave thee, rescued from that bitt'rest woe,
   To live uninjur'd, and unplunder'd die:
To *Him,* who yet hath other gifts in store,
   Whom further deeds of worth shall render great:
Who still shall blend humanity with power,
   The parent, not the ruler of the state.
Yet, not confin'd to legislation's sphere,
   'T is *He* shall bid fair science too take root;
Shall nurture ev'ry plant that she may rear,
   And teach her tender scyons how to shoot:
And haply animate some vent'rous eye
   T' explore the mysteries conceal'd so long:
To trace where learning's earliest sources lie,
   And ope the fountains of *Sanscritian* song.
Weep as thou wilt, thy sons will bless his name,
   When thou art mingled with thy kindred earth;
And consecrate the happy hour to fame
   Of *Pollio*'s[14] greatness, and of freedom's birth.''[15]

Halhed left Bengal in 1778 and, back in England, became one of the most vocal defenders of Hastings' Indian
policies. He published in 1779 an anonymous tract in de-

fense of Hastings' Maratha policy.[16] His involvement with East Indian politics grew even stronger in 1782, when he helped John Scott (Hastings' agent in England) and Joseph Price to wage a press campaign to refute the accusations leveled against Hastings by parliamentary committees. Under the pseudonym "Detector" he published from October 1782 to November 1783 a stream of letters in the *Morning Herald* [17] and in separate pamphlets.[18] John Scott described him to Hastings as "indefatigable upon this, as upon every other occasion, and he is esteemed the first political writer in England."[19]

It is in this atmosphere that our second poem originated. It was written on 8 June 1782 and therefore antedates the war of pamphlets. The combativeness, however, is already present. A paean to Hastings, the poem has a totally different tone from the preceding one. It has no peaceful scenes of flourishing arts and trade, no mention of science and Sanskrit learning; all these concerns are swept aside by a sudden burst of military enthusiasm. Hastings is no longer a "guardian," "the parent, not the ruler of the state," but "great arbiter of Hindostan." Although the lines resound with names of Indian princes and their cities, the mood is not Indian. It is a poem composed in England to extol military victories over barbaric rulers. The feeling emerges that, even though the Indian enemies have been defeated, the battle is not over; the British Commons remains to be conquered. The poem bears no title but announces itself as a paraphrase of an ode by Horace:[20]

What thanks, O Hastings, from the chair,
    What ballot of impartial names,
What vote of commons shall declare
    The meed exerted virtue claims?
O first in rank! in merit first!
    Whose influence *Poona*'s restless hord,
Alien from law, in rapine nurs'd,
    Hath felt, hath trembled, and ador'd.

For late, by thy strong legions back'd,
  Hath Goddart[21] hewn their armies down:
Where o'er the widely subject tract
  Bassein's insulting bastions frown,
Bassein, for long resistance stor'd:
  But fenceless to a British foe.
Nor long, ere Coote[22] unsheath'd the sword,
  And laid the proud *Mysôrean* low.
Eager of fight, how fierce he prest
  To struggle in the manly strife;
And harrass out each stubborn breast
  Sworn to quit plunder but with life.
Rapid he rush'd resistless forth,
  And drove along the surge of war.
Like some black storm, when West and North
  Sweep o'er the verdure of *Bahar.*
As foams swol'n Ganges on the sides
  Of some frail bank in rich *Nattore.*
Sudden it bursts—th' impetuous tides
  Destruction o'er the meadows pour.
So rag'd he 'gainst each adverse line;
  Now charg'd the rear, now storm'd the van;
The troops, the auspices were thine,
  Thine the campaign's digested plan.
For thee, on that important hour
  When *Guallior* wide its portal threw
(A conquest for an empire's power)
  To Popham[23] and his daring few,
(While light'ning-wing'd the wond'rous tale
  Thro' Asia's farthest regions ran)
Astonished millions join'd to hail
  Great arbiter of Hindostan!
The *Peshwâ* trembles at thy nod;
  And stubborn *Hyder* bends the knee;
The Lama, king at once and god,
  Hath bow'd to virtue and to thee.
To thee hath roll'd obedient waves
  The Ganges of uncertain source;
And frequent *Carumnassa* laves

Thy laurels in her lengthen'd course.
Thy voice the stern *Marattah's* hear,
    With hands in purple slaughter dy'd:
Fearless of death, yet thee they fear,
    "And lay their vanquish'd arms aside.[24]

Halhed returned to Bengal in 1784 and was supposed to be appointed to the first vacancy on the Council of Revenue. When he reached Calcutta in July, Hastings was on a trip to Oudh and Banaras. He joined Hastings in Banaras in October and learned of his intention to resign and return to England. Hastings, anxious to have several of his supporters accompany him home to help fight the attacks that he knew were to continue, arranged that Halhed be made the agent of the nawab of Oudh in England.[25] While Hastings returned to Calcutta, Halhed stayed behind and wrote Hastings three letters,[26] all of which contain poems. Two of these poems have Indian themes.[27]

The letter in which the first "Indian" poem is inserted deals mainly with the technicalities of obtaining the agency for the nawab of Oudh. Toward the end, Halhed is reminded that all these dealings are caused by Hastings' impending departure. He voices concern for India. Hastings—not any British administration—is viewed now as India's sole protection against anarchy. Halhed reverts to the tone of the poem, quoted earlier, written during his first sojourn in Bengal: Hastings is again pictured as a considerate parent for India. The poem bears no title but links immediately with the paragraph that precedes in the letter:[28]

> I am rendered exceedingly happy in the observation that each successive packet from England brings an addition of strength, or at least a presumption of such addition to your arm and to your cause. The prospect of daily invigorating influence will at all events throw a brighter lustre on the remaining products of your labours, and cast a rich tint of sunshine on your final arrangements.

But ah! when from the parting vessel's stern,
A nation's woes shall in your bosom burn;
While, as Calcutta fades beneath your eye,
That breast shall heave the last parental sign,
To think that o'er this strife-devoted plain,
So long reposing in your cares—in vain,
Uprais'd by mammon, and by faction nurs'd,
So soon the storms of anarchy must burst.
Say can a frail exotic's tender frame
Repel the torrent, or defy the flame?
Your gardener hand, dear Sir, first gave it root,[29]
Your kindly[30] influence bade its buds to shoot;
Can it but wither, when those beams are gone,
In air ungenial, and a foreign sun?

The poem included in the third letter, written during Halhed's trip to Oudh, is a very curious production and one in which the scholar comes to the fore. It does not touch upon East Indian politics, either in India or in Britain, but focuses exclusively on India and Hinduism. Although couched in less reserved terms than is usual, it is a fairly representative example of the westerner's uneasiness with popular Hinduism. Modern scholars make a distinction between philosophical and popular Hinduism; eighteenth-century scholars used to posit a historical development: the pure—and monotheistic!—religion of pristine ages had been debased to a gross, idolatrous superstition at the hands of a cunning Brahman priesthood. Halhed's tone is all the more raucous, his disgust for the practices he witnessed in Banaras is all the more profound, because he feels genuine admiration for what he considers to be the only real, unadulterated, elevated Hinduism. The *Bhagavadgītā* figures prominently in the poem as the symbol of "the most ancient and pure religious principles of the Hindoos." Halhed's enthusiasm had been fanned by his visit to his friend Charles Wilkins, who was completing his English translation of the text at that precise time.[31] The letter in which Halhed forwarded the poem to Hastings is nothing more than a note of explanation—and apology—for the theme he struck:

> I arrived here at 1 P.M. at Mr. Magrath's bungalow, and scribble a copy of the enclosed while dinner is getting ready. In excuse for it I can only say, that I really intended to speak of the learning, the integrity, the virtue, the philosophy and the disinterestedness of Bramins. But that when I came to *"sweep the sounding lyre,"* the devil of one of them could I find—and Mrs. Melpomene or whoever is the proper officer on these occasions obliged me to say what I have said. As a poet I might plead the privilege of fiction. But alas it is all sober fact! and therefore I cannot possibly have hit the sublime. I believe there might have been more of it, but the accursed dawk bearers have obliged me to walk so much (not being able even to drag the palanquin after me in some places,) that I was tempted to bestow all my iambics upon them.[32]

Halhed describes the poem[33] as an "ode on leaving Benaras" and dedicates it pointedly to what he considers alternative names for one primordial notion of the divine, now abandoned:

To *Brăhm* or *Kreeshna*[34]

Who shall, O Brăhm, thy mystic paths pervade?
   Who shall unblam'd the sacred scenes disclose,
Where ancient wisdom's godlike sons are laid
   Immortal sharers of divine repose?
Ōm! Veèshnû! Brăhm![a] or by whatever name
   Primeval Reshees[b] have thy power ador'd:
They worshipp'd thee, they knew thee still *the same*,
   One great eternal, undivided lord!
Tho' now, in these worn days, obscur'd thy light,
   (Worn days, alas, and crazy wane of time!)
Tho' priest-crafts' puppets cheat man's bigot sight
   With hell-born mockeries of things sublime,
Ages *have* been, when thy refulgent beam
   Shone with full vigour on the mental gaze:
When doting superstition dar'd not dream,

And folly's phantoms perish'd in thy rays.
Yes, they *have* been, but ah! how fallen, how chang'd
  Behold, on Caushee's[c] yet religious plain,
(Haunts where pure saints, enlighten'd seers have rang'd)
  The hood-wink'd *Hindu* drag delusion's chain.
What boots it, that in groves of fadeless green
  He tread where truth's best champions erst have trod?
Now in each mould'ring stump, and bust obscene,
  The lie-fraught bramin bids him know a god.
What boots it, that on *Gunga's* hallow'd shore
  He sees *Dwypáyan's*[d] earliest scroll unfurl'd,
Where the proud turrets of *Benàras* soar,
  And boast acquaintance with a former world?
For *him*, misguided wretch! nor ear nor eye
  Perceives in hearing, nor beholds in sight:
Else might he still at *Kreeshna's*[e] camp supply
  His blunted organs with caelestial light.
He rather glories at some flow'r-strew'd fane
  Of *Hánumàn*, baboon[f] obscene, to bow:
Or blind his blank existence in the train
  Of gaping suppliants to a pamper'd cow!
'T is night—from yon low door, in hallow din,
  Bell, drum, and voice th' affrighted ear assault.
Hush—'t is a temple—*Doorgah's* rites begin:
  What pious *Hindu* hails not *Doorgha's* vault?
Nich't in an angle of the seven-foot space
  Stands a gaunt semblance of th' ill favour'd hag:
Her drizzling carcase and unseemly base
  Veil'd in a squalid yard of scanty rag.
A silver'd convex marks each garish eye,
  Her hideous visage shines imbrued with ink:
And as the bramin waves his lamp on high
  The satisfied adorer sees her wink.
Here, as in silent horror we survey
  The priest-rid mis'ry of the blinded throng,
A lip-learn'd *yogee* opes the choral lay,
  And writhes and labours in a *Sanscrit* song.
Not far, a wretch with arms erect and shrunk
  Full thrice-ten-years god's image hath defac'd:

Till like some age-worn *Peepul's*[g] leafless trunk
  His very vegetation is a waste.
Here, in one spot, the dying and the dead
  For rites funereal wait their sev'ral turn:
While the yet-gasping victim, from his shed,
  Smells the parch'd bones, and sees his brother burn.
Where'er we tread 't is consecrated mould,
  Streets choak'd with temples—God's at ev'ry door—
But canst thou, *Kreeshna!* not inceas'd behold
  Thy bramins grind the faces of the poor?
Thy bramins, did I say?—degen'rated herd,
  Offspring of Nārāk,[h] lucre-loving race,
Who crush thy *Geeta's*[i] more than human word
  T'exalt some pagan *pootee*[35] in its place.
Accurst *Benāras,* wherefore are endus'd
  Such foul misdeeds to taint pure *Gunga's* stream:
Wherefore have idols, heifers, apes, obscur'd
  The simple science of the one supreme?
God of all good! yet once events controul!
  Snatch yet thy volume from the night of time!
Let not this precious balsam of the soul
  Waste all its virtues in a thankless clime!
E'en yet there is, whose spirit soars above
  This finite mansion of distemper'd clay:[j]
Who leaves to groveling minds the wealth they love,
  Nor stifles conscience in the lust of sway.
Him in thine essence late absorb! and here
  Illumine, worthy, with thy truths divine!
So shall *thy sastra* see-girt nations chear:
  So Kreeshna's light in northern darkness shine.

Back in England, Halhed led the easy life of a gentleman of independent means, traveling, appearing at court, and eventually becoming a member of Parliament in 1791. He was, however, deeply disappointed with England, which did not appear to appreciate the achievements of Hastings in Bengal. Together with John Shore, and several other devoted friends of Hastings', he participated in the preparation of his patron's defense presented before the House of Commons in 1786. His rancor kept growing throughout the impeachment, particularly vis-à-vis Edmund Burke, who requited Halhed's hostility.[36] Halhed gave vent to his feelings in a series of poems written at every step of the legal proceedings. Although these poems refer to events in India, their theme is the struggle of the Hastings faction in Britain; India is only the background for matters debated at home. These poems are therefore peripheral to the concerns analyzed here.

For Halhed, only a few special people—not Britain at large—could understand and carry out the policies that were needed in India. His friend and fellow defender of Hastings, John Shore, was such a person, and Halhed was delighted at his appointment as governor-general in 1792. He wrote on that occasion a congratulatory poem in imitation of an epigram by Martial:[37] Halhed's loss will be Indian's gain:

> To parch'd Bengal's Brahminical domains,
> Where floods of Ganges fertilize the plains,
> Go, virtuous Shore! I urge thy journey—go!
> A nation's welfare compensates my woe.
> Go!—I can court regret on such a plea;
> The bliss of millions should be bliss to me.
> Thy patriot toils a few short seasons claim:
> Guard but thyself, and leave the rest to Fame.
> Go!—and imbibe incessant suns once more.
> We rate not merit by complexion, Shore.
> Nay, if inglorious ease can feel concern,
> Thy fairer friends shall blush at thy return:
> One British winter Asia's tint shall chase,
> And feed thy glory, as it clears thy face.

As the years went by, Halhed's alienation grew. His tragic involvement with Richard Brothers, who prophesized the imminent end of the millennium and destruction of London, completed the process which had been initiated with his bitterness over the trial which Hastings had to endure. Halhed was an object of ridicule for his defense of Brothers and had to relinquish his seat in Parliament. He severed all ties with society and lived as a recluse from 1796 to 1808. He wanted no contact with what he named "Sclerocardia," the hardhearted city of London. Even when he emerged from his self-imposed confinement, he did not make his peace with his British surroundings. His friends, his concerns, even the employment he obtained in the home administration of the East India Company, were all linked to his India days. His letters to Hastings attest to his patient study of the *Mahābhārata*. His intimacy with Hastings and the Daylesford circle became stronger, more exclusive. Halhed was not the only member of the group who dabbled in poetry, but he was the undisputed judge in this field. There were endless exchanges of verses, particularly with Hastings. Halhed usually offered Hastings verses when he arrived for a visit and again when he left. He dedicated poems to him on his successive birthdays. Two such poems, in which the indologist comes to the fore, are published here. They testify to Halhed's continuing captivation with Hinduism.

The poem written to celebrate Hastings' eighty-third birthday uses the theory of *yuga*s, the concept of cyclical time which fascinated Halhed throughout his life, from his first indological publication[38] to his last work in manuscript.[39] The poem, dated 17 December 1815, is provided with a note of explanation by the author:[40]

Firm on four feet the *Sati-yûg* behold!
　As symboliz'd (and wherefore?) by a bull!
　'T is *Taurus*—whence the sun in vigour full
First through the zodiac his fixt period roll'd,
Op'ning with joy the pristine age of gold.
　Trīta less stedfast under virtue's rule,
　Stands but on three. From these another pull
'T is *Dwāpar:—Kali* reels on one, grown old.

To mortals scriptures four-score years assign.
Youth's *satya* then compute at thirty two
For *Trīta* twenty-four are manhood's due:
Sixteen mark *Dwāpar*, verging tow'rd decline:
Eight the decrepitude of Kali close.
Hastings, at eighty three, a *second satya* knows.

The poem offered to Hastings on the occasion of his last birthday, on 17 December 1817, draws a simile from the stages of life recommended for the orthodox Brahmans, "the sages whom we both admire." Halhed's admiration for philosophical, monotheistic Hinduism remains intact:[41]

Hastings! The sages whom we both admire,
  Offspring, so fable wills, of *Brahmā's* head,
  When of their century the first half is fled,[a]
Narrowing their labours, as the *Vēds* require,
Burst all mundane obstructions, that so higher
  Their intellect's expansive force may spread,
  Till like the poles, with *Brăhm*[b] concentrated,
They move in thought the universe entire.

This heav'n-taught Hindûs life-directing rule,
  Hadst thou, illustrious friend, long since in view,
  Renouncing empire's cares at *fifty-two*,
To dwell with wisdom in her spiritual school.
Tow'rds its true center *there* thy mind gains way,
Year after year advanc'd—and eight-five to day.

Some of Halhed's poems appear to be irretrievably lost, together with most of his private papers. According to Grant, Halhed wrote "a series of Sonnets on the ten incarnations of Vishnu."[42] Grant prints one of these sonnets as "a specimen of the mode in which he associated our sacred writings with those of the Hindoos."[43] The blending of Christian and Hindu myths was a common preoccupation in the late eighteenth and early nineteenth centuries and was pursued by Halhed with particular vigor. The trend appears indeed to have grown stronger with the years; the pages of his last work[44] are replete with far-fetched parallels between biblical, classical, and Indian data. The only sonnet in the series on the incarnations of Viṣṇu that has been preserved pursues the same line of thought. It is devoted to the dwarf Vāmana, the fifth incarnation of Viṣṇu, who is likened to Christ:

Vaman

O'er the three worlds when Vali's[45] empire spread,
Vaman, a holy dwarf, before him bow'd.
"Take what thou wilt" exclaimed the monarch proud.
"Space his three steps to cover," were, he said,
"Enough." The sovereign's priest opposed, in dread
Of latent mischief: but the king allow'd.
Vaman strode twice and spann'd (a god avow'd)
The universe. The *third* took Vali's head.
So Christ, a dwarf in reason's lofty eyes,
Two steps had trod, where Satan's glories swell,
The first, his cross, o'erstriding death and hell;
The next his resurrection clear'd the skys.
For his *last step*, his second advent know
To bruise the serpent's head, and chain him down below.[46]

Grant gives no indication as to the date of this series of poems. It is probable that they are late in Halhed's life, possibly in the 1810s, if they are related to his renewed indological activities after his period of reclusion. If this is the case, they would follow the hymns to Hindu deities of Sir William Jones,[47] although the latter do not seem to have occasioned them.

Hastings died in 1818. Halhed resigned his post with the home administration of the East India Company less than one year later. His very last poem, entitled "Mes adieux," dated 23 July 1819,[48] not only takes leave of the company, but at the same time bids farewell to poetry. Although he lived on for more than a decade, he was not heard from any more. The death of his patron and the end of his involvement in Indian affairs signified the close of his active life.

For years his existence had been led under the sign of past Indian days. For better or for worse he was a "Nabob," a returned Anglo-Indian, who never could call England home again.[49]

NOTES

1. See the latest addition to the literature on the subject: Benita Parry, *Delusions and Discoveries: Studies on India in the British Imagination 1880-1930* (Berkeley, 1972).

2. See, recently, P. J. Marshall (ed.), *The British Discovery of Hinduism in the Eighteenth Century* (Cambridge, 1970), published in a series with the revealing title "The European Understanding of India."

3. William Jones to Viscount Althorp on 18 August 1772: "I do not know whether you ever heard me mention a schoolfellow of mine named *Halhed:* I received a letter from him the other day, partly *Persian* and partly Latin, dated *the Cape of Good Hope.* He was in his way to Bengal. . . . " Garland Cannon (ed.), *The Letters of Sir William Jones* (Oxford, 1970), vol. 1, pp. 114-115.

4. *The Love Epistles of Aristaenetus: Translated from the Greek into English Metre* (London, 1771).

5. Samuel Parr, *Works; with Memoirs of His Life and Writings and a Selection from His Correspondence,* ed. John Johnstone, (London, 1828), vol. 1, pp. 469-470 n.

6. Hastings had it published by the East India Company: *A Code of Gentoo Laws, or, Ordinations of the Pandits. From a Persian Translation, Made from the Original, Written in the Shanscrit Language* (London, 1776).

7. Reprinted in Marshall, *British Discovery of Hinduism,* pp. 140-183.

8. *A Grammar of the Bengal Language* (Hooghly, 1778).

9. British Museum Add. MSS 5657-9; Asiatic Society, Calcutta, MS E. 48.

10. The importance of Hastings' role in this regard has been highlighted recently by P. J. Marshall, "Warren Hastings as Scholar and Patron," *Statesmen, Scholars and Merchants: Essays in Eighteenth-Century History Presented to Dame Lucy Sutherland,* ed. Anne Whiteman et al. (Oxford, 1973), pp. 242-262.

11. Virgil *Aeneid* 2.291-292: "If a hand could save Troy, this hand would have."

12. *Bedes,* corrected into *Vedes* = Vedas. In 1774, when the poem was written, Halhed consistently reproduced the Bengali pronunciation of

Sanskrit. By the time the collection which preserves this poem was made, after Hastings' death, Halhed had occasion to eliminate spellings influenced by Bengali pronunciation.

13. Illegible.

14. Pollio, Roman politician and patron of the arts, friend of Virgil. Here Pollio = Hastings.

15. British Museum Add. MS 39,899, ff. 2–3.

16. *A Narrative of the Events Which Have Happened in Bombay and Bengal, Relative to the Maharatta Empire, Since July 1777* (London, 1779).

17. *Morning Herald*, 7, 9, 12, 16, 18, 21, 23, 28 October and 1, 2, 11, 18, 20, 25 November 1782; collected and reprinted in *The Letters of Detector on the Reports of the Select Committee of the House of Commons Appointed to Consider How the British Possessions in the East-Indies May Be Held and Governed with the Greatest Security and Advantage to This Country and How the Happiness of the Natives May Be Best Promoted* (London, 1782). *Morning Herald*, 28 April and 1, 5, 15 May 1783; collected and reprinted in *The Letters of Detector, on the Seventh and Eighth Reports of the Select Committee and on the India Regulating Bill* (London, 1783). *Morning Herald*, 17 July and 7 November 1783, the latter also printed as a separate pamphlet and distributed at a meeting of proprietors of East India stock.

18. *A letter to Governor Johnstone . . . on Indian Affairs* (London, 4 January 1783); *A Letter to the Rt. Hon. Edmund Burke, on the Subject of His Late Charges against the Governor-General of Bengal* (London, 18 October 1783).

19. British Museum Add. MS 29,160, f. 170.

20. Horace *Odes* 4.14.

21. Thomas Goddard, who defeated Mahadaji Sindhia and captured Bassein in 1781.

22. Sir Eyre Coote, who defeated Haidar Ali at Porto Novo in 1781.

23. William Popham, who stormed the fort of Gwalior in 1780.

24. British Museum Add. MS 39,899, ff. 4–5.

25. Hastings to his wife on 20 November 1784: "Halhed is at Lucnow, busied in the Execution of a Plan which I have concerted for his Return to England. I wish he was there, but I hope to precede him. His Talents were always of the first Rate; but they are improved far beyond what you knew them, and I shall still require them in Aid of Scott's Exertions." Sydney C. Grier (ed.), *The Letters of Warren Hastings to His Wife* (Edinburgh, 1905), p. 368.

26. Dated Muzaffarpur, 9 November 1784; Banaras, 12 November; Kanpur, 18 November. Printed in John Grant's "Warren Hastings in

Slippers: Unpublished Letters of Warren Hastings," *Calcutta Review* 26 (1856):76–80. When printing the last letter, Grant omitted—or did not have—the poem.

27. The poem in the letter dated 12 November, not reproduced here, is introduced in the following terms: "I have hit upon a source of perpetual amusement on an inexhaustible subject: 'The abuse of language in modern poetry, by introducing the idioms and expressions of the poetic language of the antients into modern verses.' I have taken the liberty to subjoin a few stanzas by way of specimen: and I hope I am not presumptuous in requesting your assistance, when you feel a necessity of relaxing a little from the toils of empire, in adding to my humble effort, which has only the merit of being so lax and disjointed, that it will admit a stanza on any subject in any part where you may be pleased to put it." Grant, "Hastings in Slippers," p. 77.

28. Grant's article "Hastings in Slippers" is our only source for the text of Halhed's letter. The poem printed in Grant's article, from Halhed's private papers, is also included in the collection which Halhed made of his poems to Hastings "that happen to have been preserved" and offered to Hastings' widow (British Museum Add. MS 39,899, f. 6). There are some variants in the two copies of the poem. The text reproduced here is that in Grant's article; the variant readings in the British Museum manuscript are mentioned in notes. It is probable that, when Halhed collected his poems after Hastings' death, he emended some verses which he felt could be improved. Grant may have committed minor mistakes while copying the poem, but he is not likely to have changed the wording. The version quoted in Grant's article has therefore a better chance to represent the original poem written in 1784.

29. "Your animating hand first gave it root" (British Museum Add. MS 39,899, f. 6).

30. "quick'ning" (British Museum Add. MS 39,899, f. 6).

31. Charles Wilkins, *The Bhăgvăt-Gēētā* (London, 1785). The letter dedicating the translation to Hastings (reprinted in Marshall, *British Discovery of Hinduism*, p. 192) is dated 19 November 1784, one day after Halhed wrote his poem.

32. Grant, "Hastings in Slippers," p. 80.

33. Preserved only in British Museum Add. MS 39,899, ff. 6–8.

34. Halhed's spelling of Indian names is not consistent. Since the terms are generally clear, however, it would be superfluous to add to Halhed's glosses (marked a through j):

   a. "names of the deity."
   b. "saints or prophets."
   c. "Benāras."

    d. *"Dwypáyan* (i.e. *Vyás* the great Hindo legislator and hierophant and sacred penman)."

    e. "i.e. in the Geeta."

    f. "a sacred ape."

    g. "a species of tree."

    h. "Hell."

    i. "a book containing some of the most ancient and pure religious principles of the Hindoos."

    j. "a Sanscrit phrase for the body."

35. Book.

36. See a letter from Burke to Dundas dated 7 April 1787: Holden Furber (ed., *The Correspondence of Edmund Burke* (Chicago, 1965), vol. 5, pp. 323–324.

37. Halhed published, anonymously, *Imitations of Some of the Epigrams of Martial* (London, 1793–1794). The poem to John Shore, in imitation of Martial *Epigrams* 10. 12, is published in pt. 4, pp. 23–25. It is also quoted in Lord Teignmouth, *Memoir of the Life and Correspondence of John, Lord Teignmouth* (London, 1843), vol. 1, pp. 225– 226.

38. Preface to the *Code of Gentoo Laws* (reprinted in Marshall, *British Discovery of Hinduism*, pp. 158–159).

39. Translations from and notes on the Persian *Mahábhárata,* which he made from 1811 to 1813, with an additional note in 1816 (Asiatic Society, Calcutta, MS E. 48).

40. British Museum Add. MS 39,899, f. 32:
"The *proportions* of the four Hindú Yugas.

Satya	32
Trita	24
Dwapar	16
Kali	8
	80."

41. British Museum Add. MS 39,899, f. 37. Halhed provides his poem with explanatory notes (marked a and b):

    a. "The quadripartite subdivision of human life—supposed to consist for each individual among the bramins of a 100 years—is thus allotted. In the first 25 years the person is a *Brahmachári,* or pupil; in the next quarter he is called *grahasta,* or a house-holder; at the close of 50 years he becomes a *vánaprasta* or a dweller in the woods; and after 75 he is a *saniási* or pilgrim."

    b. "The One omnipotent."

42. "Hastings in Slippers," p. 137.

43. Ibid.

44. Asiatic Society, Calcutta, MS E. 48.

45. Bali.
46. Grant, "Hastings in Slippers," p. 137.
47. William Jones, *Works* (London, 1799), vol. 6, pp. 313–392.
48. British Museum Add. MS 39,899, f. 42.
49. I thank the authorities of the British Museum for permission to publish Halhed's poems preserved in manuscript in the Hastings papers in their collections.

Holden Furber at Work

Blair B. Kling

In his preface to *John Company at Work* Holden Furber suggests the basis for his own contribution to the historiography of European expansion in Asia. "The ideal historian for modern India," he writes, "should doubtless be neither a European nor an Asian, but that ideal historian does not exist. Yet I have felt that a work on this period should be written by an American."[1] As one of the first Americans to work in Indian history, Furber is keenly aware of the juxtaposition of India and America in the eighteenth-century world. Both countries were part of the same British empire and both were frontiers of an expanding Europe. In his first published article on European life in eighteenth-century India, Furber observed the similarity between the European community in India and American frontier society:

There was the same overshadowing presence of danger, the diversity of opportunity, the chance to scramble for wealth quickly acquired, the lack of settled law and order, the possibility of easy shift from one way of life to another, the scope for building a new life in a new land after disgrace in the old, and finally the presence in a community primarily of British stock of elements from other nations of Europe.[2]

In some respects, however, the differences between the two frontiers were more important than their similarities. The European in India had little opportunity to develop and exercise political freedom to match his economic freedom; and, further, while the American frontier gradually became settled, the Indian frontier was perennial, "ever young, and never stable."[3]

The bond between India and America in the eighteenth century was more than political. Both were parts of a complex commercial network in which, for example, the tea and slaves imported into America were paid for with Indian exports to China and Africa. The merchant-adventurers of whom Furber writes saw themselves as members of a single commercial system, and many pursued careers in both India and America. Those who went to India to seek their fortunes were not much different from Holden Furber's own ancestors who came to New England in the seventeenth century and established themselves as sea captains, lumbermen, and merchants. Furber's sympathy with these adventurers and his disposition to view the empire from its underside has led him to appreciate the crucial role of ordinary people in the establishment of British dominion in the east. The foundations of the empire, he writes in his latest book, "were as much laid by sea captains, supercargoes, country merchants and agency houses as by military officers and administrators."[4]

Furber was the first historian to understand fully the importance of one kind of adventurer, the "country" trader. In *John Company at Work* he pays tribute to the role of these free traders who, in the eighteenth century, captured from indigenous merchants the lucrative trade between ports in the Indian Ocean and the China Sea.

This obscure and unsung soldier of fortune charted new trade routes in the Eastern Seas and redeveloped old ones. With a crew of obedient lascars at his back, he dared undertake voyages which few Mohammedan commanders would attempt. Whenever several such voyages were successful, he was able to buy a ship of his own and become independent of the Indian or European merchant prince who employed him. His widespread operations had their share in bringing about a commercial revolution in the Indian Ocean in the mid-eighteenth century.[5]

This commercial revolution, whose significance was first noticed by Furber, was essentially a tremendous expansion of the trade between India and China at the expense of the trade between eastern and western India. It led to the "certain triumph" of the British country trader, who controlled these routes, over private traders of other European nationalities.

In Europe the counterpart of the country merchant was the "clandestine" trader who, like the merchant-heroes of Revolutionary New England, respected no trading company monopolies and traded alike with the friends and enemies of the British crown. Furber's typical clandestine trader is Robert Charnock, who was born in Lancaster and lived for periods of his life as a merchant in France, Holland, and Belgium before finally settling in London. While trading illicitly as a merchant of Flushing, Charnock presented a memorial to the States-General protesting the monopoly of the Dutch East India Company in which he referred to himself with pride "as a burgher of the whole world."[6]

Though these clandestine and country traders had their part in the process that swept the British into power in India, Furber sees them as the precursors of laissez faire rather than as the perpetrators of "Plassey plunder" or the harbingers of imperialism. He leaves to others the job of condemning or defending the European record. The source of his interest in India is romantic rather than polemic, and he is not ashamed to admit his susceptibility to "the lure of the East" or to share with us that his first introduction to India was "through the tale of an American youngster kidnapped and spirited away to India were he was seized from his abductors, protected, and sheltered by a heroic and faithful Indian bearer."[7] Although Furber is aware that from the Indian perspective Americans are "Europeans," he tries to emphasize, particularly with Indian audiences, the special historical and cultural ties between India and America.[8] He is more at home in the eighteenth than the nineteenth century because he sees the imperialist era as an unhealthy episode in international relations. One recurrent theme in his recent writings is that relations between Asia and Europe are now returning to their happier eighteenth-century form of relations between equals.

Holden Furber's academic entry into South Asian history was through his dissertation on Henry Dundas, Viscount Melville. Dundas, the political manager of Scotland in 1784, helped elect the Younger Pitt to power and was rewarded with the newly created post of president of the Board of Control (later called secretary of state for India). Through a London bookseller Furber gained access to a section of the Melville papers that dealt with Indian affairs, and, in his own words, "a study of Scottish politics turned into a study of the foundations of the Indian empire." Within the collection it was the correspondence between Dundas and Shore, governor-general of India from 1793 to 1798, that first gave Furber the idea of writing a history of eighteenth-century British India from the perspective of what was going on in Asia rather than in Europe. He also discovered that much of the Shore correspondence dealt not with the grandiose themes of "wars, conquests and annexations" but with revenues, trade, and remittances. From that discovery came the insight that most Europeans went out to India not to build an empire but to build a personal fortune.[9]

The great depression hit just as Furber received his Ph.D.

from Harvard in 1929. It meant ten years of struggle to find a permanent position while alternating between temporary instructorships at Harvard and travel abroad. His first trip to the orient was in 1934 to see the empire about which he wanted to teach. He traveled to Asia across the Pacific, visiting colleagues and looking into local archives. While in Colombo he first saw the possibility of working in Asian archives on the East India trade and the advantages of using Dutch, Danish, and French sources in conjunction with British.

The idea of making use of the archives of continental East India companies—Dutch, Danish, and French—was reinforced when he married Elizabeth Chapin in 1936. Mrs. Furber was a historian of medieval France, and the Furbers researched together in The Hague, Paris, and elsewhere. They first visited India almost immediately after their marriage and spent the winter of 1936–1937 traveling around the country from the Khyber Pass in the north to Trichinopoly in the south, stopping to work in the archives at Bombay and Madras. The period was heavy with history, dominated by Gandhi, Nehru, and Jinnah and the elections of 1937. It left its imprint on Furber, who now began to focus more of his interest directly on India itself, and the experience infused his later work with a flavor of timeliness.

Step by step Furber was bringing together the components of his distinctive historical approach—the perspective from Asia, the importance of the country trade, the focus on the merchant-adventurer, and the use of continental European sources to build a more accurate picture of the economic world of late eighteenth-century India. He had also shaped the historical problem that would give his work meaning and direction: the economic basis for the rise of British power in India.

Furber found the final ingredient of his research while in England on a Guggenheim fellowship in 1937–1938. A messenger at the India Office Library showed him a box of ledgers whose value no scholar till then had realized. They consisted of the financial records of the East India Company and dealt with sums taken in and disbursed, commodities sent to and from the east, prices paid, and contracts entered into. These records dealt primarily with the trade between London and India, but they included records of the major Indian ports as well. By using the ledgers and the attached invoices, a historian could trace the fluctuations in demand and supply of any commodity, the level of prices, wages, and expenses over a series of years, and the rise and fall in the prosperity of various Asian ports. Each product had its own story, and the changes in its fortunes over time required explanation. If imaginatively used, these records could link together the economic, social, and political history of eighteenth-century India.[10]

Furber's pioneering use of this kind of material from British and continental archives prefigured the quantitative work on European expansion in Asia now in progress. He did his research on John Company before the availability of photocopying, electronic calculators, and computers and thus did not have the facilities for quantitative economic history which depends on the collection and analysis of complete series of data. Instead he used his economic data to indicate the direction of economic change and to integrate the economic into the larger social and political picture.

But even if Furber had had the tools for cleometrics, he probably would not have used them. His style is literary, his approach is empirical, and his analysis comes only after he has tried to recreate the historical scene with precision and accuracy. The individual is the unit of Furber's history. Even in his ledger books he sees not only columns of figures but the pain and hardship of the "prodigious amount of clerical work . . . done by Indian clerks as well as the young 'writers' sent out to India from Britain in their 'teens.''[11] He tries to capture what the individual actor sees and feels. *John Company at Work* opens with a portrayal of Warren

Hastings on his final voyage home to face his enemies in Britain. "As Warren Hastings worked among his papers," writes Furber, "he perhaps thought of these invoices which Captain John Johnston held in safekeeping." The invoices refer to the cargo that lay "far beneath his feet . . . 5000 pounds of Bengal saltpeter . . . 90,000 pounds of redwood dunnage . . . 209 bales of raw silk, 54 boxes of indigo."[12] And thus Furber captures the reality of what first brought Hastings and most other Europeans to India.

In his attention to the individual, Furber has followed the philosophy of his own mentor, Wilbur Cortez Abbott, who saw all institutions as "gatherings of personalities" and as "groups of living individuals."[13] Although Furber writes of "the economic and social forces . . . at work under one guise or another"[14] and of the "inexorable" forces[15] that eventually resulted in British supremacy in India, he is equally strong in his belief in the contingencies of history. It is obvious from his work that by "forces" he means the way in which history takes its direction from "the interaction of countless human life stories upon each other."[16]

The historian of the Indian frontier is himself a pioneer. He has pioneered in writing the economic and social history of a period where previous historians had dealt primarily with the exploits of the great. He was a pioneer in the use of the archives of continental European East India companies. He saw how the humble invoice could enhance our understanding of the foundations of empire. From all this emerged his thesis: The money that enabled John Company's armies and navies to dominate the coasts of India—from which they would in time conquer the entire subcontinent—was supplied by countless country traders of all nationalities. These country traders had learned from experience that British bottoms were safe places in which to freight their goods and that the British East India Company in London would honor its debts without discrimination.

Holden Furber's scholarship represents a transition period in South Asian studies. Although his original contributions have been in the area of European expansion in Asia, he is usually acknowledged as the founder of modern Indian historical studies in America. He has directed more than a score of students, some of whom have followed his example and worked on European expansion, but most of whom have dealt with the internal history of South Asia. Beyond those of us who have formally received their degrees under his guidance is an even larger constituency of students and mature scholars in many parts of the world who, because of Furber's reputation for integrity, his unselfish interest in the advance of historical studies, and his legendary generosity, have sought his guidance as both friend and mentor.

WORKS OF HOLDEN FURBER

Books

Henry Dundas, First Viscount Melville, 1742-1811. London: Oxford University Press, 1931.

The Private Record of an Indian Governor-Generalship: The Correspondence of Sir John Shore, Governor-General, with Henry Dundas, President of the Board of Control, 1793-1798. Edited with an Introduction and Notes. Harvard Historical Monographs, no. 2. Cambridge: Harvard University Press, 1933.

John Company at Work: A Study of European Expansion in India in the Late Eighteenth Century. Harvard Historical Studies, vol. 55. Cambridge: Harvard University Press, 1948; reprinted 1951, 1970.

The Correspondence of Edmund Burke. Vol. 5: July 1782–June 1789. Edited with the assistance of P. J. Marshall (general editor, Thomas W. Copeland). Cambridge and Chicago: Cambridge University Press and Chicago University Press, 1965.

Bombay Presidency in the Mid-Eighteenth Century. Bombay and New York: Asia Publishing House, 1965.

Rival Empires of Trade in the Orient, 1600-1800. Vol. 2 of *Europe and the World in the Age of Expansion.* Editor, Boyd C. Shafer. Minneapolis: University of Minnesota Press, 1976.

Articles

"How William James Came To Be a Naval Historian." *American Historical Review* 38(1)(October 1932):74–78.

"The East India Directors in 1784." *Journal of Modern History* 5(4)(December 1933):479–495.

"Fulton and Napoleon in 1800: New Light on the Submarine *Nautilus*." *American Historical Review* 39(3)(April 1934):489–494.

"An Abortive Attempt at Anglo-Spanish Commercial Cooperation in the Far East in 1793." *Hispanic American Historical Review* 15(4)(November 1935):448–463.

"The Beginnings of American Trade with India 1784–1812." *New England Quarterly* 11(2)(June 1938):235–265.

"The United Company of Merchants of England Trading to the East Indies 1783–1796." *Economic History Review* (London) 10(2)(1940): 138–148.

"Madras in 1787." In *Essays in Modern English History in Honor of Wilbur Cortez Abbott*. Cambridge: Harvard University Press, 1941.

"Constitution-Making in India." *Far Eastern Survey* 18(8)(April 1949): 86–89.

"The Letters of Benjamin Joy, First American Consul in India." *Indian Archives* 4(2)(July–December 1950):219–227.

"British Conquest and Empire, 1707–1947" and "India and Pakistan 1947–1950." In *India, Pakistan, Ceylon*. Ed. W. Norman Brown. Ithaca, N.Y.: Cornell University Press, 1951. Articles on the Indian subcontinent and Ceylon reprinted in *Encyclopaedia Americana*.

"Pakistan." In *The State of Asia*. Ed. L. K. Rosinger. New York: Alfred A. Knopf, 1951.

"The Overland Route to India in the Seventeenth and Eighteenth Centuries." *Journal of Indian History* 29(August 1951):105–133.

"The Unification of India 1947–1951." *Pacific Affairs* 24(4)(December 1951);352–371.

"The East India Company's Financial Records." *Indian Archives* 7(2) (July–December 1953):100–114.

"Edmund Burke and India." *Bengal Past and Present* 76(January–June 1957):11–21.

"In the Footsteps of a German 'Nabob': William Bolts in the Swedish Archives." *Indian Archives* 12(1, 2)(January–December 1958):7–18.

"Plassey: A New Account from the Danish Archives." *Journal of Asian Studies* 19(2)(February 1960):177–187. With K. Glamann.

"The Theme of Imperialism and Colonialism in Modern Historical Writing on India." In *Historians of India, Pakistan, and Ceylon*. Ed. C. H. Philips. London: Oxford University Press, 1961.

Article on History in *Resources for South Asia Area Studies in the United States*. Ed. Richard D. Lambert. Philadelphia: University of Pennsylvania Press, 1963.

"The Country Trade of Bombay and Surat in the 1730's." *Indica* 1(1) (March 1964):30–46.

"Historical and Cultural Aspects of Indo-American Relations." *Journal of University of Bombay* 34(July 1965–January 1966):95–116.

"Glimpses of Life and Trade on the Hugli 1720–1750." *Bengal Past and Present* 86(152)(July–December 1967):13–23.

"Asia and the West as Partners before 'Empire' and After." *Journal of Asian Studies* 28(4)(August 1969):711–721.

"The History of East India Companies: General Problems." in *Société et Compagnies du Commerce en Orient et dans l'Océan Indien.* Ed. Michel Mollat. Paris: SEVPEN, 1970.

"Madras Presidency in the Mid-Eighteenth Century." In *Readings on Asian Topics: Papers Read at the Inauguration of the Scandinavian Institute of Asian Studies, 16-18 September 1968.* Scandinavian Institute of Asian Studies Monographs, no. 1. Lund: Studentlitteratur, 1970.

NOTES

1. Holden Furber, *John Company at Work* (Cambridge, 1948), p. viii.

2. Holden Furber, "Madras in 1787," in *Essays in Modern English History in Honor of Wilbur Cortez Abbott* (Cambridge, 1941), pp. 292–293.

3. Ibid.

4. Holden Furber, *Rival Empires of Trade in the Orient, 1600–1800* (Minneapolis, 1976), p. 297.

5. *John Company at Work*, p. 161.

6. Ibid., p. 159.

7. Holden Furber, "The Theme of Imperialism and Colonialism in Modern Historical Writing on India," in *Historians of India, Pakistan, and Ceylon*, ed. C. H. Philips (London, 1961), p. 341.

8. Holden Furber, "Historical and Cultural Aspects of Indo-American Relations," *Journal of University of Bombay* 34(July 1965–January 1966): 95–116.

9. The Shore-Dundas correspondence is found in Holden Furber (ed.), *The Private Record of an Indian Governor-Generalship* (Cambridge, 1933).

10. Holden Furber, "The East India Company's Financial Records," *Indian Archives* 7(2)(July–December 1953):100–114.

11. Ibid., p. 100.

12. *John Company*, pp. 3–4.

13. Charles Seymour, "Forward," in *Essays in Modern English History in Honor of Wilbur Cortez Abbott* (Cambridge, 1941), pp. ix–x.
14. *John Company*, p. vii.
15. *Rival Empires*, p. 239.
16. From a letter to the author, 30 August 1956.

Contributors

SINNAPPAH ARASARATNAM is professor of history and head of department at The University of New England, Armidale, New South Wales. He is the author of *Dutch Power in Ceylon 1658-1687* (1957); *Ceylon: Modern Nation in Historical Perspective* (1964); *Indians in Malaysia and Singapore* (1969); *Memoirs of Julius Stein von Gollenesse, Governor of Ceylon 1743-1751* (1974); and numerous other books and articles.

C. R. BOXER is professor emeritus of Portuguese, University of London; professor emeritus of history, Yale University; and has frequently been visiting professor of history, Indiana University. He is the author of over 260 articles, editions, and monographs dealing primarily with the Portuguese and Dutch colonial empires. His most recent works are *The Portuguese Seaborne Empire, 1415-1825* (1969), *Women in Iberian Expansion Overseas, 1415-1815* (1975), and *The Church Militant and Iberian Expansion, 1440-1770* (1978).

JOSEPH JEROME BRENNIG received his Ph.D. in history from the University of Wisconsin in 1975. His dissertation was entitled "The Textile Trade of Seventeenth-

Century Northern Coromandel: A Study of a Pre-Modern Asian Export Industry."

ASHIN DAS GUPTA is professor of history at Visva-Bharati University, Santiniketan, West Bengal. He is the author of *Malabar in Asian Trade* (1967).

BLAIR B. KLING, a professor of history at the University of Illinois, was one of Holden Furber's first doctoral students in Indian history. He is the author of *The Blue Mutiny: The Indigo Disturbances in Bengal, 1859-1862* (1966) and *Partner in Empire: Dwarkanath Tagore and the Age of Enterprise in Eastern India* (1976).

PETER MARSHALL is a reader in history at King's College, London, and the author of *The Impeachment of Warren Hastings* (1965); *Problems of Empire: Britain and India 1757-1813* (1968); *The British Discovery of Hinduism in the Eighteenth Century* (1970); and *East Indian Fortunes: The British in Bengal in the Eighteenth Century* (1976). He served as co-editor with Holden Furber of the *Correspondence of Edmund Burke*, vol. 5.

M. N. PEARSON, who taught at the University of Pennsylvania before moving to his present position at the School of History, University of New South Wales, is the author of *Merchants and Rulers in Gujarat: The Response to the Portuguese in the Sixteenth Century* (1976).

OM PRAKASH is a reader in economic history, Centre for Advanced Study in Economic Development and Economic History, Delhi School of Economics, University of Delhi. He has written numerous articles on seventeenth and eighteenth-century Indian economic history.

ROSANE ROCHER is associate professor of Indo-Aryan languages, University of Pennsylvania. She has published extensively in Indian linguistics, the history of indology and linguistics, and British orientalism in eighteenth and nineteenth-century India.

☥ *Production Notes*

This book was designed by Roger J. Eggers and typeset on the Unified Composing System by the design and production staff of The University Press of Hawaii.

The text and display typeface is Garamond.

Offset presswork and binding were done by Halliday Lithograph. Text paper is Glatfelter P & S Offset, basis 55.

This material is reproduced following ... pass

CHINA

SEA

Nangasak

Kyongchang
Singan
Ho-nan kay-fong
Que-te
Yu-ning
Ho-heyngan
Fong-yang
Chonkiar
Pau-king
Suang-yang
Nan-king
Nai-king
King-chen
King-po
Shangtu
Quey-chen
Yuen-tu
Nan-king
chi-in
Ha
Tenchen
Lequeas
Ching-tu
King-chen
Kyen-kyang
Swichen
Chong-king
Shwi-chen
Win-chen
Yong-ing
Chingche
Se-nan
Fu-chen
Fu-chen
Ching-kyang
Tong-chveng
Chang-sha
Yven-chen
Yen-ping
I. dos Reys Magos
Yung-ning
Pau-king
Kan-chen
Hing-wha
Yong-cha
Yunnan
Lyau-chen
Cha-chen
Chau-chen
King-wha
Sin-chen
Chauking
Kai-ton
Hey-chen
Tay-wan
Formosa I.
Ao
Meng
Kircho
TUN
QUIN
Laychen
Macao
Barluon
Bashee I.
LUCONIA or
MANILLA
Porceloue
Kyongchen
Segovia
P. of Casiguran
Thoanoa
Falso C.
Haynan I.
Cochinchina
Triangles
PHIL
IPPINE
SIAM
Pekin
Quinin
Pracel
Shoals
Manilla
Str. of Manilla
Louvo
Siam
Mindora
Philipina or
Tandaya
Cambodia
Lamalhan
Falip
Ciampa
Paragoa I.
I. Layta
St. John Pays I.
Bay of Siam
ISLANDS
MINDANAO
Mindanao
Ligor
Tigana I.
C. Henry
Caldero
Tanda
Carud
Patana
Sanguin
Sion
Nattina
Pera
Anamba I.
Borneo
MOLU
C
A
Malacca
BORNEO
Manado
C. Romania
Sambas
Lava
Celebes
Gilole
Andragin
Banca
Lao
Strait of Macassar
BES
Bilaton
Buro
Ceram I.
Palambam
Vase P.
Madura
Jan
Amboyna
NDA
ISLANDS
JAVA
ISLAND
Engano I.
Sunda Str.
Bantam
Batav.
Mataram
Palambuan
Bally I.
Loubec
I. Cumbava
Flores I.
High I.
TIMOR
EAN
Sandelbosch I.
Roth I.
Concordia

10 0   11 0   12 0   13 0